Archaeozoological Analysis of the Fortified Settlement of Sand (10th Century AD, Lower Austria)

Early Medieval faunal remains from Sand an der Thaya

Konstantina Saliari

BAR International Series 2892

2018

Published in 2018 by
BAR Publishing, Oxford

BAR International Series 2892

Archaeozoological Analysis of the Fortified Settlement of Sand (10th Century AD, Lower Austria)

ISBN 978 1 4073 1637 6

BAR titles are available from:

BAR Publishing
122 Banbury Rd, Oxford, OX2 7BP, UK
EMAIL   info@barpublishing.com
PHONE   +44 (0)1865 310431
FAX   +44 (0)1865 316916
www.barpublishing.com

Dedicated to my family and my husband.
With special thanks to my mother.

Acknowledgements

I am very grateful to Erich Pucher for sharing his great archaeozoological experience and knowledge. Many thanks to Michael Doneus for very helpful insights and comments and to Sabine Felgenhauer-Schmiedt for entrusting me with the material from Sand and for very important feedback.

Special thanks to Daniel Makowiecki for providing me with crucial literature and entrusting me with valuable data. I would also like to thank Kerstin Pasda, Umberto Tecchiati, and Karl Kunst for their important scientific contribution, Claudia Theune-Vogt, David Ruß, Martin Obenaus, and Alexander Pollak for our interesting discussions during the writing of this work.

I wish also to thank Karina Grömer, Gabriela Russ-Popa, Ursula Göhlich, and Andreas Kroh for their cooperation and support. Many thanks to Frank Emmanuel Zachos, Anton Igersheim, Matthias Kucera, Soledad De Esteban-Trivigno, and Chris Klingenberg for their interest in my work and suggestions as well as to Michael Stachowitsch for his help improving the language of the text.

Additionally, I would like to thank Irene Forstner-Müller, Christine Neugebauer-Maresch, Irmtraud Hellerschmid, Monika Griebl, Peter Ramsl, Bendeguz Tobias, Peter Trebsche, Oliver Schmitsberger, Martin Penz, Nikolaus Hofer, Franz Sauer, and Florian Fladerer, who entrusted me with material for archaeozoological interpretation. Special thanks to Michaela Kronberger, Kristina Adler-Wölfl, and Martin Mosser for useful insights.

Many thanks to my professors, teachers, and colleagues Lilian Karali, Efterpi Koskeridou, Konstantinos Moraitis, Konstantinos Kopanias, Despoina Kalesopoulou, Panagiota Kassi, Alexandros Faskianoudakis, Emi Paraskevaidou, Despoina Glyka, and Despoina Stamatiadou.

Special thanks to my family and especially to my mother for all their trust and continuous support. I am very grateful to Erich Draganits for his guidance and encouragement. Many thanks to my friends Konstantinos Chondroyiannis, Athanasios Papantonopoulos, Caroline Truffinet, Benjamin Huet, Michael Weissl, Alexander Preh, Mario Aigner-Torres, Susanna Hitzel, Dominik Hitzel, Gerhard Draganits, Monika Draganits, Ingrid Leser, Iris Leser, Julia Leser, Marko Leser, and Anton Leser.

Konstantina Saliari
Κωνσταντίνα Σαλιάρη

naturhistorisches museum wien

Contents

List of Figures

List of Tables

Abstract

Sand was a fortified 10th century site located at a river bend of the German Thaya, in the northern part of the Waldviertel (Lower Austria). The site was built very soon after Henry I signed a nine-year peace treaty with the Hungarians in 924 AD. For this reason, it has been proposed that the building of the site was enabled by this peace treaty. Sand fulfilled vital productive and economic functions, which makes it a *central site* in this period. Based on the regional relationship with other important settlements (e.g. Gars, Holzwiese/Schanze) and on its location, Sand may have been part of a supra-regional network. The archaeological data show that the site suffered an unexpected, violent event, probably involving the Magyars, after the battle of Lechfeld (955 AD). Thus, the site existed for only a very short period and the material excavated there provides a well-defined time window to the Early Middle Ages.

The excavations brought to light five distinctive areas: a) the central structure, b) the upper settlement terrace (Sand 1), c) the lower settlement terrace (Sand 2), d) the Westwall area, and e) the Nordwall area. The archaeological finds indicate that Sand was a production centre, with intensive activities taking place in some of the areas. The most intensive economic activities were detected at the upper settlement terrace and the Westwall area. The analysis of the archaeological material points towards a relatively self-sustaining way of life and indicates that the inhabitants tried to serve their own daily needs. The finds and the architectural elements witness different social hierarchies. Precious archaeological objects including a metal bridle, a horseshoe, and parts of metal armour indicate the presence of an elite group, probably mounted cavalry.

In total, 9830 animal bones were identified and analysed. They were found in the two settlement terraces (Sand 1, Sand 2) and the Westwall area. The archaeological and archaeozoological material was unearthed inside the objects (structures) at the ground level of each area. The animal bones were retrieved at a very good state of preservation. Most of the faunal remains represent food and production waste.

The faunal assemblages from Sand exhibited key characteristics for the analysis and interpretation of the material. Firstly, they can be placed in a very specific historical context. The site existed for less than 50 years and it was never again occupied. Moreover, the animal bones constitute primary waste, suggesting that the faunal remains were found where they were used and discarded.

The investigated faunal assemblages exhibit patterns of high social status for its inhabitants. Important features that suggest general prosperous conditions and consumers who enjoyed luxurious meals are: hunting activities for big-sized game, a wide spectrum of wild species, and several domesticated taxa slaughtered at the best age for meat consumption. These observations are in accordance with the archaeological interpretation, which points to the presence of an elite group.

Several indications suggest internal social hierarchies. Most of the evidence for elite behaviour derives from the upper settlement terrace (Sand 1). Many horse bones, which are usually connected to elite groups, were found here but only at a lower frequency in the other two areas. Also, the wild species are mostly represented by large, robust male individuals, symbols of prestige and bravery.

The analysis of the spatial distribution additionally highlights the various activities that took place at different areas of the site. In particular, Westwall is the only area where artefacts made of antlers were found and where more than 60% of the osseous artefacts were recovered, together with production waste. Moreover, the species representation, skeletal element distribution, and modifications point to further exploitation of skin and fur.

The quantitative results showed that the percentage of wild animals in Sand is almost 40%, which is a high value. In this work, it is suggested that hunting activities were mainly aimed at acquiring meat and raw materials. The presence of big-sized game shows that hunting for trophies cannot be excluded, but it apparently did not constitute the first priority.

Among the domesticated species, the prevalent taxon is cattle, followed by pigs, horses, and sheep/goats (only goats have been securely identified). Dogs and domesticated birds are very rare. The age and sex distribution of the economically most important species (cattle, sheep/goat, pig) suggests that the domesticated animals were imported to the site. These profiles also reveal an economic organisation that has rarely been observed elsewhere. An exception is the 16th century AD military camp at the ruins of Hauenstein in Styria (Austria).

The biological profiles (age and sex distribution) at Sand differed decisively from comparable sites. The most distinctive difference is the absence of a logistical balance. Most sites usually exhibit a mutual compromise between consumers and producers (peasants). This balance is important for a sustainable animal economy. In Sand, however, all the economically important domesticated species were slaughtered at a young age stage (immature animals and young adults); this might guarantee ideal meat quality, but it demonstrates the absence of an economic regulation between consumers and producers. Therefore, it is suggested that the inhabitants of Sand conducted an opportunistic requisition of animals, significantly influencing the long-term economy of the producers. Interestingly enough, the osseous artefacts and the analysis of the butchery marks from Sand show that the residents had comparably little experience in handicrafts.

The combination of the archaeological and archaeozoological observations suggests that the inhabitants of Sand exhibited more similarities to a military group than to farmers, traders, or an elite group. The historical record of this period would support the idea of a military group that acted carelessly and conducted raids against simple people, like peasants. An interesting analogue derives from the 10th century chronicle *Res gestae Saxonicae* by Widukind of Corvey.

Chapter 1

Introduction

1.1 Archaeozoology

Archaeological finds, written sources, and the pictorial record are some of the major sources that help us to better understand the past human societies and their way of life. Still, life is complicated; it has many different aspects, and the archaeological record offers only a fragmentary picture of the past. Thus, the interpretation of an archaeological site requires gaining as much information as possible from the finds discovered during the excavation campaigns.

A specific category of finds is biological (or environmental) remains, which include human and animal bones along with botanical remains. The focus of the present study is the analysis of animal bones, the field devoted to the investigation of the faunal remains known as archaeozoology. The investigation of animal bones is a fascinating but also demanding work and it can become even more challenging when certain important requirements are not fulfilled. The existence of a good and well-organised reference collection, space availability, and sufficient light sources are key requirements.

Studying faunal material is crucial for archaeology because it can bring to light a rich spectrum of information. Animal bones signify cognitive abilities, technological level and know-how, social status (inequality and differences), and economic structures (exchange and trading); they are markers of identity (rituals and taboos related to animals), they can visualize power (precious animal fur as visual symbols), and they can carry emotional meanings (emotional relationship between animals and people). Even if it is not always possible to find evidence for all the aforementioned aspects, it does not mean that they did not exist.

The analysis of faunal remains must be systematic and follow certain basic steps. The first crucial step is the identification. This process is a combination of knowledge and experience and can cost lot of time and energy. Archaeozoologists usually have to deal with large amounts of fragmented pieces that might represent a very wide spectrum of domesticated and wild species. The next steps are quantification, age and sex estimation, body part representation, study of modifications, and morphometric investigation. The information gained during the analysis of the material is of great significance for the final results and their interpretation.

The interpretation of the material can be influenced by many factors; taphonomy is one of them. The study of the taphonomic processes offers a vital contribution to archaeozoological studies. Significant information can be gained about the local environmental conditions and accompanying organisms, changes in the bone morphology and structure, and human practices. The taphonomic processes could be divided in three major categories: a) physicochemical processes, b) biological processes, and c) anthropogenic factors. The physicochemical processes include the environmental parameters that affect the material, such as weathering, soil, and marine/fluvial environment. The biological processes include the effect of plants (roots) and animals (carnivores, rodents, herbivores, and marine organisms) on the bones. The anthropogenic processes include diet (butchering marks etc.), manufacture of artefacts, burial customs (fire etc.), and the excavation techniques.

The interpretation of the material can become even more complicated considering that the recovery site is sometimes not the place where the material was primarily used or processed. This means that the recovery site is only the site of final deposition. These factors make it difficult to interpret and reconstruct the biography of archaeological finds.

Dating and the stratigraphic sequence are two major factors that can strongly influence any interpretation. In cases where characteristic finds are absent, such as pottery (e.g. in graves) it is difficult – and sometimes expensive – to correctly date the material. Conversely, it is equally possible that the dating of faunal remains and material culture differs. When significant archaeological information is missing (i.e. the archaeological context), it is sometimes better to avoid analysing (or over-interpreting) the material.

Moreover, it can be difficult to understand the formation of the material in terms of time. This means that it is not always possible to determine whether an assemblage was accumulated within weeks, months, or even years. Additionally, the amount of the material studied should be sufficient for statistical processing. Small assemblages might be random, and new material can significantly change the results.

Finally, many additional factors can influence the interpretation of faunal assemblages, including personal scientific interests. Archaeozoologists, similarly to archaeologists, are people with a specific social and scientific background, opinions, and experiences, which might influence the approach, the methodology, the scientific questions, and ultimately the results.

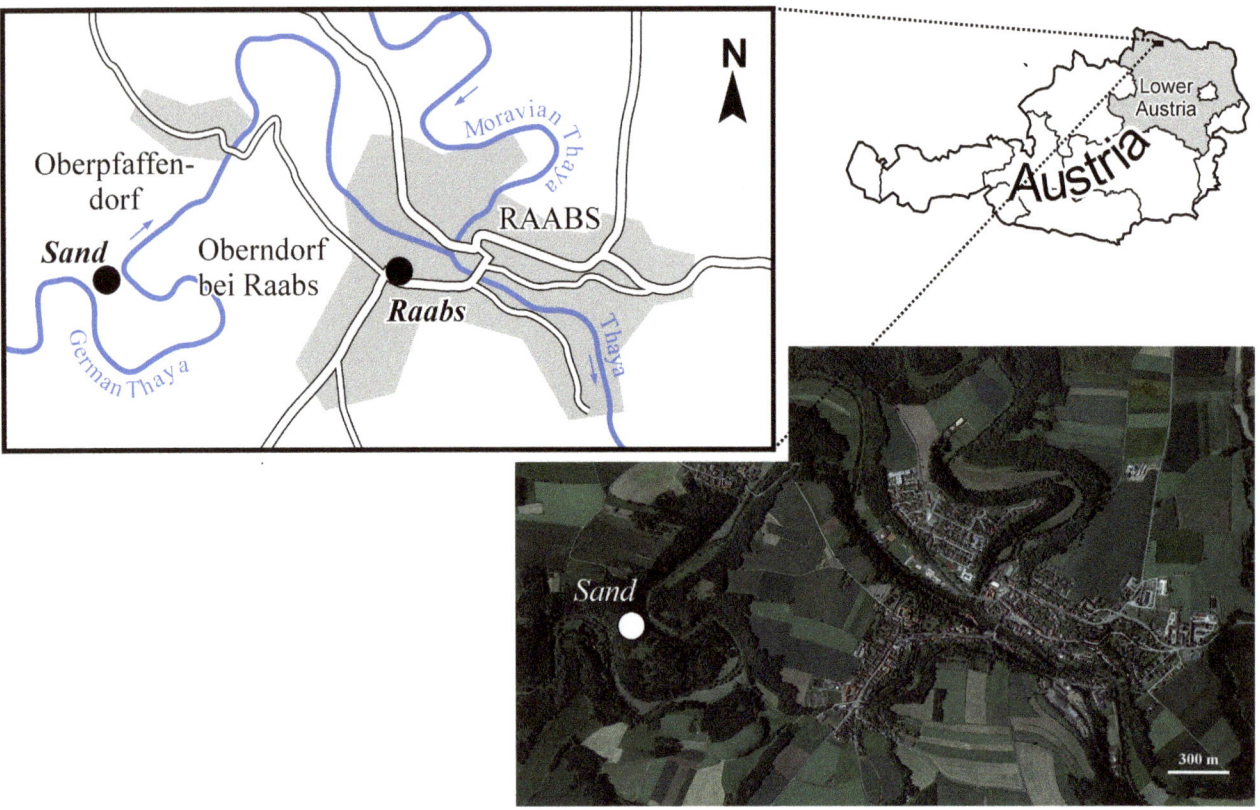

Figure 1. Location of Sand in a river bend of the Thaya (Waldviertel, Lower Austria). Source: Satellite image: Google Earth (6th June 2014).

1.2 The site of Sand and its archaeozoological context

Sand was an early medieval stronghold in Lower Austria that was erected around 930 AD and it was destroyed in the second half of the 10th century (Figure 1). The site was discovered by Kurt Bors in 1992 and excavations were conducted by Sabine Felgenhauer-Schmiedt (Institut für Urgeschichte und Historische Archäologie,[1] Universität Wien) from 1993 to 2008.

Sand combines practical and scientific characteristics that make the site a very interesting case study. To begin with the practical factors, the material derives from a well-defined period of the Early Middle Ages based on dendrochronological analysis (Grabner 2002, 975–976). Moreover, the destruction of the site some years after its erection indicates that the observable trends and patterns pertain to a very short period of maximally 50 years. This helps place the material in a very specific historical context. Another practical reason was the quantity of the faunal remains. In total, Sand produced more than 9000 animal bones, which is significant for statistically processing the material. Finally, the material represents mainly primary waste, which is important for the discussion, interpretation, and conclusions.

Additional factors concern the interesting archaeological and historical background of the site. The role of Sand in the political scenery of the early medieval period is enigmatic. Questions related to the identity of the inhabitants of the site, their political connections, and the reasons for the erection of the stronghold remain unknown; written sources are absent.

Finally, a preliminary investigation of the faunal remains by Pucher and Schmitzberger (1999b, 111–121) exhibited a high scientific potential. In their analysis of the material from the upper settlement terrace (Sand 1), the authors concluded that many vital questions regarding the economic strategy and logistical organisation of the site remain to be answered.

1.3 Research questions and structure

The main aims of this work are to understand the socio-economic organisation of the site, the strategies employed for the exploitation of the natural resources, and the interaction between providers (peasants) and consumers (inhabitants of the stronghold) based on the faunal material. Information on the socio-economic structures is crucial and can deliver important evidence for the way of life and the identity of the inhabitants. Thus, another major challenge is to approach historical questions through the study of animal bones. In order to meet these aims, the present work has been divided into five main chapters.

- Chapter 1 includes a brief introduction, the archaeozoological context of the site, and the research questions.

---

[1]   Former Institut für Ur- und Frühgeschichte.

- Chapter 2 presents information about the site, the archaeological background, the historical context, and the animal bones.
- Chapter 3 contains the methodology.
- Chapter 4 presents the analysis of the material per species and is subdivided into two major parts, where the domesticated and wild animals are separately treated.
- Chapter 5 contains the discussion and interpretation.

Chapter 2

Site and Material

2.1 Site

2.1.1 Location

Sand is located at the northern part of the wooded area of Waldviertel, which is the north-western region of Lower Austria (Niederösterreich) near the Austrian border with Czech Republic (Figure 1). Important landscape features of the region include the rivers Thaya and Kamp. The site of Sand was erected in the woods at a bend of the Thaya River, which offered natural protection. The Thaya has two major tributaries, the Moravian and the so-called German Thaya; both tributaries meet at Raabs, 1.6 km from Sand. The distance from Sand to the modern Czech border is just 8 km.

The location of Sand at the later border between Germans and Slavs[1] is of key significance for understanding the role of the site in the political scenery of that period. According to Dingley (2006, 95–104) the Thaya River formed a sort of *limes* between Germans and Slavs, where a number of forts and/or fortresses existed. Based on the present state of research, the location of Sand in a previously unsettled area of Waldviertel might indicate efforts of expansion, probably in connection to an important trade route (Kühtreiber & Obenaus 2017, 189). In this context, Sand´s location close to the river increased security, provided an abundant water supply and connection possibilities along the German Thaya Valley towards the north and towards the east, as well as along the nearby Kamp River towards the south.

2.1.2 Environmental setting

The biography of the investigated site is constrained not only by the historical horizon (see below), which incorporates the political, social, economic, and cultural part, but also by the natural framework in which the historical and social events took part. In this context, the fields of ecology, geology, and climate are essential in better understanding and reconstructing the environmental conditions under which the inhabitants of Sand lived and acted. Concerning the archaeozoological interpretation, understanding the environmental setting is important in order to comprehend the existence, dominance, absence, and combination of species.

2.1.2.1 Geology

Geologically, Waldviertel is part of the Bohemian Massif that forms a plateau extending from northern Austria into Czech Republic and Germany, comprising metamorphic rocks of the Variscan orogeny. This region is mainly characterized by a relative hilly topography with an average altitude of 750 m and several deeply incised valleys. The most common rock types are granite and gneiss, followed by granulite, marble, and amphibolite (Schuster et al. 2015). Sand is located in the Moldanubian tectonic unit and is locally situated on gneiss (Kollmitzer Gneis); the area directly on the opposite side of the river (right-hand side) comprises an alternation of biotite gneiss and amphibolite (Raabser Serie) (Jenček et al. 1987). An overview of the lithologies and mineral resources can be found in Steininger (2008).

The Waldviertel is characterized by a basement plateau, dissected by rivers, including the rivers Zwettl (west), Thaya (north), Kamp (at the middle and at the eastern part), Krems (south) and Ypser (south). The Thaya River comprises the so-called German Thaya, originating in Waldviertel, and the Moravian Thaya originating in the Czech Republic. Both rivers have their confluence close to castle (Burg) Raabs, where the Thaya River has a mean run-off of about 44 m³/s. The hydrological setting is clearly a very important component of Sand, located at a narrow river bend of the German Thaya River, where the river is incised more than 40 m into the surrounding plateau.

The soils mainly reflect existing rock types and climatic conditions. Generally, soils of the Waldviertel are dominated by different types of brown earth and podsol (Kilian et al. 1993, 56; BFW 2016), which are not regarded as being very rich concerning agricultural productivity.

Soil type and the climatic conditions[2] also created the abundant peat bogs once present in the Waldviertel, which are no longer visible after amelioration efforts during the Second World War. The same factors have a great impact on the flora and fauna of the region as well. The peat bogs were adjoined by low-growing woody vegetation. The landscape is dominated by mixed woodland of spruces, firs, beeches, and oak trees; the name Waldviertel describes the general landscape (German *Wald* = woods). Concerning climate and soil, until today the Waldviertel is regarded as an agriculturally poor region. Important crops include

---

[1] 11th century AD.

[2] The process of weathering is important in that case.

potatoes, rye, oat, flax, and poppy. The timber industry is also quite important.

2.1.2.2 Present-day climatic conditions

Based on its variable topography and especially the Alps, Austria shows many different climatic regions. Sand is located at an altitude of c. 450 m above sea level (asl) in the eastern part of the Bohemian Massif, which forms an undulating plateau ranging from c. 200-1400 m asl. The climate of Sand is classified as cool boreal (Kilian et al. 1993, 55) and is a result of its location in Central Europe in a marginal area on the plateau close to areas influenced by Pannonian climates towards the east. The closest climate data collected by the Zentralanstalt für Meteorologie und Geodynamik (ZAMG) are those from Japons, about 9 km southeast of Sand at an altitude of 520 m. The mean daily temperature in January, the coldest month, is -2.7°C and the mean daily temperature in July, the warmest month, is 16.8°C. The mean annual precipitation is 588.8 l/m², with main precipitation between June and August (ZAMG 2002).

2.1.2.3 Palaeo-climatic conditions – The Medieval Warm Period (MWP)

Sand dates into the 10th century AD, which is within the so-called Medieval Warm Period or Medieval Climatic Anomaly or Medieval Climate Optimum, all of which refer to a favourable climatic period of the European Middle Ages, with the warmest period between c. 950 and 1250 AD (Glaser 2001, 61–92; Mann et al. 2009, 1256–1260). A series of studies based on the investigation of tree rings, sediments, pollen, glaciers, and even historical written sources indicate that during this period Europe experienced climatic stability consisting of milder winters, less extreme conditions, and drier summers.

It is difficult to call this period a global phenomenon because different spatial and temporal patterns have been recorded. Favourable climatic events have appeared at different times for the various regions worldwide (e.g. Xoplaki et al. 2016, 229–252). The investigation of ice cores shows that Greenland experienced a warm event at around 1000 AD, whereas Eastern China exhibited warm conditions during the 11th and 12th centuries (Mann 2002, 514–516). Local differences have been observed also in Europe, demonstrating regional variability (Markonis et al. 2012; Büntgen & Tegel 2011, 14–15). For instance, severe winters were recorded for the Eastern Mediterranean during that period. Differences in the hydro-meteorological conditions between the western and eastern part of Mediterranean have been also observed (Markonis et al. 2012).

The geological record of the Alps confirms favourable climatic conditions for Central Europe during the MWP. According to Luetscher et al. (2013, 1073–1081), coarse crystalline cryogenic cave carbonates (CCC$_{coarse}$) from the Western Alps can provide valuable information concerning hydrology, melting, and warm events. That study suggests

that the thawing of ice-filled cavities and subsequent flow of water through ice-free conduits is a perceivable result of warming climate. Similar results have been suggested by Mangini et al. (2005, 741–751). The isotopic composition of a stalagmite from the Spannagel cave in the Central Alps showed that the highest temperatures of the investigated period occurred during the MWP, the lowest during the period 1400-1850 AD (Little Ice Age).

The Medieval Climatic Optimum is characterized by humid and mild summers along with milder winters. These results are confirmed by the tree-ring data, which exhibit distinct warmer and drier periods for Central Europe (Büntgen & Tegel 2011, 14–15). In contrast, the following Little Ice Age (LIA) (Grove 2004) is characterized by extreme and cold winters and a much higher precipitation, which have been associated with historic catastrophes in Europe (Glaser 2001, 61–92). Similar to the MWP, the LIA also shows regional and temporal differences.

2.1.3 Archaeological research and interpretation

Sand covers an area of 0.7 ha and it consists of five different parts (Felgenhauer-Schmiedt 2001, 85–106; 2006, 253–268; 2011, 551–559; 2012, 57–81): a) the central structure (*Burghügel*), b) two settlement terraces, the upper (Sand 1) and lower terrace (Sand 2) in the SE part, c) the Westwall (WW) and Nordwall (NW) areas. In these parts, 28 settlement features (termed objects by the excavator) have been totally excavated. The archaeological finds show that the end came suddenly; a major fire event took place and its traces can be detected especially at the two settlement terraces.

This chapter provides a short description of the areas of Sand along with information on and when possible an explanation of the settlement features. A detailed view is provided by Figure 3.

At the **central structure (*Burghügel*)** the excavation yielded stone foundations, which suggest the existence of a wooden house. Importantly, the house at the *Burghügel* is built at the highest part of the stronghold. This is also where precious findings (e.g. jewellery) have been retrieved. The distinctive location of this structure has been interpreted as a tendency for separation of the elite groups that later developed (Felgenhauer-Schmiedt 2011, 551–559). All the other settlement features that have been excavated at the two settlement areas and at the areas of Westwall and Nordwall are never solitary and they are located at the interior side of the fortification. Apparently, the central structure (*Burghügel*) was inhabited by the lord of the stronghold and thus held a special position (Felgenhauer-Schmiedt pers. comm.).

The **upper settlement terrace** (Sand 1) was protected by a strong fortification at the southern part. A ditch and a dry stone wall constituted the fortification. The settlement features were found at the interior side of the fortification and they were destroyed during a violent conflagration.

Object 6 at the western part of the terrace indicates that the construction was done with great care; at the interior of this object, the largest hearth has been found. This object has been interpreted as the residence of a local administrator (Felgenhauer-Schmiedt pers. comm.). Objects 2, 3, 4, 5, 7 and 8 were significantly smaller. Two cupola furnaces have been found in Object 3.

The findings that have been unearthed indicate intensive economic activities. In particular, objects 3, 4, and 5 provided abundant pottery and pottery waste, suggesting production at the site. Intensive economic activities related to pottery processing took place at Object 7 too; there, the excavation brought to light unbaked and baked pieces of pottery. Finds from objects 4, 5, 6 and 7 indicate that metal (slags) and textile (spindle whorls) processing was also done in this area. The highest number of spindle whorls was found in Object 5. Most of the botanical remains (Popovtschak 1998, 758–762; Kohler-Schneider & Vitalos 2009, 1258–1262) were excavated at Object 3 and especially Object 5 (Felgenhauer-Schmiedt forthcoming).

The **lower settlement terrace** (Sand 2) was protected by a massive fortification at the southern part. The fortification was consisted of a ditch (outer side), a dry stone wall, and wooden blocks filled with stones and soil (inner side). The architectural features were erected at the interior side of the fortification, similar to the upper settlement terrace. Object 13 at the western part presents special characteristics, similar to Object 6 at the upper settlement terrace. This object has been interpreted as the residence of another administrator, who would have been responsible for this part of the site (Felgenhauer-Schmiedt forthcoming).

At this part of the site the material culture indicates significantly less economic activity as opposed to the upper settlement terrace and Westwall area. The excavation yielded post holes, grindstones (Objects 10-14), botanical remains, including cereals (Object 9), and a few spindle whorls (Objects 9, 11, 12, 13, 14). The objects of this terrace have been interpreted as resting rooms (Objects 11, 12, 14), but also as places where products might have been stored for trading (Object 10) (Felgenhauer-Schmiedt forthcoming).

Westwall area (WW) exhibited only a stone wall as fortification. However, the archaeologist of the site assumes that wooden blocks, which have not been preserved, would have supported the stone wall. In some areas of Westwall, intensive economic activities have been noted, but it remains challenging to interpret the function of Objects 18, 19, 20 (Figure 2), 22, and 23 (Felgenhauer-Schmiedt forthcoming). The main finds include pottery and animal bones. Metal processing, as demonstrated at the upper settlement terrace, has not been documented. At Objects 16 and 17, economic activities took place; in Object 16 spindle whorls and grindstones came to light; fragments of rock crystal indicate that it was processed at the site. Fewer findings were recorded from Object 17 (Felgenhauer-Schmiedt forthcoming).

Figure 2. Westwall area, Object 20. Source: Felgenhauer-Schmiedt.

Object 21 produced a high concentration of spindle whorls and one loom weight, indicating textile production. In this object, faunal remains with a high concentration of cranial elements have been excavated. Note that in Object 21 the soil was – in comparison to other finds – glossy and greasy. The Objects 24 and 25 seem to be connected to the central structure (*Burghügel*); they contain hearths and a clay floor (Felgenhauer-Schmiedt forthcoming).

The Westwall area is the only location where artefacts made of antlers were manufactured and where a high frequency of bone artefacts have been yielded (63%). The presence of semi-finished bone artefacts and of production waste indicates that they were made on-site. One bone needle, appropriate for skin processing, was also discovered. The potential processing of skin and fur has been indicated by the faunal remains (Saliari & Felgenhauer-Schmiedt 2017, 95–114). In summary, this area produced evidence strongly related to the intensive processing of animal material (Felgenhauer-Schmiedt forthcoming).

Similarly to Sand 2, the fortification at the **Nordwall area** (NW) consists of a dry stone wall and wooden blocks filled with stones and soil. No finds indicating economic activities were discovered here. Object 15 yielded neither slags nor spindle whorls (Felgenhauer-Schmiedt pers. comm.).

In **Sand**, the archaeological finds indicate that each area had a different character. Often the architectural features of these areas indicated a multifunctional role (Felgenhauer-Schmiedt forthcoming). The characterisation of these features is not always simple, but it seems that the rooms excavated in Sand are apparently related to economic activities (workshops, production places) as well as to other aspects of daily life (resting rooms, depots, etc.).

Based on the processing of the different materials, Sand 1 seems to hold a special place in comparison to Sand 2 and the Westwall area; for instance, even if non-ferrous metals have been retrieved in limited number, they mainly derive from Sand 1 (Felgenhauer-Schmiedt forthcoming). Although the political power under which the inhabitants of

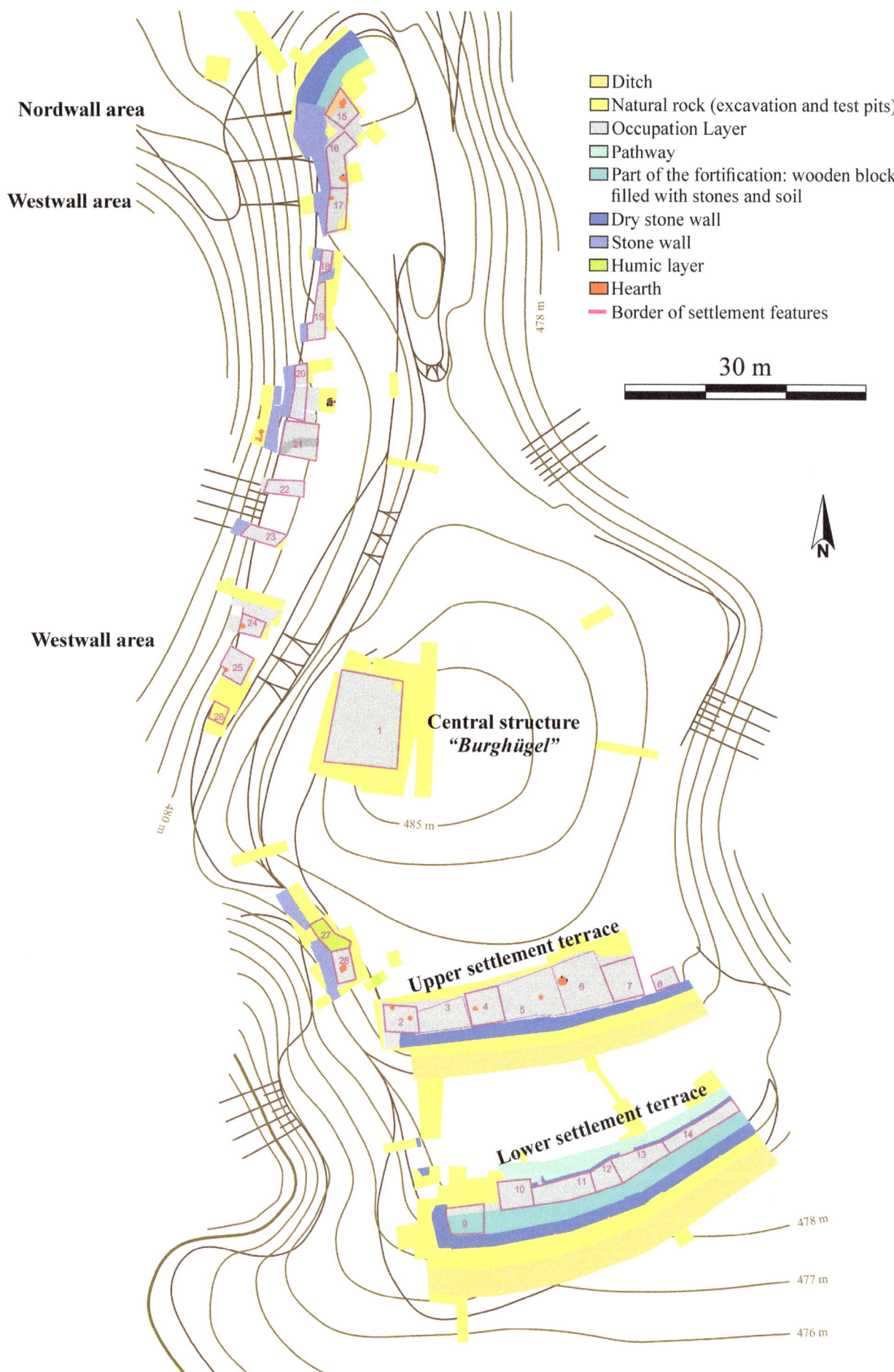

Nordwall area

Westwall area

Westwall area

Ditch
Natural rock (excavation and test pits)
Occupation Layer
Pathway
Part of the fortification: wooden blocks filled with stones and soil
Dry stone wall
Stone wall
Humic layer
Hearth
Border of settlement features

30 m

N

Central structure *"Burghügel"*

Upper settlement terrace

Lower settlement terrace

478 m

480 m

485 m

478 m

477 m

476 m

Figure 3. Overview of excavation areas at Sand. Source: Felgenhauer-Schmiedt.

Sand acted remains unknown, the material culture indicates strong connections to the north (Slavic populations) but also to the south (Felgenhauer-Schmiedt pers. comm.). An interesting observation concerning the archaeological finds was the huge amounts of retrieved pottery (750 kg). According to the excavator, this phenomenon has been observed at some Slavic castles. Other important materials, beyond clay and metals, were wood, plants, and materials from the animals such as bone, fur, and skin. The amount of carbonised plant remains is impressive, indicating a rich diet for the inhabitants of Sand, including wheat, barley, emmer, oat, and millet.

The analysis of the archaeological findings shows that the residents tried to cover most of their own needs. In Sand, production played a central role; raw materials were imported from the surroundings, and imported objects indicate small-scale trading activities (Felgenhauer-Schmiedt 2001, 85–106). The excavated defensive walls and houses as well as the archaeological finds suggest that Sand harboured different social hierarchies and that some type of elite group was present. Significant archaeological finds including a metal bridle, a horseshoe, and parts of metal armour were retrieved. These finds are an important indication of hierarchy because they did not belong to everyday equipment. They were special pieces that suggest complicated processing and limited access. The existence of such finds points to a group of mounted warriors (Felgenhauer-Schmiedt 2012, 57–81).

2.1.4 Archaeozoology of Sand: previous investigations and state of research

The first study on the [There has been prelim analysis] conducted at the Natural History Museum of Vienna and focussed on material from the upper settlement terrace (Sand 1) (Pucher & Schmitzberger 1999a, 355–378; 1999b, 111–121). The comparison of these results with faunal remains from castle Raabs shows considerable differences related to the socio-economic organisation and structure (Riedel & Pucher 2008, 159–194).

In total, 3172 bones have been identified and analysed from layers of the upper settlement terrace (Pucher & Schmitzberger 1999a, 355–378; 1999b, 111–121). Those investigations showed that, based on the number of identified specimens (NISP) and the weight analysis, the wild animals accounted for more than 40% of the total material; the minimum number of individuals (MNI) proved that the wild fauna prevails (54.6%). The dominant animals among the wild species were red deer, wild boar, and European bison. A high number of the most significant big-sized wild species was represented by male adults, suggesting noble hunting activities (Pucher & Schmitzberger 1999a, 355–378; 1999b, 111–121).

Among the domesticated taxa the prevalent species was cattle with 64.1% (NISP), followed by pig (23.2%), goat (7.3%), horse (3.6%), and fowl (1.8%). The analysis of age at death and sex ratio provided strong indications

for the existence of socially privileged meals (Pucher & Schmitzberger 1999a, 355–378, 1999b, 111–121). Morphometric examination of the material yielded some interesting observations regarding the domesticated cattle: a very small number of cranial fragments suggested the existence of a second cattle group (Pucher & Schmitzberger 1999a, 355–378).

The first results of the archaeozoological investigation corroborate those produced during the archaeological study, supporting the existence of an elite group in Sand. Nonetheless, these preliminary observations regarding the general composition of the material (including the prevalence of species, quantification, and age/sex estimation) were surprising for the region and the period because there are scarcely other parallel examples. Many key questions related to economic and social aspects remained open (Pucher & Schmitzberger 1999a, 355–378; Pucher 2009a, 259–272). A preliminary investigation of the new material from the lower settlement terrace (Sand 2) and the Westwall area showed important differences to the material from Sand 1, making the study of the material fascinating yet challenging.

2.1.5 Historical context

Many factors have influenced the emergence and evolution of medieval Europe. Sand is part of the early medieval world, making it important to understand the political landscape of the 10th century in order to better appreciate the decisions that lead to the erection and ultimate destruction of Sand. Finding an answer in such historical questions is never easy, especially when written sources are absent, but it is inconceivable to exclude the historical scenery from an interdisciplinary approach that benefits from an additional or alternative interpretation through the archaeozoological analysis.

The historical overview clearly proves that every historical event is influenced not only by the political situation in a ferocious game of power, but also by other factors such as the environmental and geographic framework, the existence of local populations, waves of newcomers, previously well-established or fragile traditions and tendencies. All these factors are compounded by the fights among the existing forces in Europe between the Franks, Lombards, Byzantine Empire, and Bulgarians, along with the antagonism between the Roman Catholic Church and Byzantine Christianity, and the different economic systems. Sand belongs to a period that is still fluid, and the balances have the potential to change under a new alliance or by taking advantage of other parameters.

The early 10th century starts with the alliance of Germans and Slavs in an effort to defeat the Magyars (902 AD). During the first half of the 10th century, many Hungarian expeditions were in response to calls from the Byzantine Emperor, the Germanic and French kings (Molnár 2001, 17). During the Hungarian raids, the Kingdom of Moravia fell (906) and the Bavarians were seriously defeated twice

– in 907 (Pressburg) and in 910 (first battle of Lechfeld). The typical warfare strategies of the Magyars proved to be a significant factor promoting their expansion. At the Italian, French, and German monasteries, people were praying: *De sagittis Hungarorum libera nos, Domine* (Benda et al. 1988, 21).

The Sand site was also destroyed probably by the Magyars in the second half of the 10th century. According to the dendrochronological analysis (Grabner 2002, 975–976), the erection of the site took place only a few years earlier, at around 930 AD; this was a peaceful period for the Germans and the Magyars. In 924, Henry I "the Fowler", the first of the Ottonian Dynasty, agreed to pay the levy in return for a nine-year peace. Usually, the Magyars plundered an area until the local ruler agreed to pay an annual levy. This situation was favoured by an array of internal problems and the instability that Western Europe had to face; even Byzantium accepted to pay a kind of annual tribute (Molnár 2001, 16).

During this period, Henry gained some time and improved and re-equipped his military forces (Cartledge 2011, 9). Nine years later, in 933, Henry I rejected renewing the payment of the annual tribute, a decision that resulted to the Battle of Merseburg in 933, where the Hungarians were defeated. The key consequence of this loss was the termination of the levies (Kontler 2002, 47). Nevertheless, the Magyars were still tempted by the wealth of other groups and continued their attacks in southern Germany, France, Switzerland, Italy, and Constantinople. The situation began changing in 936, under Otto I the Great, King of Germans (Makkai 1990, 13; Cartledge 2011, 9–10).

In the mid-10th century, namely in 951, Henry of Bavaria defeated a Magyar troop in northern Italy, and several years later, in 955, Otto I, after successfully resolving internal problems and difficulties, achieved a decisive victory at the well-known battle of Lechfeld (Majoros 2008, 55–56). Bulcsu and Lél, the Magyar leaders, were hanged as common criminals (Makkai 1990, 14) and, according to a legend, only seven survivors were able to return to Hungary (Cartledge 2011, 11). The victory at the battle of Lechfeld nearly terminated the raids into the West and also had enormous social consequences, especially for the Hungarian society. The destruction of Sand apparently took place after 955 AD (Felgenhauer-Schmiedt pers. comm.).

An interesting question is the role of Sand in this specific historical context. This issue presents many difficulties, partly due to the absence of written sources and the short life-span of the stronghold. As noted above, the site was erected during a period of peace between the Germans and the Magyars (Felgenhauer-Schmiedt 2006, 253–268). The assumption is therefore that those responsible for the erection of the site probably took advantage of the peace-treaty (Felgenhauer-Schmiedt pers. comm.). During this period Henry tried to consolidate his power by erecting fortifications and sites with important economic and

military roles, while the Magyars continued their attacks and raids.

In general the 10th century is characterized by many new castles in Bavaria and strongholds in Bohemia, indicating efforts of expansion (Felgenhauer-Schmiedt forthcoming). The emergence of fortified settlements during the 9th and 10th centuries in Central Europe indicates important socioeconomic and political changes (Herold 2016). It nonetheless remains difficult to understand who was responsible for the organisation of Sand; as already mentioned, there are indications that suggest connections to the north (Slavic populations), such as pottery and construction techniques (Felgenhauer-Schmiedt 2008, 298–321), but also to the south; moreover, the area would have been of great interest for the Germans as well. According to Daim (2007, 38), Sand might have been part of a network of fortifications against the Hungarians, probably by Henry I.

One essential clue is the location of Sand, which indicates its importance (see chapter 2.1.1). This is also suggested by the erection of castle Raabs in close proximity several years later (Figure 1). Additionally, the archaeological finds and the preliminary archaeozoological investigation reveal patterns of wealthy behaviour, indicating the presence of an elite group. Therefore, despite the limited information, the site apparently played a multiple and important role.

2.1.6 Archaeological evidence for early medieval settlements in Lower Austria

During the early medieval period, a number of fortified (hilltop) settlements are documented in Lower Austria (Figure 4). These sites have been summarized under the term *central sites* (*Zentralorte*) in order to underline their economic role. Some of the most important sites, which have been thoroughly excavated and studied, are Gars-Thunau and Raabs. According to the present state of knowledge, there are a total of 16 early medieval *central sites* (Wawruschka 2009, 135–136).

Sand, as a fortified stronghold, has been included as a *central site*. Its characterization is based on applying the criteria proposed in the model of Gringmuth-Dallmer (2011, 431–440). According to the excavator, the functions recognized in Sand underline the importance of the site, which was probably part of a network with a supra-regional radius (Felgenhauer-Schmiedt forthcoming). This network could be imagined as a chain in which Sand is one knot in a complicated and well-organised system. This is an important approach, because it could help to better understand the political and economic scenery of Lower Austria and the role of the so-called *central sites* – particularly of Sand.

However, a better appreciation of the dynamics and the historical processes that took place in this part of Austria during the early medieval period requires more than

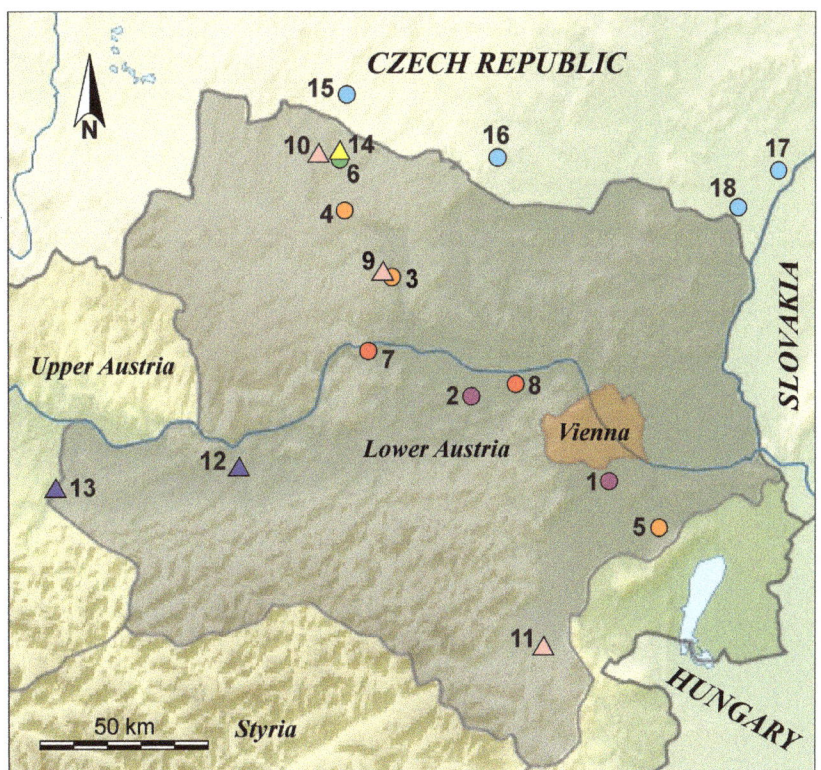

Figure 4. Topographical map with important early medieval sites from Lower Austria and the Czech Republic. Some sites from the Czech Republic have been added, due to their proximity to Lower Austria and to Sand. This map is based mainly on a) the publication of Herold (2007, 77–92), b) the work of Obenaus (2011, 529–549), c) pers. comm. with the archaeologist Pollak A. Map source: http://www.basemap.at/application/index.html.

studying strongholds and significant fortified settlements. A variety of different types of sites have been found in the region, including former Roman enclosures, open settlements, and single finds (Herold 2007, 77–92).

The role and significance of unfortified settlements is sometimes underestimated due to a lack of research. Many of the open rural sites remain unpublished or are only partly available in the form of preliminary reports (Wawruschka 2009, 9–13). Moreover, sometimes even if information is available on the existence of possible open settlements, they are not archaeologically documented (Purgstall). These finds are, however, important for our research, especially because we currently lack clear data on potential rural settlements in close proximity to Sand.

According to Wawruschka (2009), there are 36 remains of open settlements (e.g. Eggendorf, Hollabrunn, Michelstetten) and 135 (known and published) single finds, including pit houses, store pits, and wells (e.g. Bisamberg, Fugnitz, Rosenburg).

Due to the very limited amount of data, it is not always possible to interpret the spatial structure of the early medieval settlements or to find a pattern for the distribution of the sites. Some were apparently built on top of mountains and hills, along ancient routes, on former Roman sites, and close to rivers or other water sources (Wawruschka 2009, 129–134). This suggests known routes of trading and communication that were still active and did not lose their significance during the early medieval period. The March and Thaya rivers are characterized by a number of stretches

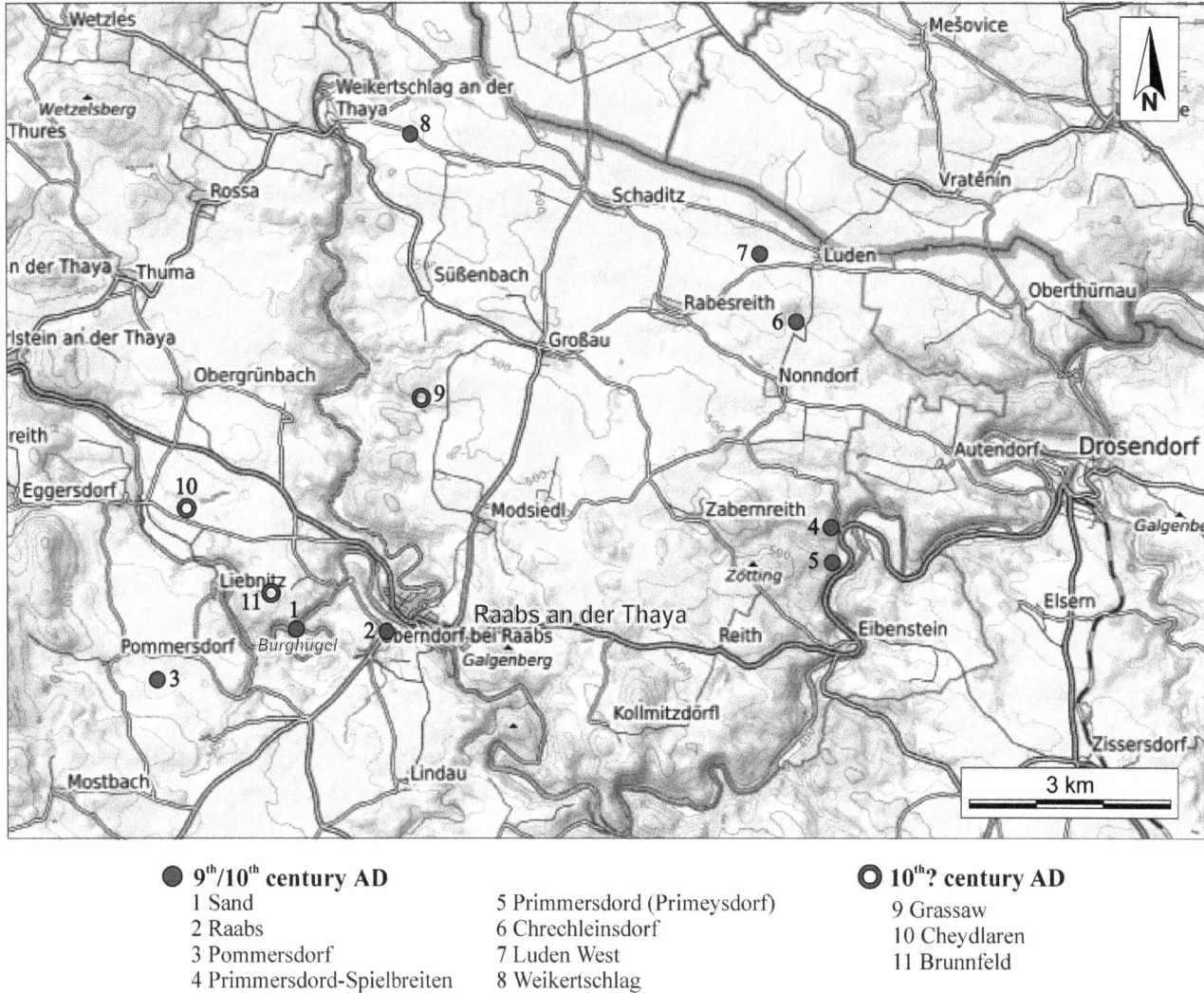

9ᵗʰ/10ᵗʰ century AD

1 Sand	5 Primmersdord (Primeysdorf)
2 Raabs	6 Chrechleinsdorf
3 Pommersdorf	7 Luden West
4 Primmersdord-Spielbreiten	8 Weikertschlag

10ᵗʰ? century AD

9 Grassaw
10 Cheydlaren
11 Brunnfeld

Figure 5. Topographic map with important sites from the 9ᵗʰ and 10ᵗʰ centuries AD around Sand (modified after Bors & Felgenhauer-Schmiedt 2000). Map source: http://www.basemap.at/application/index.html.

that were partly used even up until the 20ᵗʰ century. This strengthens the argument for a well-organised system of exchange as has been expressed after studying the fortified settlements.

The findings indicate that husbandry and agriculture were very important for the inhabitants of the open settlements (Wawruschka 2009, 132–134). Animal bones illustrate that pigs, cattle, small ruminants, and domestic fowl were the main domesticated species. The lowland forests were used to find food, fodder, and raw materials such as wood. Finally, the material culture suggests a great variety of activities including pottery production along with the processing of metals, textiles (abundant spindles), bones, and antlers (artefacts).

2.1.7 Archaeological finds from the immediate region of Sand during the 9ᵗʰ and 10ᵗʰ centuries AD

Sand might belong to the *central sites*, but its isolated character in the middle of the woods and the absence of a settlement potentially associated with the stronghold raise many questions about its actual character. This chapter is

therefore designed to understand how the historical landscape of the immediate region was formed during the 9ᵗʰ and 10ᵗʰ centuries AD. It presents finds that suggest human presence and activities (e.g. settlements) close to Sand (Figure 5).

However, as it has been previously discussed such an effort involved practical difficulties. One of the most crucial was the dating difficulties, due to the very low number of finds. Moreover, written sources are usually absent and when they exist, they do not always deliver information about the life of simple people (Bors & Felgenhauer-Schmiedt 2000, 9). In spite of these challenges, efforts were made to reconstruct the surroundings of the immediate region. Important material derives from the study conducted by Bors and Felgenhauer-Schmiedt (2000), who show that some sites close to Sand can be dated between the 9ᵗʰ and 10ᵗʰ centuries AD (Figure 5). These sites are:

- The unfortified site of Spielbreiten. Finds here indicate the existence of a small settlement probably inhabited by craftsmen. Part of the material has been dated to the 9ᵗʰ century AD (FÖ 36/1997, 895; 38/1999, 876–880; Bors & Felgenhauer-Schmiedt 2000, 84).

- Fragments of pottery have been retrieved 500 m away from Spielbreiten (Primeysdorf), suggesting the presence of a settlement. The finds indicate similarities to the pottery retrieved in Sand; accordingly, the existence of a settlement during the 10th century AD cannot be excluded (FÖ 35/1996, 568; Bors & Felgenhauer-Schmiedt 2000, 85).
- In Luden West, fragments of pottery and slags have been found, indicating the presence of a small settlement probably dating to the 10th century AD (Bors & Felgenhauer-Schmiedt 2000, 85).
- Between Luden and Nonndorf (Chrechleinsdorf), pottery sherds indicate the existence of a small settlement (Bors & Felgenhauer-Schmiedt 2000, 85).
- One ceramic fragment was found 900 m east of Pommersdorf (Pommersdorfer Graben) (Bors & Felgenhauer-Schmiedt 2000, 85).
- One ceramic fragment that can be probably dated to the 10th century AD derives from the area east of Weikertschlag (Bors & Felgenhauer-Schmiedt 2000, 86).
- The fortified site of Raabs yielded pottery fragments dated to the early medieval period (Bors & Felgenhauer-Schmiedt 2000, 84).

Additional sites were dated to the 10th century, but not with great certainty, including:

- Grassaw (10th?, 11th-13th century AD), 500 m away from the castle Oeden Grossau (FÖ 32/1993, 78; 34/1995, 746).
- Cheydlaren (10th /11th-16th century AD) (FÖ 33/1994, 640), 1 km east of Speisendorf.
- Brunnfeld (10th? 11th-15th/16th century AD) (FÖ 32/1993, 797), 700 m west of Oberpfaffendorf.

Although some evidence points to human activities close to Sand during the 9th and 10th centuries, no rural settlement can currently be chronologically associated to the site with certainty (Bors & Felgenhauer-Schmiedt 2000; Ruß, D. pers. comm.).[3] The available evidence shed more light on the character of the site, but future research is crucial for a better understanding of the cultural landscape of the region (Obenaus, M. pers. comm.).

2.2 Material

2.2.1 Quantification

Faunal assemblages have been found in the upper and lower settlement terraces and the Westwall area. In the framework of this work, 6658 bones and bone fragments weighing almost 158 kg have been analysed and investigated. The faunal material derives from the Westwall area and the lower settlement terrace (Sand 2) and is archived at the Museum of Natural History, 1. Department of Zoology, Archaeozoology. The material from the upper settlement

terrace (Sand 1) that has been already studied (Pucher & Schmitzberger 1999a, 355–378) is also included in order to deliver a more thorough analysis and interpretation of the site. The material from Sand 1 consists of 3172 animal bones (total weight 95 kg). Therefore, overall, the present work examines 9830 faunal remains weighing ca. 253 kg.

2.2.2 Archaeological context

According to the excavator Felgenhauer-Schmiedt the vast majority of the faunal assemblages represents primary waste. This indicates that the material was found in the context where it was used and discarded; it has not been disturbed since its original deposition (Figures 6, 7). Accordingly, an undisturbed context can offer valuable information concerning the time that it was created. Thus, the animal bones from Sand, which mainly represent food and production waste, can provide important information including the organisation of the site,[4] the social status of the people living and acting in the different areas,[5] and

Figure 6. Animal bone (radius of a horse) found in a hearth in Object 3 at the upper settlement terrace (Sand 1). Source: Felgenhauer-Schmiedt.

Figure 7. Upper settlement terrace (Sand 1), Object 5: occupation layer with archaeological findings and animal bones. Source: Felgenhauer-Schmiedt.

---

[3] More evidence derives mainly from the late 10th and especially the 11th century AD (Bors & Felgenhauer-Schmiedt, 2000).

[4] E.g. ways of dealing with rubbish.
[5] E.g. food waste can be used as a marker of social status.

the functional character of (at least) some architectural features.[6] The short lifespan of the site offers an additional advantage. Combined, these factors make Sand an archaeologically rare opportunity to trace behavioural patterns of a group of people in a specific time and space.

The excavations in Sand have been complicated by its topography and location, as well as by the site's irregular stony surface. The excavations were limited mostly to surface layers because there were very few indications for stratigraphy above the bedrock; traces of repairs have been observed on some architectural features and walls. The archaeological and archaeozoological material was found inside the Objects (structures) at the ground level of each area. Outside of these areas, in the open space of the stronghold, no finds have been retrieved, with only some exceptions. Gnawing marks by carnivores on the animal bones indicate that the material was lying on the surface. The big amount of waste inside the structures, where people worked and lived, raised many questions regarding the organisation of the daily life. The widespread material suggests lack of care and management (Felgenhauer-Schmiedt pers. comm.). Finally, the animal bones were in a very good state of preservation, as evidenced by numerous fragile bones of small-sized animals and of young individuals. Sieving was done during the excavation, which also supported the discovery of smaller fragments.

---

[6] E.g. the existence of workshops.

Chapter 3

Methodology

3.1 Identification

Identifying the material is the first important step in gaining an initial impression and to understand the composition of any archaeozoological assemblage. The identification process took place at the Museum of Natural History (1. Zoological Department, Archaeological Zoological Collection) by using the Adametz Collection, the Osteological Collection, and other archaeological material already studied and archived at the Museum.

In Sand, each bone was separately studied. The identification was firstly conducted at an element level (i.e. cranium, humerus, tibia, etc.). Doubtful fragments were excluded from the process of identification and therefore from all the other steps. Some fragments were impossible to identify even at an element level. This material was kept separately and stored under the label *unidentified*. Sometimes an element could be broadly identified, but not more concretely. For instance, a number of fragments of metapodials (especially from the diaphysis) were difficult to identify as metacarpals or metatarsals; therefore they are recorded as metapodials.

After the material was identified at element level, the next step is the species identification. The high numbers of wild animals made this process very challenging and thus some bones were difficult to categorize; for instance vertebrae, ribs, cranial fragments, and abundant fragments of long and flat bones resemble each other closely in several big-sized species.

There are also some species, which traditionally present difficulties in identification. Almost every assemblage requires using special criteria in order to separate the small ruminants (sheep/goat). A considerable amount of literature was available for this separation, including Boessneck et al. (1964, 1–129), Schramm (1967b, 107–133), Kratochvíl (1969a, 483–490), Payne (1969, 295–306), Prummel & Frisch (1986, 567–577), Pucher & Engl (1997), Helmer (2000, 29–38), Halstead et al. (2002, 545–553), Zeder (2006, 87–118), Zeder & Lapham (2010, 2887–2905), Zeder & Pilaar (2010, 225–242), and Salvagno & Albarella (2017).

In Sand, some species made this process even more complicated. A case in point is the wild Bovidae. A separate chapter discusses the identification process and the criteria of separation between European bison (*Bison bonasus*-BB) and aurochs (*Bos primigenius*- BP), or between domesticated pig (*Sus scrofa* f. *domestica*- SD) and wild boar (*Sus scrofa*- SS).

In order to present an as objective approach as possible, categories were added to indicate that separation was not always feasible. For example, there is a category termed sheep/goat (O/C), which summarizes unidentified fragments of small ruminants, and a category wild Bovidae because it was not possible to group all the fragments as European bison or aurochs.

3.2 Quantification

The quantification of the material is the next step and it reflects the general scenario concerning the economic organisation of the site. NISP (number of identified specimens), MNI (minimum number of individuals), and weight analysis have been mainly used. Each of these methods was applied during different stages of the analysis, depending on the question set. The biases inherent in each method are taken in mind when interpreting the results.

Important factors that bias NISP and MNI are related to identifiability, taphonomy, and cultural practices. In Sand the butchery marks were very intensive, resulting in a high number of fragments. Moreover, the recovery techniques and the processing of the material can also affect NISP (Reitz & Wing 2008, 192–193). The weight analysis is another method to evaluate the role of the species as meat suppliers (Ziegler 1990, 1–46). This is based on the close correlation between bone weight and meat weight. However, as the weight of the bones is related to the weight of the animal, the results favour the big and heavy animals.

The quantification methods yield only the relative frequencies of the taxa. Archaeozoologists study a very small and fragmentary piece of information that has survived taphonomic processes, excavation techniques, and laboratory treatment. This calls for critically viewing the sources. The material from Sand is considered to be representative; the excavation has been terminated and test pits did not bring to light evidence for more finds (Felgenhauer-Schmiedt pers. comm.).

3.3 Skeletal element representation / body part representation

The analysis of the skeletal element distribution offers valuable information including the way animals were transported to the site[1] and the existence of possible

---

[1] If they have been imported as whole individuals or if portions of the carcasses have been delivered.

activities.[2] This is an important step because the representation of the different body parts can be connected to aspects of daily life including the logistic organisation, possible socio-political changes, etc. (Müller 1978, 101–170). In this work the skeletal element representation is based on NISP and MNI; in Sand, comparing the weight analysis with other well-established models is risky because of difficulties in species identification. In some cases in order to interpret the distribution of the anatomical elements, the results have been compared with other case studies.

The frequency of skeletal elements is influenced by various factors including taphonomy, fragility of bones, excavation techniques, and cultural practices (Reitz & Wing 2008, 191). Compact bones such as mandibles have a better potential to survive than the soft and fragile parts of the cranium; usually crania are found in numerous pieces. Concerning long bones, parts of the forelimbs are better preserved than those of hindlimbs. Mechanically, the bones of the forelimbs carry the weight of the animal and are therefore more robust than the hindlimbs. The hindlimbs are mainly responsible for locomotion, which influences the nature of the bones and thus the state of preservation. Nonetheless, some differences have been also observed among these groups. For instance, radius and tibia are thought to be very robust elements, which survive better. Still, these bones have parts that are found more often than others. Generally, most tibia fragments derive from the distal epiphyses, and this is also the case in Sand.

Small compact bones such as tali, calcanei, and phalanges usually survive better and are therefore often used to calculate MNI. This explains why many statistics are based on such bones. Other small elements such as carpals and tarsals might also survive, but they are sometimes overlooked during excavations, as are certain other bones such as sesamoidea. Patellae, although small, are robust and survive better. The most common tarsal found in Sand is the os centroquartale, which is relatively big and robust.

Concerning cultural practices, factors that can affect the body part representation are butchering techniques, manufacture of artefacts out of osseous material, skinning etc. In the particular case of skinning various studies have shown that the different techniques and stages of this process have an impact on the presence or absence of specific skeletal elements (Prummel 1978, 399–422; Noddle 1994, 117–128; Bartosiewicz 1995; 2006, 457-478; Deschler-Erb 2012, 113–137; Rehazek & Nussbaumer 2012, 65–69).

3.4 Sex ratio and age at death

Numerous publications are based on age and sex reconstruction in order to address questions concerning human-animal relations (Marciniak 2014, 186–205).

Sex estimation and age at death are two very important parameters that help better understand the economic exploitation of the animals; the results that derive from such analyses are decisive for interpreting the lifestyle of a society and the character of the site (Zeder 2006, 87–118; Fischer 2014, 84–121). Many technical advances regarding aging and sexing of ancient animal bones have been achieved, and there is abundant literature that deals with further methodological improvements (O' Connor 2006, 1–8).

3.4.1 Sex ratio

The criteria used for sexing the faunal remains can significantly vary depending on the species. Importantly, it is generally possible to sex only adult individuals because they have fully developed all the anatomical features that need to be investigated.

Most ungulates (especially ruminants) can be sexed by studying the morphological features of pelvic bone (Figure 8), which is strongly influenced by the process of birth (Boessneck et al. 1964, 89; Lemppenau 1964, 20, 33–36; Pucher 2004, 363–403). Nonetheless, the morphological criteria used for the pelvic bone should be applied with caution, especially for domesticated animals, because many factors can influence the sex assessment, such as age, population´s variability, breed, exploitation, number of births, etc. For instance, cows that have been used as labour animals might bear better developed muscular marks than expected. Another important factor is population size. Populations of large-sized animals tend to exhibit more masculine characteristics than animals from populations comprising smaller individuals (Pucher 2013, 9–36). Finally, pelvis is a preferable element because it can survive many taphonomic processes.

Sex estimation can be also addressed on cranial elements (Degerbol & Fredskild 1970, 160–170), but this can be a demanding and difficult task. One important reason is the fragility of the cranium. Additionally, complete horn cores (cattle, sheep, goat, wild Bovidae) are scarce and usually exhibit a great variation in form and shape. For instance in the case of castrated cattle the age of castration affects the development of the bones and of the horn cores, complicating the identification. Cervidae can be also sexed based on their antlers. However, antlers are usually excluded from the quantification process because their presence is not always related to hunting but also to gathering activities, which considerably influences the interpretation.

Teeth or – for some species – alveoli (tooth sockets) can also be used for sexing animals such as pigs, wild boar, and horses (Hillson 2005; Pucher et al. 2007, 107–114). Some animals can also be sexed based on the penis bone (Carnivora), but this bone is very rarely found at excavations; its absence however, does not indicate lack of males. Dogs can be also sexed by the dimensions of the sacrum (Pucher pers. comm.).

---

[2] There are many publications that associate the over- or underrepresentation of specific parts with specific activities.

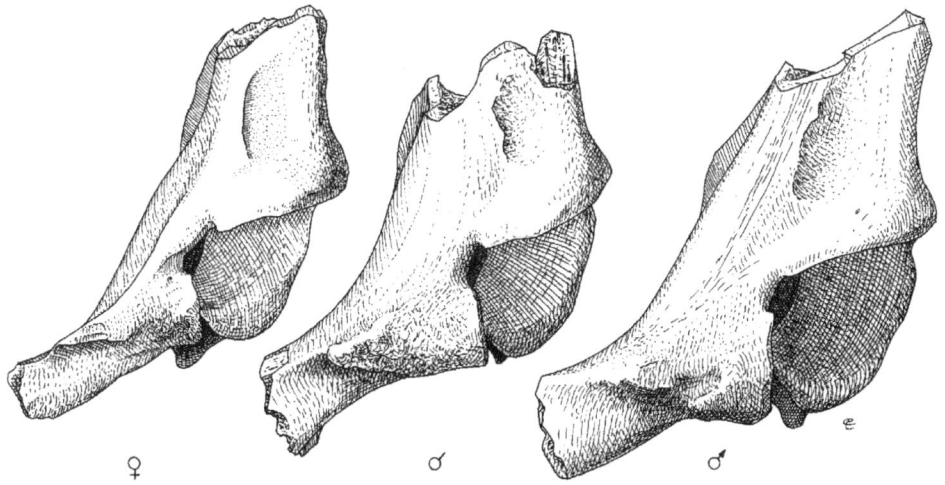

Figure 8. Pelvis of domesticated cattle representing (from left to right) a female, a castrated, and a male individual. Source: Pucher 2004, 363–403.

Estimating the sex distribution by the metapodials is challenging, because of the delicate differences that should be observed and due to the occasional presence of complete metapodials. Still this method is widely used and ancient DNA studies have often confirmed the osteometrical identification of sex based on metapodials (Fock 1966; Degerbol & Fredskild 1970, 160–170; Wiig 1985, 495–503; Albarella 1997, 37–47; Telldahl et al. 2012, 121–127; Davis et al. 2012, 1445–1454). This method has been additionally used in the case of Sand.

The analysis of cattle metapodials indicates that the size and proportions differ significantly among the sexes. Females have a relatively slender, thin and fragile corpus, whereas males are more robust, shorter in length, and have a wider corpus. Castrated animals are more elongated and relatively robust, but not as wide as the males. Castrated individuals might present a wider variation, depending on the age of castration. The distal epiphysis of the females is the narrowest and smallest. Males exhibit quite wide and robust epiphyses, whereas the castrated individuals have a relatively higher and more compact distal part, not as wide as the males. Publications such as Pucher 2013 (9–36) and Abd el Karem 2013b (97–104), which deal with local material, present the statistical processing of the metric data, in order to identify the sex by using metapodials.

In Sand, the sexing of fragments of metapodials was done macroscopically in comparison with other local material and whenerver possible by comparing with the existing metric data from other well-studied sites. The statistical processing of the material could not always take place, due to the low number of finds. Of course not all finds could be identified with certainty (in this case a questionmark is noted) and other finds remained unidentified.

The general proportions and size of other bones, such as the long bones, might also contribute to understanding the sex distribution of a population, but only as a tendency. This method is generally avoided.

Birds also bear some diagnostic features for sexing (Reitz & Wing 2008, 83–84). A relatively good indicator for sexing Galliformes (chicken, turkey, pheasant etc.) is the presence of a spur on the tarsometatarsus. Female individuals usually do not develop such a spur, although it is known to occur. In males it is well-developed and increases in size with age. Another method is by plotting measurements of various bone elements (especially of the maximal length).

Even if domesticated and wild fauna sometimes share common criteria for sexing, the wild fauna can be additionally sexed based on metric data due to the intensive sexual dimorphism that they present.[3] The metric data of some bones of domesticated animals are more difficult to interpret due to the presence of castrated animals. Identifying castrated animals is difficult and not possible for all the domesticated species.

The interpretation of sex distribution calls for caution because elements such as teeth, horn cores, and antlers are not necessarily related to the economic organisation of the site; they might indicate craft contexts (manufacture of artefacts, tanning activities) or they might have been used as prestige symbols (wild boar teeth). Finally, for the statistic processing a sufficient number of finds is necessary. In Sand, when the number of finds (for both the sex and age distribution) was low the statistical analysis was done with caution or in some cases was even avoided.

3.4.2 Age at death

The methodology followed for the assessment of age distribution is common for almost all the species that are analysed in this work. Aging can be conducted by examining the epiphyseal fusion, the eruption and wear stages of the deciduous and permanent teeth (Habermehl 1975, 1985), the morphology and texture of the horn cores/antlers, and by investigating other characteristics such as

---

[3] Usually males are larger, but in some species females might be larger (species dependent).

the texture of the bones, and the development of muscle marks.

The epiphyseal fusion is important, especially when the number of other elements such as teeth is low. However, it presents some difficulties. The proximal and distal epiphyses are fused for some bones at a different stage and thus one bone might be recorded twice if the different parts are found separately, as adult and as immature/subadults (depending on the stage of fusion). Moreover some stages of the immature individuals, such as the neonati, are underrepresented because they are included in the group of immature animals.

Other elements, such as horn cores are very rarely used for age estimation. Their development is related to a series of factors such as population or even utility. Only broader categories can be made, such as senile, mature, and immature. Even more uncertain is the age estimation based on bone texture. This is often avoided because it is also influenced by the experience and abilities of the researcher.

One of the most trustworthy methods is the examination of the deciduous teeth, premolars Pd^4/Pd_4 and the permanent teeth, molars M^3/M_3. This method is used in the present dissertation for the most important domesticated and wild species. These two teeth are preferred because their identification is relatively easy and the two teeth share only a small period of coexistence on the mandible. When M_3 erupts, Pd_4 is replaced shortly thereafter, significantly reducing double counts of the same individuals.

After identifying the deciduous from the permanent teeth, the wear stage is noted, namely how high the crown of the tooth is in combination with the dentine exposure. During the life of an animal, tooth height decreases and more dentine is revealed as the enamel (the visible part) is reduced. The different wear stages are linked to a specific age phase of the individual. Nonetheless, other factors can influence the speed of the wear, such as sandy ground, or hard and inadequate fodder.

The system followed for noting the wear stage is the one used at the Natural History Museum of Vienna at the Archaeological Zoological Collection and is based on four different stages: 0 (no wear), + (slightly), ++ (medium), and +++ (significantly) (Schmitzberger 2009, Figure 2). The creation of more categories, as proposed by Wilson et al. (1982, 1–268), is thought to be impractical because it causes difficulties during the statistical analysis of the material (Schmitzberger 2009, 17). Additionally, the study of the roots can help estimate the mortality profile; the roots are gradually elongated and tend to close when the animal is old enough.

3.5 Butchery marks

The butchery techniques express cultural practises and changes (Marshall 1989, 7–26; Doll 2003; Seetah 2005, 1–8). Thus, they offer important evidence about the people of the past and their activities. Such information is a valuable key for the archaeological interpretation. Cut and chop marks on bones from Sand contribute to a better understanding of the site organisation. Their study involved systematically recording their location, orientation, and type. A considerable amount of literature was available for interpreting the marks, including the work of Binford (1981), Batrosiewicz (1995), Berke (1995, 343–369), Pucher (1999), Strid (2000), Knight (2002), Fairnell (2003, 2008, 47–60), Seetah (2005, 1–8), Kunst & Fitzgerald (2011, 155–164), Saliari & Kunst (2015, 123–134).

3.6 Morphometric analysis

Morphological observations were conducted using the comparative collections at the Museum of Natural History, including the Adametz Collection, the Osteological Collection, and the archived archaeological material. The collections of the Museum also offered a vital background for the comparison of the measurements from Sand with other sites, especially when the number of finds was low.

Metric data follow the standard published by Driesch (1976). Whenever it was possible and the number of finds adequate the metric data were statistically processed. The size of the animals was calculated according to the height at withers, following the factors set for each species (Matolcsi 1970, 155–194; May 1985, 368–382; Schramm 1967a, 89–105; Teichert 1969, 237–292; 1975, 51–69; 1999, 447–454; Teichert et. al. 1997, 181–191). Sometimes these factors were calculated based on modern material, requiring the final estimation to be corrected for the archaeological finds in some cases.

Finally, although bones are usually found at large quantities, it was not always possible to define the limits of the variation range of a population due to the few well-preserved fragments, which are important for the morphological and metric observations.

3.7 Spatial analysis

Spatial analysis is another important step for interpreting the final data and understanding differences in the organisation of the space. The results can indicate social status and/or different activities. In Sand the material derives from different areas of the stronghold. One important question is related to the distribution of the material. The faunal remains of each region were examined separately in order to better recognize similarities and differences related to species, element representation, age and sex distribution, and traces of manipulation. Smaller units (such as objects) have been taken into consideration only in very special cases where a specific accumulation of bones was present. This is because the very low number of bones in such smaller units usually does not allow statistical processing or interpretation (the sample might be random). Finally, the information from each area was combined to better interpret the character of the entire site.

Chapter 4

Analysis by Species

4.1 Quantification and analysis of the archaeozoological material

The animal bones that have been unearthed from the three areas in Sand –upper settlement terrace (Sand 1), lower settlement terrace (Sand 2), and the Westwall area – were found inside the Objects (structures) at the ground level of each area. This is also confirmed by the presence of gnawing marks (Carnivora) on the surface of the bones. In total, 9830 animal bones are presented, corresponding to an overall weight of almost 253 kg.

4.1.1 Domesticated species

According to the weight analysis the domesticated taxa prevail in Sand 1 (58.7%). The dominant domesticated species is cattle (78.3% of the domesticated species, 45.9% when also including the wild fauna), followed by horse, pig, and goat. In Sand 2, domesticated animals are represented by an even higher percentage (66.4%). The dominant species is cattle (76.6% of the domesticated species, 50.8% including the wild fauna), followed by pig, small ruminants, horse, and dog. In the Westwall area the weight analysis shows that domesticated taxa reach 47.4%. The prevalent species is cattle (74.2% of the domesticated species, 35.2% including the wild fauna), followed by pig, small ruminants, horse, and dog. Domestic fowl contributed only minimally to the faunal assemblages of Sand.

The above profiles indicate that a significant difference concerns the ratio between domesticated and wild taxa; the material from the Westwall area exhibits the highest number of wild animals. Concerning the prevalence of taxa, the domesticated species in Sand 1 indicate a higher percentage of horses. In contrast, pigs seem to be more important in Sand 2 and the Westwall area.

4.1.2 Wild species

The weight analysis shows a 41.3% representation of wild species in Sand 1. The prevalent species are red deer and European bison, followed by wild boar and other species, which are found in limited numbers. In Sand 2 wild species made up 33.6%, the lowest value of all three areas. Dominant species are wild Bovidae (mainly European bison) followed by red deer, wild boar, and other species at a lower frequency, similar to Sand 1. In the Westwall area, wild taxa reach 52.6%. Wild Bovidae (mainly European bison) and red deer dominate, followed by wild boar. Wild birds and fish remains were found at a very low frequency.

Accordingly, wild species played a very important role in the daily life of the inhabitants; this result raises many questions regarding the interpretation of the wild fauna. In total, the main wild species in Sand are wild Bovidae (mainly the European bison), red deer, and wild boar, which constitute the so-called big-sized game.[1]

DOMESTICATED SPECIES

4.2 Cattle (*Bos primigenius* f. *taurus*)

4.2.1 Quantification

Cattle bones constitute the most numerous domesticated species in Sand with 3399 bones weighing a combined 104439.0 g (Table 1).

Table 1. Cattle: number of identified specimens (NISP) and weight analysis

Bos primigenius f. *taurus*		
Area	NISP	Weight (g)
Upper settlement terrace (S1)	1204	43588.0
Lower settlement terrace (S2)	745	18232.4
Westwall area (WW)	1450	42618.6
Total	3399	104439.0

The weight analysis showed that cattle make up 76.3% of the domesticated taxa in Sand (41.4% when the wild fauna is considered as well). In Sand 1 the corresponding values are 78.3% and 45.9%. In Sand 2, cattle constitute 76.6% of the domesticated animals and 50.8% of the total fauna. In the Westwall area the corresponding values are 74.2% and 35.2%. In all the three areas, cattle attain more than 70%, showing its clear dominance among the domesticated and wild species.

The analysis of other early medieval assemblages shows that in many sites cattle were the main domesticated species (Pohansko, Stillfried, Gaiselberg, Gars-Thunau). Nonetheless, the very high frequency of cattle in Sand – more than 70% – was unexpected. Such a high percentage has rarely been recorded. Two well-known examples yielding similar results derive from the salt mining site of Dürrnberg (La Tène A-C) and the Roman Castellum Traismauer/ Augustiniana (1st-4th century AD).

---

[1] Hochjagd in German.

In the case of Dürrnberg the presence of cattle has been interpreted as an external supply for the workers of the salt mining operations; meat trading might have been also possible, especially when considering the preservation possibilities that salt offered and the high percentage of cattle (Pucher 1999, 2014b, 65–93). The high frequency of cattle in Traismauer/Augustiniana has been explained as being the best dietary option for the military personnel: cattle are large and their meat was cheaper than that of pig (Riedel 1993, 179–294).

In order to understand and interpret the significance of cattle in Sand, further investigation has been conducted, including the reconstruction of age and sex distribution, the body part representation, the study of manipulation marks, and the morphometric analysis.

4.2.2 Sex ratio

4.2.2.1 Results

The examination of pelves in Sand demonstrated that castrated animals and females are represented by 44.5% each, males by 10.7% (Table 2). Due to the limited number of pelves, however, the sex distribution has been also addressed using metapodials (Table 3). The analysis of the total number of metapodials shows similar results, namely the prevalence of castrated/males. 48.6% of the individuals are oxen, 40.4% females, and 11.0% males (Figure 10).

The sex distribution among the areas indicates certain differences. According to Figure 9, 52.6% of the animals in Sand 1 represent castrated animals, 36.8% females, and 10.5% males. In Sand 2, the percentage of castrated

animals is higher (58.3%), followed by females (25%) and males (16.7%). The Westwall area exhibits a different ratio with a higher frequency of females (49%) compared with the other two areas; castrated individuals follow with 41.5% and males with 9.2%.

4.2.2.2 Interpretation

Overall, the material indicates the dominance of male/ castrated animals (Figure 10). The question now is what the interpretation is in terms of economy. Understanding the organisation suggested by the sex ratio requires some general remarks on patterns of behaviour at autarchic rural settlements. Similarities or important differences compared with the economic organisation of the peasants provide a preliminary impression of the site's logistic organisation.

First, the normal birth rate of cattle is 50% females and 50% males. The study of archaeozoological records has shown that the peasants have to regulate this ratio in order to be able to survive and gain some profit. Faunal assemblages from various sites in Austria (e.g. Göttlesbrunn: Pucher 2006b, 197–220) indicate that, at an autarchic peasant economy, female animals reach a high percentage – around 70%. The remaining 30% is represented by males; oxen usually constitute the vast majority of males. The reason why the number of bulls drops significantly below the 50% is because of their minimal utility. Bulls offer no long-term economic advantage. Concerning reproduction, one male can copulate with many females, making a high number of males unnecessary. As labour animals, bulls are not preferred due to their hot-tempered character and consequently the lack of obedience. Males usually have to be castrated or slaughtered at a young age. This is not easily

Table 2. Cattle: sex determination based on pelvis fragments (NISP and NISP%)

Area	Male	Male %	Castrated	Castrated %	Female	Female %	Total
Upper settlement terrace (S1)	2	7.1	13	46.4	13	46.4	28
Lower settlement terrace (S2)	1	12.5	6	75.0	1	12.5	8
Westwall area (WW)	3	15.0	6	30.0	11	55.0	20
Total Sand	6	-	25	-	25	-	56
Total Sand (%)	-	10.7	-	44.5	-	44.5	100

Table 3. Cattle: sex determination based on metapodials (NISP and NISP%)

Area	Element	Male	Male %	Castrated	Castrated %	Female	Female %	Total
Upper settlement terrace (S1)	Mc	4	14.8	15	55.6	8	29.6	27
	Mt	2	6.7	15	50.0	13	43.3	30
Lower settlement terrace (S2)	Mc	4	36.4	7	63.6	0	0.0	11
	Mt	0	0.0	7	53.8	6	46.2	13
Westwall area (WW)	Mc	5	15.2	13	39.4	15	45.5	33
	Mt	1	3.1	14	43.8	17	53.1	32
Total Sand	Mp	16	-	71	-	59	-	146
Total Sand (%)	Mp	-	11.0	-	48.6	-	40.4	100

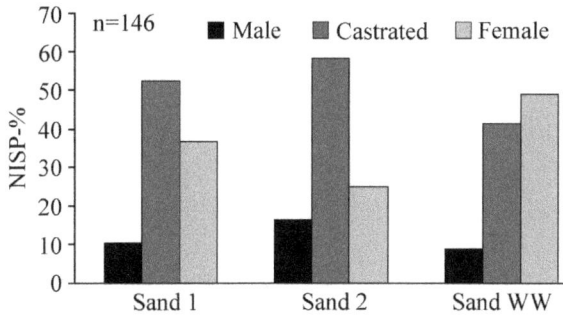

Figure 9. Cattle: sex determination based on metapodials–per area (NISP%).

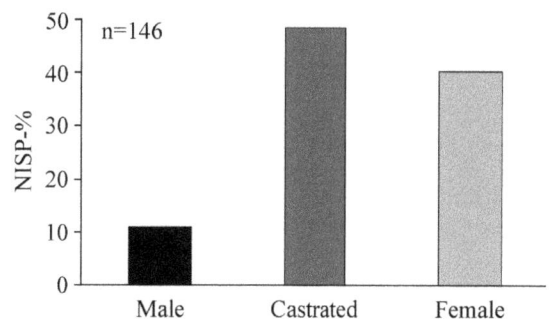

Figure 10. Cattle: sex determination based on metapodials – Sand total (NISP%).

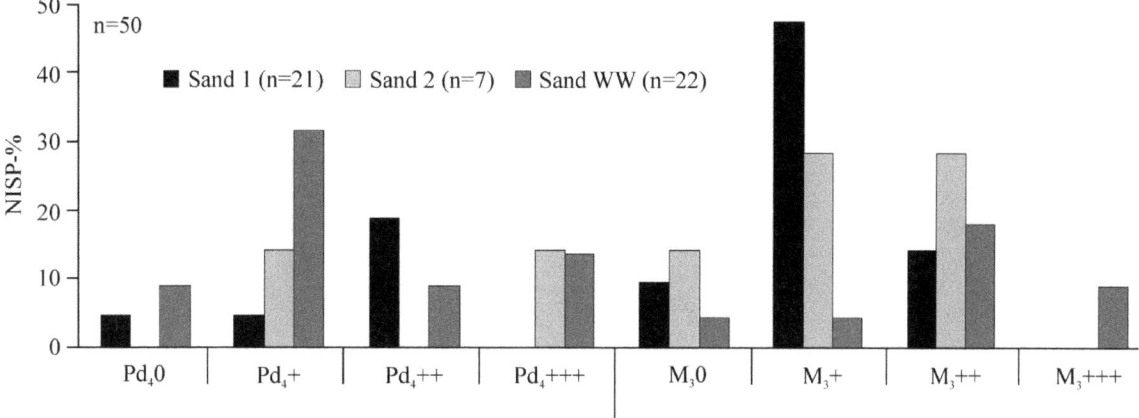

Figure 11. Cattle: mortality profiles – per area – mandibular teeth (NISP%).

proved based on the archaeozoological record because the sex distribution can only be applied for adult individuals.

This means taking a decision on which males will be castrated and which slaughtered. For this reason the peasants let the animals live for several months to observe their evolution, and then castrate the weaker individuals. The castration can take place at an early or at a later stage. Castration at an early stage means that the individual will be physically more developed than an animal that is later castrated (Watson 1969, 164–171; Heaton et al. 2004, 130–133). Animals designated as meat suppliers are usually castrated earlier. The castrated males offer two choices: as labour animals or being sold for their meat.

In contrast, female cattle are vital for the economy and survival of the peasants (Pucher & Schmitzberger 2006, 608–623). Cows secure the next cattle generation and provide the suppliers with other secondary products such as milk. Another reason favouring the dominance of female animals is fodder regulation. Keeping males and castrated animals could be characterized as being luxurious when considering the amount of fodder needed to cover their needs. The bigger size of the males, their need for energy, and the different hormones compared with cows are responsible for a high fodder demand. Fodder availability is also related to space availability and the economic situation of the peasants. The number of animals per peasant is restricted by the capacity of the area in which the animals can move, find fodder, and be kept (Pucher 2006b,

197–220; 2014a, 73–100). Based on these considerations, cows play the major role for a sustainable economy.

The fact that males dominate in Sand has important consequences for the economy. According to Figure 10, 48.6% of the total material derives from oxen, 11% from bulls, and 40.4% from cows. The high frequency of oxen and bulls revealed by the sex determination does not suggest a sustainable autarchic economy as typically described for rural settlements. One interpretation is that the animals were imported and thus the inhabitants of Sand were the consumers. The imports show a clear selection of males and castrated animals. As noted above, a high number of oxen usually suggests meat supply or labour animals. More information concerning the role of the castrated animals in Sand can be gained by the age at death profile.

4.2.3 Age at death

4.2.3.1 Results

The age distribution is presented for each area separately (Figure 11) and subsequently for the whole site (Figure 12, Table 4). The statistical processing should be treated cautiously in the cases, where the number of finds is low. First, Figure 11 shows the number of teeth noted for every abrasion stage from Sand 1. The diagram indicates that mainly young animals are represented in this area, including immature individuals (Pd_4 stages) and young adults ($M_3 0/+$). The latter clearly prevail (57.1%).

Table 4. Cattle: mortality profile and animal exploitation (NISP and NISP%)

	Meat supply		*Secondary exploitation*		NISP (total)
	$Pd_4$0-+++	$M_3$0-+	M_3++	M_3+++	
Sand 1	6	12	3	0	21
Sand 1 %	28.6	57.1	14.3	0	
		85.7		14.3	
Sand 2	2	3	2	0	7
Sand 2 %	28.6	42.9	28.6	0	
		71.5		28.6	
Sand WW	14	2	4	2	22
Sand WW %	63.6	9.1	18.2	9.1	
		72.7		27.3	
Sand Total (%)		78.0		22.0	

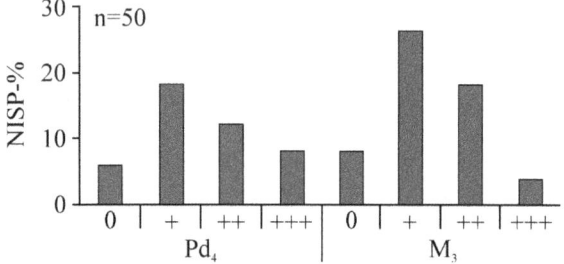

Figure 12. Cattle: mortality profile – Sand total – mandibular teeth (NISP%).

Individuals indicating older age (M_3+++) were not recorded. The tendency is similar in Sand 2. Even if the number of findings is limited, Figure 11 indicates that the remains derive mostly from young individuals. In Westwall area all the age stages are represented, but a remarkable ratio between immature and adult animals has been noted. Immature individuals dominate and this is a noteworthy difference from the other two areas. Concerning the profile of adults, slightly older individuals (M_3++) prevail.

4.2.3.2 Interpretation

According to Table 4 a very high percentage of animals derive from the young stages ($Pd_4$0-+++ and $M_3$0/+), which are mainly related to meat consumption. The frequency of animals that could be further exploited as labour animals (oxen, cows) or for milk production (cows) is low. This suggests the role of cattle as important meat suppliers for the inhabitants of the site.

Interpreting the distribution of young animals in Sand is difficult because it might be related to many factors. It can be argued that the mortality rate was higher during the medieval period than today. Nowadays, 4-5% of the newly born animals do not survive; that percentage may well have been higher in the early medieval period (Schmölcke 2004, 41). Nonetheless, the frequency of young animals is unusually high in comparison to other case studies, and it mainly involves calves between 6 months and 1 year (Pd_4+).

A study from the settlement and castle of Mecklenburg (7th-12th century AD) suggests a similar phenomenon, namely a higher presence of young animals in the castle (Müller 1984, 161–188). There are many potential reasons why young animals are found in higher numbers in castles, and this phenomenon has been interpreted in various ways. For instance, the low frequency of young animals at typical autarchic rural settlements might be related to logistical reasons, including fodder and space regulation (Teichert 1988, 143–220).

In Sand, it is important to note this similarity with the castle of Mecklenburg and to underline that the presence of immature animals usually indicates provision from outsiders. This verifies what it has already been proposed based on the sex determination. Calves are commonly related to noble meals, but also to the exploitation of very good-quality skin. Interestingly, the high number of calves comes from the Westwall area. This raises the question whether this accumulation points to some kind of selection and probably indicates regulations regarding the internal distribution and organisation.

4.2.4 Combining sex and age distribution

4.2.4.1 Discussion and interpretation

Combining the cattle sex and mortality profiles reveals the first fascinating aspects of daily life. Numerous publications comment on the distribution of sexes in age classes as a tool to interpret economic strategies and to understand the logistical organisation of a site.

The archaeozoological record indicates that usually male animals are castrated, slaughtered at a young age, or sold at the market for breeding purposes. Castrated animals are slaughtered at a young stage ($M_3$0/+), providing a very good meat quality, or they live longer and are used as labour animals (Benecke 1994). Bulls are usually slaughtered at an early stage if they are to be consumed. Older males are less tasty because of the hormones; a very small number is mainly kept for breeding and these animals can reach an old age.

Female individuals are slaughtered later – with the exception of breeds specialized in meat production – for reproduction purposes (Benecke 1994). It is important for females to survive longer so that they can secure the next generation with an offspring, which arrives relatively late compared with other animals such as pigs, which reach sexual maturity faster. The cow is about 5 years old at first birth, and its arrival signifies the beginning of milk exploitation. The female individual has to have offspring in order to start and continue with milk production. Each year a cow delivers one and very rarely two calves. 50% of the newly born animals are males, and this percentage is regulated by the peasants as discussed above (chapter 4.2.2.2). Female individuals can be also used as labour animals, similarly to oxen.[2]

These biological facts offer a great contribution in order to a) understand aspects of the economy and patterns of behaviour between providers and consumers, b) appreciate how fragile the economy could have been during those periods, especially when the peasants could not afford many cattle and c) realize the consequences of delivery (imports of animals) and the importance of a well-organised system.

These facts will be now used to interpret how the sexes were distributed within the age stages in Sand. All adult stages are represented ($M_3$0-+++), but mainly the younger ones ($M_3$0/+). Moreover the sex ratio shows a high number of males and castrated animals (Figures 9, 10). It is logical for the bulls and oxen to be mainly distributed in the earlier stages of adulthood. Young castrated adults ($M_3$0/+) provide the best meat. Some castrated animals might also be found at the older stages. Most females are expected to be in the older stages – namely M_3++/+++ – for economic and practical reasons. Older cows have already been exploited and they usually taste better than older oxen. Figure 12 however, shows a high number of young adults and thus the presence of young cows is also possible.

The combination of the sex ratio with the mortality profile shows that Sand does not present a sustainable economy. Additionally, it is suggested that the residents of the site were consumers who enjoyed a very good meat quality. This points to patterns of noble behavior. However, every system that is based on supply from outsiders also provides information about the relationship between the consumers and the providers (peasants). This information can be used to trace socio-political changes and thus to interpret the nature of this relationship. This question will be further discussed later (part 5).

4.2.5 Skeletal element distribution

4.2.5.1 Results and interpretation

The highest MNI for Sand 1 is seventeen individuals, for the Westwall area fourteen animals, and for Sand 2 nine individuals. All the investigated elements provided similar results; no dramatic fluctuations indicated an over- or underrepresentation of any particular anatomical region. This argues for a homogeneous distribution, which could be related to the fact that whole animals were delivered.

In order to test this hypothesis, the total number of NISP data from Sand has been compared with the total number of NISP from Katzentauer, a middle Bronze Age peasant settlement (Pucher Manuscript). The comparison of these two sites is justified even if they derive from a different chronological background, because the question is to understand the profile of the skeletal element distribution when whole individuals are present. In Katzentauer the NISP analysis[3] suggests that the site exhibits whole animals. This means that if whole animals were delivered to Sand, then the NISP profiles of the two sites should bear important similarities.

Figure 13 shows similar tendencies at both sites. The slight differences may reflect practical difficulties and taphonomic factors along with cultural aspects. A noteworthy observation is the few horn cores in Sand. In general, cranial elements are well represented, verifying the arrival of whole individuals. The fact that especially the horn cores are underrepresented could suggest cultural influence. Cultural factors might have also affected the high number of metacarpals. A number of artefacts found in Sand were manufactured out of metacarpals, showing that they were deliberately kept for further usage.

Finally, some differences emerge when examining each area of Sand separately (Figure 14). The highest frequency of regions rich in meat (fore- and hindlimbs) is at Sand 2 (34%). Sand 1 and Westwall area have percentages similar to each other (25.7% and 24.6%, respectively). Compared with the other two areas, Sand 2 exhibits more crania and mandibles, but fewer carpals, tarsals, phalanges, and metapodials. Small bones and metapodials are most abundant in Sand 1 and the Westwall area.

4.2.6 Modifications

4.2.6.1 Butchery marks

The analysis of chop and cut marks present interesting information concerning the processing of cattle (Figure 15).

---

[2] These observations are the result of studying the archaeozoological record. Compare with other important works (Müller 1962, 81–97; 1965, 143–153; 1978, 101–170; Benecke 1994; Schmölcke 2004 etc.).

[3] The results of the weight analysis from Katzentauer have been compared with the standard calculated by Reichstein (1991, 1–346) and it was shown that NISP and weight exhibit similar results. Although in Sand the body part distribution is based on NISP, in the case of cattle remains (which were numerous) an effort was done by the author to control if the NISP results would overlap - or not - with the weight analysis. This effort showed that the results were very similar.

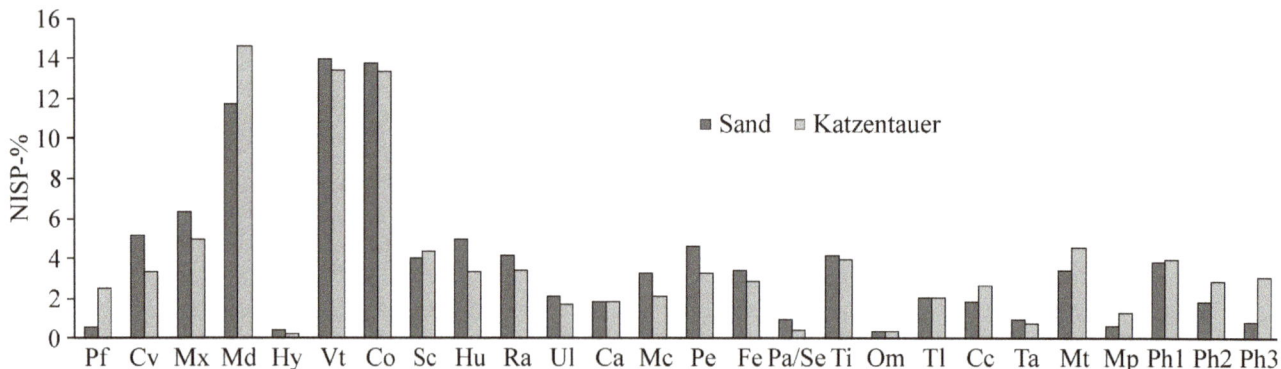

Figure 13. Cattle: skeletal element representation – Sand and Katzentauer (NISP%). Abbreviations: Pf: processus frontalia, Cv: calvaria, Mx: maxilla, Md: mandible, Hy: hyoid, Vt: vertebrae, Co: costae, Sc: scapula, Hu: humerus, Ra: radius, Ul: ulna, Ca: carpalia, Mc: metacarpus, Pe: pelvis, Fe: femur, Pa: patella, Se: sesamoidea, Ti: tibia, Om: os malleolare, Tl: talus, Cc: calcaneus, Ta: tarsalia, Mt: metatarsus, Mp: metapodia, Ph1: first phalanx, Ph2: second phalanx, Ph3: third phalanx.

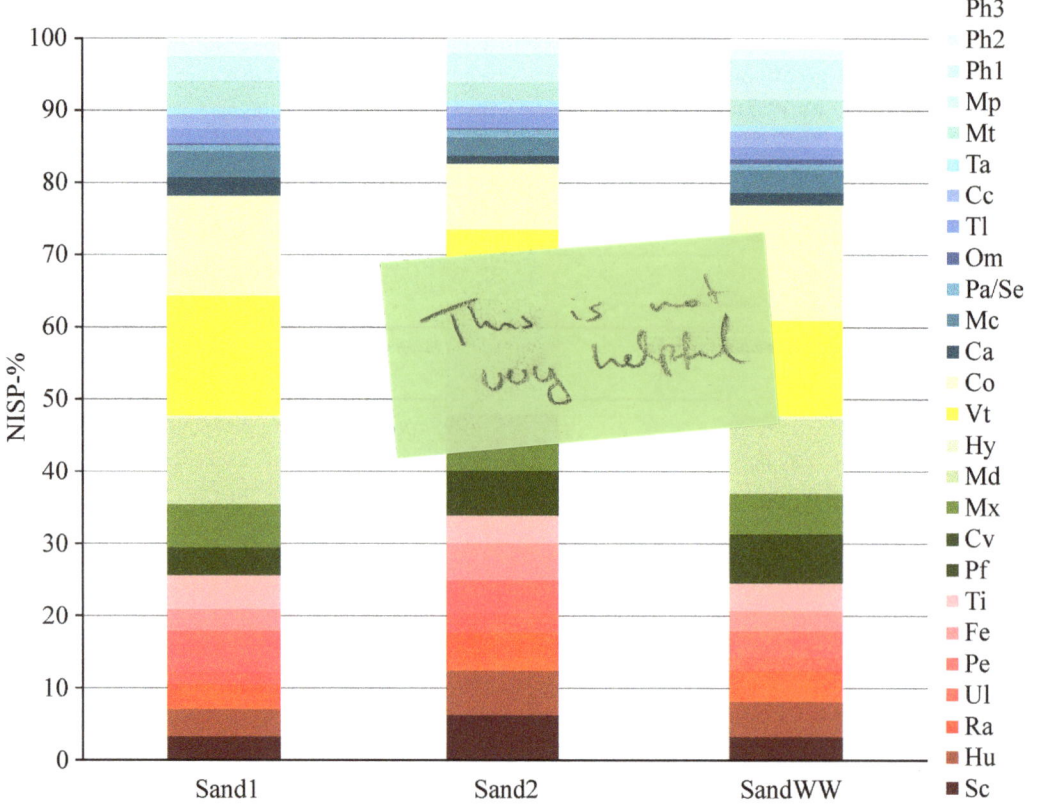

Figure 14. Cattle: skeletal element representation per area (NISP%). Abbreviations: Pf: processus frontalia, Cv: calvaria, Mx: maxilla, Md: mandible, Hy: hyoid, Vt: vertebrae, Co: costae, Sc: scapula, Hu: humerus, Ra: radius, Ul: ulna, Ca: carpalia, Mc: metacarpus, Pe: pelvis, Fe: femur, Pa: patella, Se: sesamoidea, Ti: tibia, Om: os malleolare, Tl: talus, Cc: calcaneus, Ta: tarsalia, Mt: metatarsus, Mp: metapodial, Ph1: first phalanx, ph2: second phalanx, ph3: third phalanx.

Chops on the cranium prove the removal of the horns, and further preparation is witnessed by chop marks on maxilla, zygomaticum, temporal, and the occipital condyles. Cut marks at the caput mandibulae of proc. condylaris, and at the fossa masseterica, reveal further dismemberment. Dismemberment of the head is revealed by cuts at the atlas, and sometimes such cuts are also detected at the proc. articularis cranialis of the axis. Cut marks on the hyoid could indicate slaughter at the site, but also tongue removal (Binford 1981, 101).

A plethora of longitudinal cuts and diagonal chops on the ribs show portioning and filleting. Chops on the vertebrae mainly indicate removal of the articulation surfaces or of the proc. spinosus and transversus on the lumbar and thoracic vertebrae; some cuts at the latter also indicate meat stripping. Longitudinal cuts are located across the vertebrae of the sacrum, revealing filleting and transverse chops further processing. Cut marks along the body of the scapula witness filleting and along the neck further dismemberment. The long bones have been chopped at different parts on the joints and the midshaft. These marks indicate activities related to dismemberment, marrow consumption, and portioning. Chop and cut marks are found on calcaneus, talus, and other small bones (carpals and tarsals), suggesting mainly dismemberment.

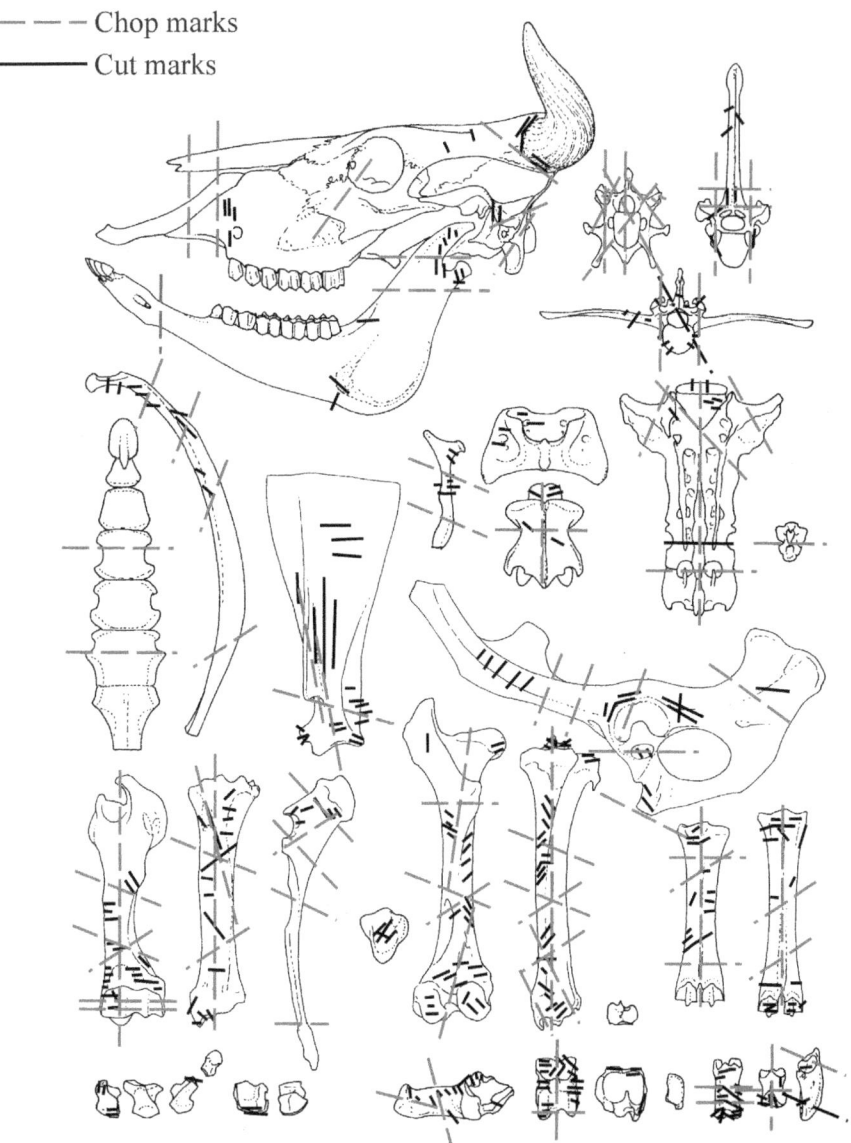

Figure 15. Cut and chop marks on cattle bones. Numerous marks were documented on the bones. Many times one bone exhibited multiple marks, indicating effort and time. No specific butchering system was noted. Cut marks indicate skinning activities, mainly for the Westwall area. Drawing provided by Pucher.

Cuts at the base of the horns and on the phalanges indicate skinning activities (Binford 1981, 101, 107, 136–142; Reitz & Wing 2008, 128–131). Interestingly, marks related to skin removal were detected on the material from Westwall area.[4] As noted above, a high number of calves were found in this region, and calves usually provide a very good skin quality (Bartosiewicz 1995, 73).

The study of the cut and chop marks indicates the full exploitation of the carcasses. From a technical viewpoint, some observations suggest how butchering was practised. The material very often demonstrates a combination of multiple chops and cuts very close to each other. Their location and orientation varies significantly and the presence of some marks cannot be always explained because they are not found at anatomically relevant positions. These indications suggest great effort during butchering and an unsystematic technique probably practised by people with no routine in butchering.

Additionally, the bones give the impression that they were intensively smashed. Similar observations derive from other sites in Germany, including the Slavic castles Mecklenburg (Müller 1984, 161–188) and Berlin-Köpenick (Müller 1962, 81–97). Other sites of the early medieval period (Raabs) and even earlier (Dürrnberg, Hallstatt) exhibited a different technique indicating a more systematic approach to butchering. These differences are part of the cultural background and are taken into consideration later in the work.

4.2.7 Morphometric analysis

This chapter identifies the cattle population(s) that was/were delivered to the site. The morphometric identification of the cattle group(s) is essential because it can provide information about the geographical distribution and

---

[4] Although such marks are a strong indication for skinning activities, their absence cannot exclude this possibility (Knight 2002, 68).

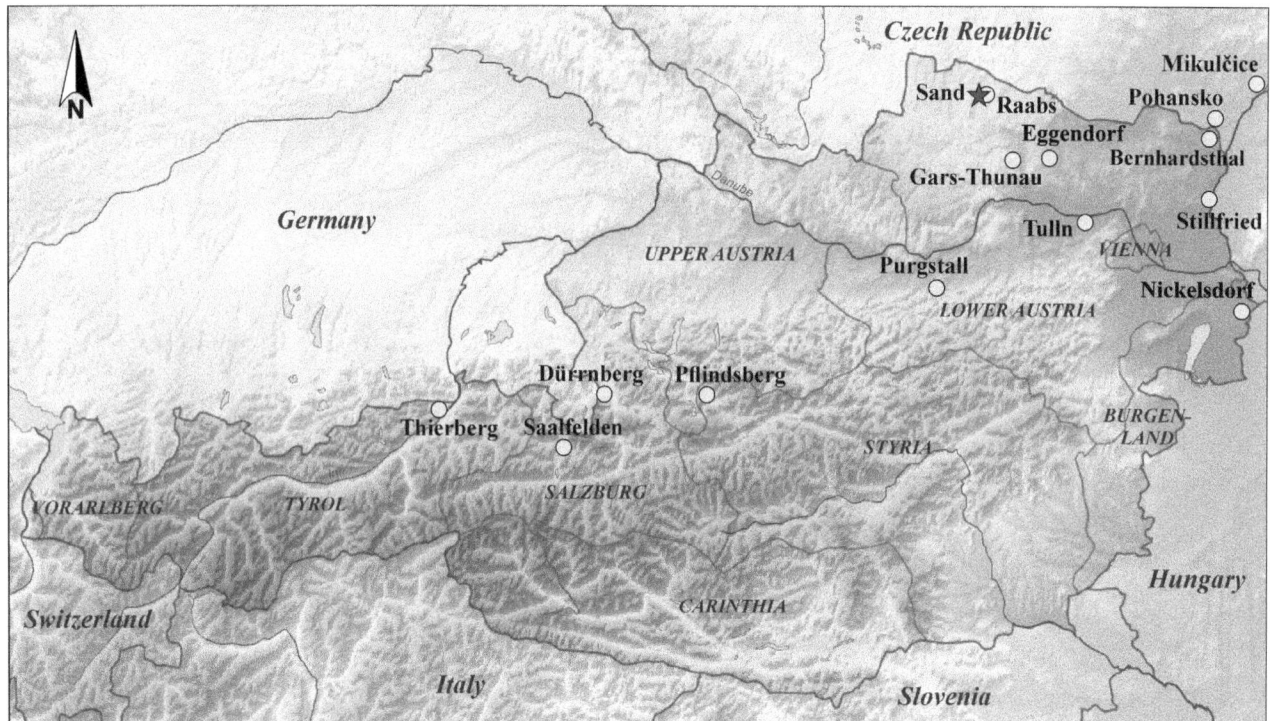

Figure 16. Sites mentioned in the text during the comparative morphometric analysis. Source: https://commons.wikimedia.org/wiki/File:Austria_location_map.svg.

evolution of former breeds, and it can deliver evidence concerning the radius of human activities and the interaction of different human populations.

To identify the cattle population(s), measurements and morphological features will be used to reconstruct the size and shape of the animals. The analysis of measurements can yield information on proportions and sizes. Although all the bones were metrically examined, metapodials and tali are very important for the statistical approach. Tali bones are used to distinguish between populations (Pucher 1999), whereas metapodials are used to distinguish between sexes (Fock 1966); other long bones such as humerus, radius, femur, and tibia cannot be sexed with certainty.

Combining the metric data with morphological observations can provide additional evidence to identify possible cattle breeds. Morphological traits are very important to distinguish among animal populations, especially when different breeds might fall in the same size variation range or when the number of measurements is insufficient for statistical analysis.

One of the most significant elements for morphological observations is the cranium. Cranial elements exhibit differences due to sexual dimorphism and are influenced by various factors, such as the size and shape of the horn cores; the latter might also exhibit a wide range of variation. Nevertheless, these elements bear features that are characteristic for specific populations. The cranium is not a compact entity, but it is constituted of many parts; for this reason any change has a strong influence on its form and is better detectable. Thus, cranium is one of the most trustworthy elements for morphological studies. However,

as this element is rarely well preserved, other bones bearing additional noteworthy morphological differences are also investigated.

4.2.7.1 The comparative material

In order to identify and distinguish among different cattle breeds, other populations from the surrounding regions can be used as reference material (Figure 16). Comparing cattle breeds from other sites without considering the region and the local animal population can be risky. This is because similarities among breeds can be coincidental or the result of different causes. This calls for seeing the morphometrical data in the historical context and based on state-of-the-art zoological knowledge.

The reference populations used as comparative reference material in the present study are presented in Table 5. These populations can be well compared with Sand for various reasons. The first is that these sites produced abundant bones. This is very important for the statistical analysis and the study of morphological traits because it enables creating reference populations.

The material from Dürrnberg and Nickelsdorf offered the opportunity to examine metrically and morphologically two fully developed different cattle groups and to define their characteristics. The material from Bernhatdsthal provided evidence for hybridization. Mikulčice and Gars-Thunau date to the early medieval period and are considered to be representative of the Slavic culture, similarly to Sand. Stillfried exhibits numerous findings that derive from the medieval period. Finally, Raabs played a significant role during the comparative study because it is very close to

Table 5. Date and archaeological interpretation of the sites mentioned in the text during the comparative morphometric investigation of cattle

Sites	Date	Interpretation	Literature
Dürrnberg	La Tène culture (A-C)	Salt-mining complex	Pucher 1999, 2002, 133–146; 2013, 9–36; Schmitzberger 2012, 79–138; Abd el Karem 2009, 133–154; Saliari et al. 2016, 245–288
Roseldorf	4th century BC	Celtic settlement	Abd el Karem 2013a
Bernhardsthal	2nd-3rd century AD	Germanic settlement	Riedel 1996, 55–144
Nickelsdorf	2nd-3rd century AD	Villa rustica	Riedel 2004, 449–539; Pucher 2006a, 253–268
Mikulčice	6th-10th century AD	Capital city of the Moravian Empire	Kratochvíl 1987a, 1987b, 1988a, 1988b
Gars-Thunau	9th-10th century AD	Fortified Slavic settlement	Kanelutti 1990, 1993, 169–184
Raabs	10th-12th century AD	Castle	Riedel & Pucher 2008, 159–194
Stillfried	12th-13th century AD	Stronghold	Pucher 1982
Thierberg	12th-14th century AD	Castle	Saliari this work
Pflindsberg	13th-18th century AD	Castle	Saliari this work

Sand (1.6 km away), it dates to the medieval period,[5] and the material derives from a very short time span, similarly to Sand.

Every complex is analysed separately here in order to reflect the cultural background and to include the archaeozoological analysis as part of the archaeological situation. As evident from Table 5 reference populations derive from various periods and not only from early medieval assemblages. This chronological difference among the comparative examples is important. The fact that the assemblages derive from different periods raises interesting questions concerning the evolution, the continuity (or not), and the geographical distribution of the cattle populations being studied.

4.2.7.1.1 Dürrnberg

Bad Dürrnberg is located near the town of Hallein, south of Salzburg close to the Bavarian border. The ancient salt-mining complex is one of the most famous archaeological sites of Iron Age Austria. Mining activities occurred in several periods, starting from the Late Bronze Age. Dürrnberg substituted the famous Bronze Age salt mining of Hallstatt, and covers a large period of the La Tène culture (A-C).

The salt-mining complex resulted in the excellent preservation of archaeological and biological findings, making Dürrnberg one of the most significant sites of the European Iron Age (Stöllner 2003, 164–170). Animal skin and hair have been very well preserved and their study has contributed to the identification of the cattle population.

Dürrnberg exhibited a very high percentage of cattle with more than 70% of the total material, constituting the main species in the diet of the salt-mining workers. Most of the animals are adult females that were exploited and then slaughtered at an old age.

Morphometric investigation

The morphological study yielded significant information for the identification of the population. In Dürrnberg the reconstruction and study of the cranial elements point to a small-sized type with a short, rather flat and slightly wavy frontal bone, and gracile cranium. The study of the horn cores indicates shorthorn cattle. Some female horn cores are small and gracile, but in general, they are relatively compact and robust. Long bones from Dürrnberg, and especially metapodials, also suggest a small, compact, and gracile type. The morphological features argue for a homogeneous population, which was also confirmed by the statistical analysis.

The metric analysis of the tali also suggests a homogeneous, small-sized population (Figure 19). Although the diagram is affected by the high number of female animals – which encourage the tendency to lower values – the general distribution of the metric data points to a small-sized breed. The size classes (GLl) show a distribution between 48.0-51.5 and 64.0-67.5 mm with a peak at 55-59 (Figure 19); the average for talus has been calculated at 57.4 mm.

The withers height estimation has verified that the cattle breed in Dürrnberg was a population of small-sized animals. The estimation is based on the GL of the long bones. Sizes ranged between 95 and 123 cm. For the cows the average is around 104 cm, for the oxen 111 cm and for the males 106 cm.

Comparing the morphological traits and the measurements with recent breeds reveals similarities to the alpine

---

[5] There may be a chronological overlap with Sand, but no clear evidence is available.

Bergschecken cattle.[6] The analysis of preserved organic material (hair and skin) from Dürrnberg suggested additional similarities to the Bergschecken cattle in terms of hair structure and colour (Groenman-van Waateringe 2002, 117–122).[7]

The question is whether the Dürrnberg cattle population could indicate a very early form of the Bergschecken cattle. In order to answer this question, archaeological assemblages from the eastern Alps have been studied by the author and are presented below. The faunal assemblages come from castle Pflindsberg, castle Thierberg, and castle Saaleck.

Castle Pflindsberg

The site is located on a hill in Styria close to Altausee (central Austria) and it dates from the 13th to 18th cent. The faunal assemblage was small with only 153 cattle bones, but some well-preserved bones could be further investigated.

Two female metacarpals exhibited a Bp (proximal breadth) value of 49.5 and 49.0 mm, whereas the Bd (distal breadth) value is 49.5 and 51.5 mm respectively. One female metatarsal exhibited Bp and Bd measurements of 41.5 and 45.5 mm. One metatarsus derives from a castrated animal. This metatarsal was very elongated, outside of the variation range for female cattle, but with a very thin corpus. The Bp and Bd (45.0 and 50.5 mm, respectively) were relatively low for castrated animals, but the maximal length (GLl) with 222.0 mm strongly argues for a castrated individual.[8] Additionally, one talus that survived in a very good state of preservation produced a GLl of 56.5 mm. More evidence derives from the estimated height at withers. The two female metacarpals measured 106.1 cm, the female metatarsal 106.6 cm. The height at withers for the castrated animals has been estimated at about 121 cm. All the above observations indicate striking similarities to the material from Dürrnberg. The values and the size estimation are within the variation range of the Dürrnberg cattle.

Castle Thierberg

Castle Thierberg is located in Tirol near Kufstein close to the Bavarian border (12th-14th century AD). Even though the material was limited, significant fragments of metapodials have been preserved. Three measurements were taken from three female metacarpals. The first fragment had a Bp value of 48.5 mm the two other fragments had Bd values of 49.0 and 46.5 mm. One metacarpal with Bp 52.5 could belong to a castrated individual, an interpretation supported by the wider proximal part compared with the female metacarpals. Two more measurements were

possible on two female metatarsals. The first fragment gave a Bp value 39.5, and the second fragment produced 44.5 for the Bd. The metric comparison with the population of Dürrnberg shows that the values fall within the same range of variation. Morphological observations verify similarities to the Iron Age cattle because female animals, which constituted the majority of the material in Thierberg, were small and compact.

Castle Saaleck

The last assemblage studied derives from castle Saaleck (12th-18th century AD), which is located at Saalfelden, Pinzgau, Salzburg. Metapodials and tali, which are crucial for the metric analysis, did not survive in a good state of preservation. Only one distal part of a metatarsal bears some morphological similarities to the population of Dürrnberg. Fragments of other long bones provided additional indications for the existence of a small-sized breed.

In this context, the phalanges were also very important. As small compact bones, they were very well preserved. Although there is a variation between anterior and posterior phalanges and even among the sexes, the phalanges and especially the third phalanx can be representative of an animal population. The phalange sizes from Saaleck fall within the variation range of the Dürrnberg population (DLS: 61.5 and 57.5 mm, Ld: 47.0, 47.0, and 43.0, MBS: 20.5, 19.0, and 18.5 mm), suggesting the possible existence of the same cattle group. The Iron Age cattle underwent a specific evolution, observable on the third phalanx, in adapting to the mountainous alpine environment. The phalanges are relatively large and wider, providing more stability while walking.

Results

According to the literature, the earliest evidence for this small-sized cattle group, which presents important similarities to the alpine Bergschecken cattle, can already be found during the Bronze Age (Riedel 1985, 9–25; Boschin 2006, 131–142; Salvagno & Tecchiati 2011; Tecchiati 2012, 79–138). This indicates that the material from Iron Age Dürrnberg represents animals of a fully developed breed.

In the present work, three medieval sites were studied and they exhibited a great homogeneity with the animals from Dürrnberg concerning the morphological traits and the metric data. These results were very much encouraging because all three sites belong culturally to the East Alpine circle of tradition and testify a long tradition of the Dürrnberg cattle type inside the Alpine area. In a final step, recent Bergschecken crania[9] were compared with the

---

[6]   This breed does not exist today. The last animal was slaughtered in the 20th century. Only hybrids of Bergschecken cattle with other populations exist.
[7]   The hair of this type is characterized by softness and fineness.
[8]   Differences in bone size or thickness might be related to the age at castration. This bone might represent an animal that was castrated at a very young age, which resulted in long and slender bones.

[9]   Housed at the Adametz Collection (Collection of Archaeozoology at the Museum of Natural History of Vienna). The collection is named after Professor Adametz (1861-1941), who contributed much to our knowledge about the morphology of farm animals and who collected skull series of various breeds in and outside Europe.

archaeological material, demonstrating key similarities (Figures 23, 24) and suggesting the survival of the breed until the modern times.

Bergschecken cattle population: adaptations to an alpine environment

Bergschecken is an alpine cattle form. The Alps are traditionally related to the mountain pastures referred to in German as *Almen*. Such pastures are found at the heart of modern Austria and reveal a long-lasting tradition, starting already during the Bronze Age; a tradition based on the adaptation of the animals and on human regulations (Pucher 1999). The Alps can be a very difficult environment to survive in, and the Bergschecken cattle show very interesting changes, which have been also observed at the cattle population of Dürrnberg (Pucher 1999, 2006c, 263–292; Schmitzberger & Pucher 2011, 71–77).

Bergschecken cattle have the advantage that their small size fits much better to Alpine customs. Due to the steep landscape and the lack of space to move, the feet of cattle present important changes. Interesting alterations are observed at the third phalanx, which is relatively large, in order to offer stability while climbing up steep slopes covered by slippery soil and stones. The larger size of the last phalanx reduces the ground pressure so that the feet do not sink into the ground (Pucher 2013, 9–36).

4.2.7.1.2 Nickelsdorf

Nickelsdorf lies 60 km away from Vienna, in Burgenland (eastern Austria) and is only several kilometres away from Carnuntum, the capital of the Roman province of Upper Pannonia. There, a Roman villa rustica has been excavated. Pits with abundant animal bones have been unearthed and the analysis of the material showed that cattle were the prevalent species (almost 33% of the total material).

Another important finding from the site was two very well-preserved cattle skeletons, which offered the opportunity to study two individuals in great detail. The skeletons were additionally studied and published (Pucher 2006a, 253–268). The age and sex distribution of these skeletons was estimated. They derive from young adult oxen.

Morphometric investigation

The first observations on the Nickelsdorf material and then the detailed study of the two skeletons confirmed the unusually big size and the robustness of the bones. The skull exhibited some similarities to the cranium of aurochs, indicating a population of domesticated cattle that preserved certain primitive[10] characteristics. The cranial elements show that the skull was elongated and massive. The nasal bones are relatively long, slender, and strongly convex. The face is wide and convex, especially when compared to the Dürrnberg cattle. The mandible is more

elongated and the teeth were not parallel to the corpus of the mandible. The last molar M_3 also presents important differences in the position of the talonid (Pucher 2013, 9–36).

Differences between the first and second vertebra indicate anatomical differences at the articulation surface of the axis, which presents an inclination downwards. The sacral vertebrae show that the tail is differently positioned and oriented. Most bones of this group exhibit a rather rounded appearance, even in the shape of the articulation surfaces, whereas the bones of the Iron Age cattle are much more edged and polygonal. The angle of articulation between stylopodium and zygopodium is bigger in the Nickelsdorf cattle than in the small-sized Dürrnberg cattle.[11] Additionally, the metacarpals show a more convex cross section, whereas the Dürrnberg population exhibits more concave characteristics. The distal articulation of the metapodials from Nickelsdorf is more voluminous and deeper (Pucher 2006a, 253–268; 2013, 9–36).

The metric analysis suggests a different range of variation for Nickelsdorf material. The talus measurements exhibit another range and consequently another peak (Figure 19). The range is between 55.0 and 79.0 mm. The most frequent size class is at 65.0-69.0 mm, but many individuals fall within the size class 70-74 mm.[12] More evidence derives from the height at withers with an estimated 111 to 147 cm. The average based on the radius[13] is 131 cm and the minimum 117 cm.[14]

Results

The morphological characteristics and the metric data show important differences to the Iron Age cattle of Dürrnberg. The Nickelsdorf breed showed a clearly different variation range from the Dürrnberg population (Figure 19). The reconstruction of the Nickelsdorf skeletons suggested additional noteworthy differences compared with the Iron Age cattle not only the size, but also in shape and form.

The two populations seem to be differently proportioned. This opinion has also been expressed earlier after comparing the average of the height at withers of the metapodials and of the other long bones. The metapodials of the big-sized cattle from Nickelsdorf produced lower values than the other long bones (radius, tibia), whereas the Iron Age cattle produced higher values for the metapodials (Pucher 2006a,

---

[10] Primitive in the sense of very old.

[11] It affects the estimation of height at withers.
[12] Due to the many castrated animals.
[13] Radius exhibited the highest value for the Italic cattle.
[14] As noted in the chapter of methodology the estimation of the height at withers is based on Matolcsi's factors. When using these factors it should be recollected that Matolcsi used Hungarian grey cattle. For this reason the factors are not well applicable to other populations, unless they are corrected. This became clear during the investigation of the skeletons from Nickelsdorf, after studying the angle of articulation of the different body parts. Based on Matolcsi's factors the values were lower than expected. Conversely, when using Matolcsi's factors for the Iron Age cattle, the values are higher than they should be. The re-articulation of the skeletons from Nickelsdorf produced higher values than Matolcsi's factors for the long bones.

253–268; 2013, 9–36). This suggests a major difference between the two breeds in terms of proportions and shape.

According to current knowledge, these big-sized animals were mainly connected to the Roman presence and the process of Romanisation.[15] This interpretation was already expressed during the late 19th century, and several papers have been published since then on the role of the Italic animals in aspects of daily life (Krämer 1899, Bökönyi 1974, Benecke 1994, Peters 1998, Lyublyanovics 2010, 182–193; Sykes 2015). One important question that cannot be answered yet, but which constitutes an idea for future research, is related to the evolution of the big-sized Italic cattle breed, which still remains enigmatic.

4.2.7.1.3 Roseldorf

Roseldorf is an important settlement at the northern part of Lower Austria that dates to the 4th century AD. The site offered the unique opportunity to study the lifestyle of the late Iron Age population through a wealth of archaeological finds and biological remains. The analysis of the faunal assemblages suggested the presence of Iron Age traditions, already known from Dürrnberg, including the consumption of dog and horse meat. According to the archaeozoological analysis, cattle were the most important meat suppliers, despite their somewhat reduced percentage in the assemblage.

Morphometric investigation

The study of metapodials is based on the GL (max. length)/ SD (smallest breadth of diaphysis) ratio. According to the results of the metric analysis, the vast majority of the finds represent small-sized animals. The Bp values for female metacarpals are between 45.5 and 52.0 mm and the Bd between 48.5 and 55.5 mm. The Bp values for oxen metacarpals are between 48.5 and 61.5 mm, and the Bd between 54.5 and 64.5 mm. The measurements from Roseldorf fall in the same variation range as the animals from Dürrnberg.

Nonetheless, the statistical analysis of the metapodials showed that a very small number of measurements (5%) was outside of the variation range of the Iron Age cattle and was closer to the range of the Nickelsdorf cattle, indicating the possible existence of the big-sized Italic cattle. The Bp value is between 59.5 and 61.5 mm, Bd between 66.5 and 67.0 mm.

The metric analysis of the tali (Figure 19) shows that sizes range between the classes 52.0-55.5 and 64.0-67.5 mm, with a high frequency of bones between 56.0-59.5 and 60.0-63.5 mm. The direction of the curve tends to

be closer to the lower values of the Iron Age cattle. A slight tendency to higher values probably reflects the very few Italic cattle, as already indicated by the metric investigation of the metapodials. Statistically, the two populations are clearly distinct also when analysing the measurements from other bones such as scapula (SLC). Morphological features on cranial elements and on well-preserved long bones confirm the existence of two different cattle populations.

Results

The Roseldorf material indicates a mixed cattle population consisting of the small-sized Iron Age cattle and the big-sized Italic animal. The vast majority of the remains derives from the small-sized breed. The presence of the big-sized cattle has been interpreted as exotic imports from the South, which would have been available at the market of Roseldorf for those who could afford it. It has been suggested that the faunal assemblages from this site deliver the earliest known evidence of Italic cattle breed in Austria.

4.2.7.1.4 Bernhardsthal

Bernhardsthal is a Germanic settlement located 60 km north of the Roman Limes of the Danube and it dates between the 2nd and 3rd century AD (Riedel 1996, 55–144). More than 14,000 animal bones have been unearthed, yielding significant information about the lifestyle of the people of the settlement. The composition of the remains indicates a peasant economy based on the domesticated animals, which dominate with almost 95%. According to the archaeozoological analysis, cattle are the prevalent domesticated taxon, comprising nearly 70% of the total material.

Morphometric investigation

According to Figure 19 the curve of tali does not really fall into the same range of Dürrnberg, Roseldorf, or Nickelsdorf, but there is a considerable overlapping. The metric analysis of talus exhibits a great variation range (50.0-74.0 mm). The most frequent size class is 60.0-63.5 mm, which is higher than in Dürrnberg or Roseldorf, indicating that the Bernhardsthal population exhibits slightly bigger-sized individuals. The curve shows a slight tendency to the big-sized animals from Nickelsdorf, but most values are lower, suggesting smaller sizes than the Italic breed. Only very few bones (n=3) exhibited a high GL value (maximal length) above 70.0 mm. The withers height estimation also varies considerably.

The investigation of the metapodials provided more information. Based on the metacarpals, the size of the animals from this population is calculated between 103 and 133.5 cm; the metatarsal analysis yielded animals between 111 and 126.5 cm. Note here that one of the female metacarpals had a length (GL) of 200 mm. Based on the present state of research, such a high value falls within the

---

[15] Note that there are some other big-sized populations with primitive characteristics as well. One of them is the Hungarian grey cattle. This breed has, however, been excluded because the Hungarian steppe cattle arrived much later, during the Late Middle Ages (Bartosiewicz 1996, 13–20). The study of recent breeds from Italy has revealed a group with very similar characteristics, namely the Chianina breed (Giuliani 1961).

variation range of the Italic group. No further analysis of the population based on metapodials was possible because the material was not sexed and no effort was made to identify the population(s). But some of the published measurements suggest a middle-sized cattle population (Figure 19) together with sporadic indications for a big-sized group, which could represent the Italic breed from Nickelsdorf.

The faunal assemblages from Bernhardsthal raised some crucial questions. One important topic is the time in which this middle-sized cattle population appears and if there are other sites that yield evidence for this group. One of the opinions that has been previously expressed is that this breed is the result of crossbreeding with Steppe cattle. This opinion is mainly based on the work of Bökönyi (1974), who suggested that the Steppe cattle came with the Huns, Avars, or at the latest with the Magyars. Although no reconstruction of the history of the Steppe cattle is available, evidence is lacking on their presence at this region at least until the Late Middle Ages. This indicates that the middle-sized cattle group from Bernhardsthal is much earlier than the Steppe cattle.

New findings show a different aspect regarding the origins of the middle-sized Bernhardsthal cattle. This evidence stems from the excavation at Bruckneudorf in Burgenland (Pucher in press). The site dates to 50-150 AD and it provided one of the first indications for the appearance of the middle-sized cattle population that has been recorded in Bernhardsthal.

The talus diagram[16] from Bruckneudorf shows two curves. The first curve has a peak at the size classes 60.0-63.5 mm. The second has a peak at the classes 68.0-71.5 mm and some individuals fall even within the size classes 72-75.5 and 76-79.5, similarly to the Italic breed from Nickelsdorf. These curves do not represent a sex difference because the measurements fall out of the population's variation range. Accordingly, the talus diagram argues for two populations. The study of metapodial size and proportions also suggests that most of the individuals are middle-sized, similarly to Bernhardsthal. In Bruckneudorf there were also traces of the small-sized Iron Age cattle, but due to the very limited number of finds, these animals were not visible in the statistical analysis. Thus, based on the talus diagram there is in Bruckneudorf a middle-sized population between the Iron Age and the Italic cattle.

The morphological examination of the bones contributed significantly to the study of the middle-sized cattle. The detailed morphological analysis suggested that this middle-sized population bears a mix of characteristics of the Iron Age and Italic breed. These features presented an intermediate stage of the morphological traits of the two cattle groups.

Results

The material from Bernhatdsthal points to a middle-sized population – between the variation range of the Iron Age cattle and that of the Italic Nickelsdorf breed. According to Pucher, who has studied faunal material from Bruckneudorf, there is evidence that this middle-sized population presents a hybrid form of the Iron Age and the Italic breed. Such a result is not very surprising since there are many sites, where the two cattle populations have coexisted (e.g. Pucher et al. 2015, 71–78). Traces of this hybridization have been recorded during the 1st century in the eastern lowlands of East Austria (Jaritz 2014, 47–48; Pucher et al. 2015, 71–78; in press). Today there are many opinions regarding the way and the reasons why this hybridization took place.

Based on morphological traits, this middle-sized breed could represent an earlier form of the later blond/ yellow breed. For this reason, in a final step, the cranial elements (including horn cores) of recent cattle that belong to the blond breed group have been compared with the archaeological material of Bernhardsthal, suggesting many important similarities (Figures 23, 24). Thus, it has been suggested that the material from Bernhatdsthal presents a new stabilized cattle breed.

4.2.7.1.5 Mikulčice

Mikulčice, located 7 km south of Hodońin (Göding) in the Czech Republic, was probably the capital of the Moravian Empire. The settlement dates from the 6th to the 10th century AD and it yielded very important archaeological finds that provided significant information about the life habits of the people of the past. The faunal deposits derive from the 8th and 9th centuries AD and comprise more than 70,000 cattle remains, which provided a very good material for morphometric studies.

Morphometric investigation

The talus curve suggests a homogeneous population with one major peak at the size classes 60.0-63.5 mm, similarly to Bernhardsthal (Figure 19). However, the GLl value exhibits a great range of variation, with minimum values from 48.0-51.5 mm and maximum values from 72.0-75.5 mm. This wide range probably suggests more than one population. There are however only few individuals that fall within the extreme values in both directions: one at the low end of the scale (48.0-51.5 mm) and one at the other end (72.0-75.5 mm).

The same broad variation range is also visible in the withers height estimation, which is between 94 and 127 cm for the metacarpals and between 97 and 131 cm for the metatarsals. Based on the metacarpals, the withers height for males is between 102 and 119 cm, for oxen between 107 and 127 cm, and for females between 94 and 118 cm. Female metatarsals range from 97 to 121 and oxen from 120 to 131 cm. When the extreme

---

[16] Unpublished material, not presented here.

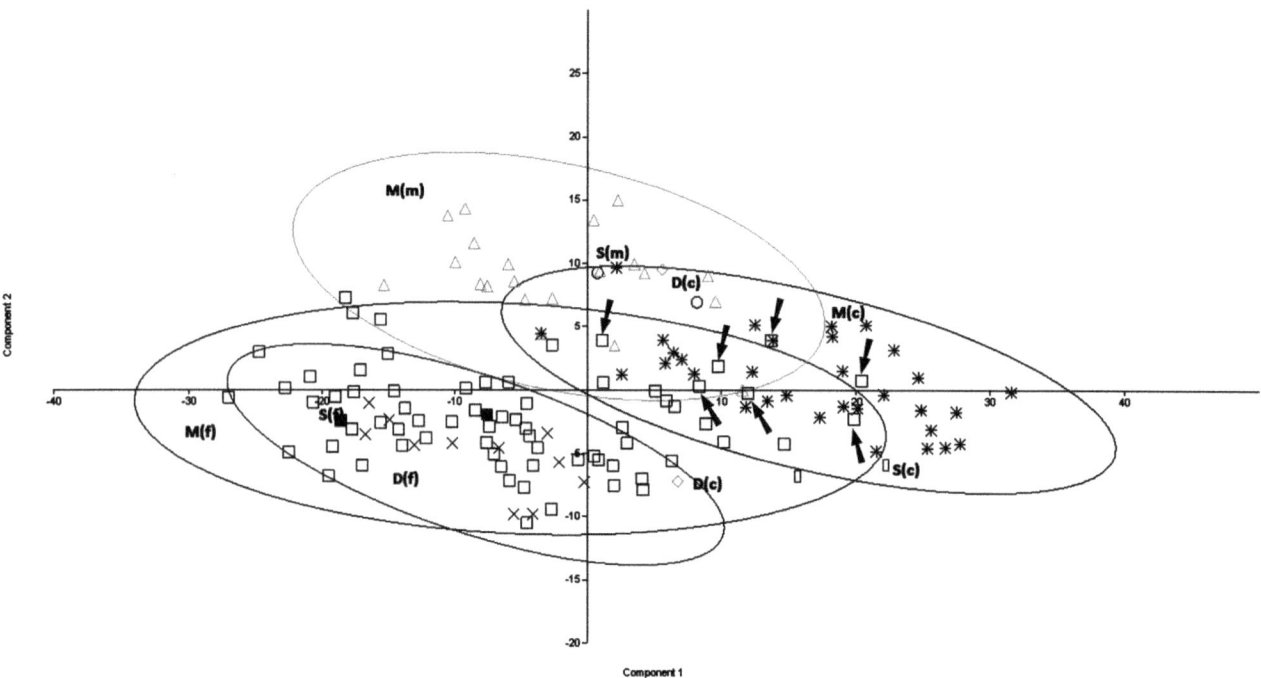

Figure 17. Principal component analysis (PCA) (Saliari). The components 1 and 2 depict the relationship between size and shape. M(m): Mikulčice males, M(c): Mikulčice castrated, M(f): Mikulčice females, D(c): Dürrnberg castrated, D(f): Dürrnberg females, S(m): Sand males, S(c): Sand castrated, S(f): Sand females.

values are excluded, the height at withers is similar to Bernhardsthal.

These data derive after the correction of published results on the sex distribution (Kratochvíl 1988a). After conducting a principal component analysis (PCA) using the Software PAST to better understand possible differences between the proportions of the different populations, it became clear that the position of some individuals from Mikulčice caused difficulties regarding the interpretation of their distribution. The PCA involved the measurements GL, Bp, KD, and Bd (Figure 17). Careful processing of the measurements revealed that some female animals should have been identified as castrated. The arrows of statistic 1 show those castrated animals that have probably been incorrectly identified as females. This correction prompted a re-assessment (Figure 18). Nonetheless, it remains uncertain whether these new results from statistic 2 are correct or whether more corrections on the old dataset are necessary. However, this work follows the results of statistic 2, since it seemed to present an improved distribution of the sexes.

Results

The metric similarities at the Bernhardsthal and Mikulčice sites point to the possibility that both exhibit the same middle-sized cattle population, probably an early form of blond or yellow breed. This indicates the survival of this group at least until the Early Middle Ages. This conclusion is further supported by a faunal assemblage that dates much later in the 15th century; the small assemblage from the Dominican monastery in Tulln (Lower Austria) provided evidence for the existence of the same cattle group (Saliari

& Kunst 2015, 123–134). The material was limited, but the talus average was around 61 mm (GLl).

In Mikulčice extreme values were recorded in both very high and very low directions. The tendency to higher values could indicate the presence or influence of the Italic breed, similarly to Bernhardsthal. Nonetheless, very few individuals exhibit low values. Such individuals were not observed in the Bernhardsthal population, with which the cattle population from Mikulčice bears remarkable similarities. The question is if these animals represent the small-sized Iron Age cattle. The same question will be addressed later when analysing the material from Sand.

4.2.7.1.6 Gars-Thunau

Gars-Thunau is a fortified Slavic settlement of the early medieval period dating from the 9th to the 10th century AD. The animal assemblage exhibited the prevalence of cattle (> 30% of the total material). The faunal remains from Gars raised interesting questions concerning the identification of the cattle population, specifically whether new breeds, which might have arrived with the Slavic culture, could be identified.

Morphometric investigation

According to Figure 19 the GLl of tali ranges from 48.0-51.5 and 60.0-63.5 mm with a peak at 52.0-55.5 mm. A similar distribution was recorded in Dürrnberg. The size classes vary between 48.0-51.5 and 64.0-67.5 mm (GLl). The talus average (Figure 19) from Gars-Thunau is 56.0 mm (GLl), similar to Dürrnberg (57.4).

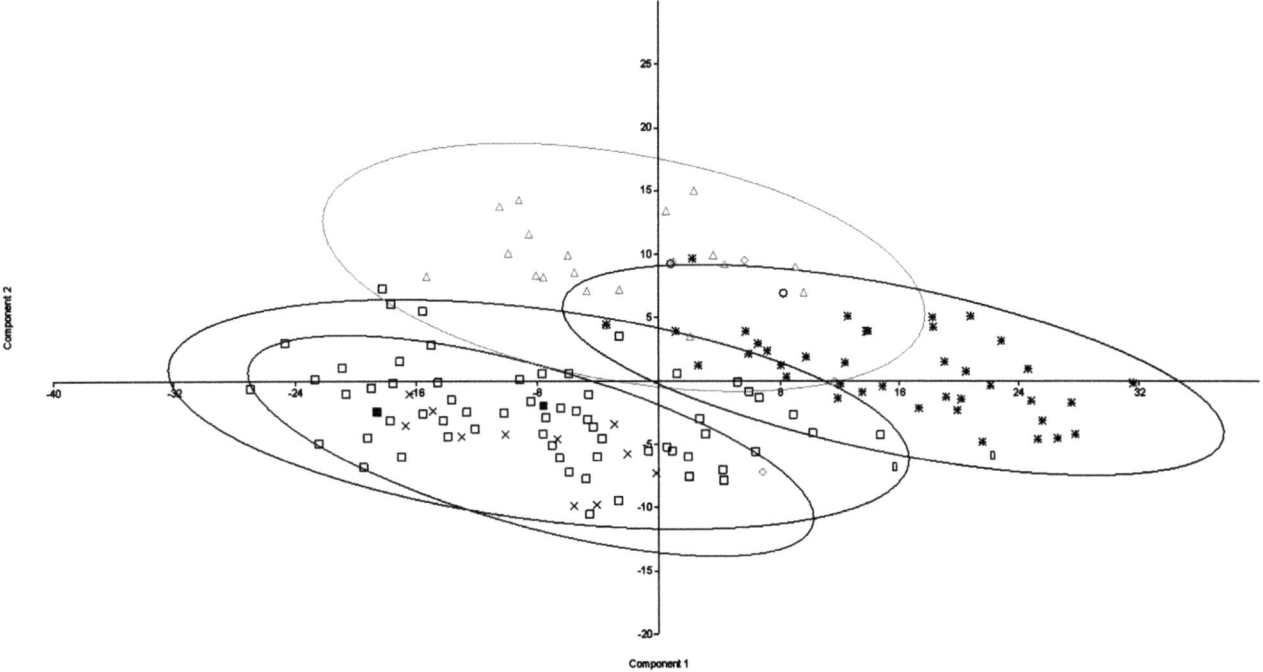

Figure 18. The new PCA after the changes suggested at this work (Saliari). M(m): Mikulčice males, M(c): Mikulčice castrated, M(f): Mikulčice females, D(c): Dürrnberg castrated, D(f): Dürrnberg females, S(m): Sand males, S(c): Sand castrated, S(f): Sand females.

Metrically and morphologically the material revealed no exotic cattle remains, although Gars-Thunau is a Slavic site. This is supported by other studies from Germany, where cattle populations at sites related to the Slavic culture show no change to the cattle populations of previous periods. When Müller analysed the assemblages from Köpenick (early German and Slavic period), he wrote that the faunal assemblages from both stratigraphic groups typically show the same range of variation. The same author continues by saying that most of the cattle of the early German period do not differ in size or form from those of the Slavic period (Müller 1962, 81–97).

Results

According to Kanelutti (1990), the bones indicate small-sized cattle individuals. They apparently bear significant similarities to the Dürrnberg material and thus to the alpine stock kept by the Bavarian settlers. Historical records confirm a very close relationship between the people of Gars-Thunau and the Bavarians (Brunner 2003, 907–1156). Pucher has suggested that the Bavarians probably supplied the inhabitants of Gars-Thunau.

4.2.7.1.7 Raabs

Raabs is one of the most famous Austrian castles; the site gave its name to Austria (Rakousko) at the Czech Republic. The archaeological remains derive from the 10th to the 12th century AD but the animal assemblages come from a very short time span of approximately 50 years in the 11th century. The archaeozoological examination showed that animals were delivered to the castle residents by the

peasants who settled around the castle. The prevalent species was pig.

Morphometric investigation

Figure 19 indicates that the most frequent talus size class is 52.0-55.5 mm, suggesting small-sized animals. The average value is 57.5 mm, similar to the material from Dürrnberg and Gars-Thunau. Additionally, the metatarsals yield a Bp value from 38.0-44.5 mm and a Bd from 45.5-51.5 mm. Further metric analysis of the measurement averages of the long bones suggests that the Raabs and Dürrnberg values are similar. The withers height estimation is 112.2 cm for a female metacarpal, and 100.2, 105.3 and 112.5 cm for three female metatarsals. One metacarpus of a castrated animal yielded 108.8 cm. These values are significantly lower than those at Bernhatdsthal, where the middle-sized cattle breed was represented.

More evidence for the group identification derives from the morphological analysis of the horn cores. Horn core size at Raabs suggests significant differences from Mikulčice and Bernhatdsthal, which exhibited elongated horn cores. The horn cores from Raabs are significantly smaller. Their form and orientation more closely resemble those from Dürrnberg. Despite their small size, they seem to be relatively compact and robust.

Results

The morphological and metric investigation of the material from Raabs argues for the presence of the alpine cattle breed. Raabs and Gars-Thunau belong to the archaeological complexes that offer additional evidence for the long

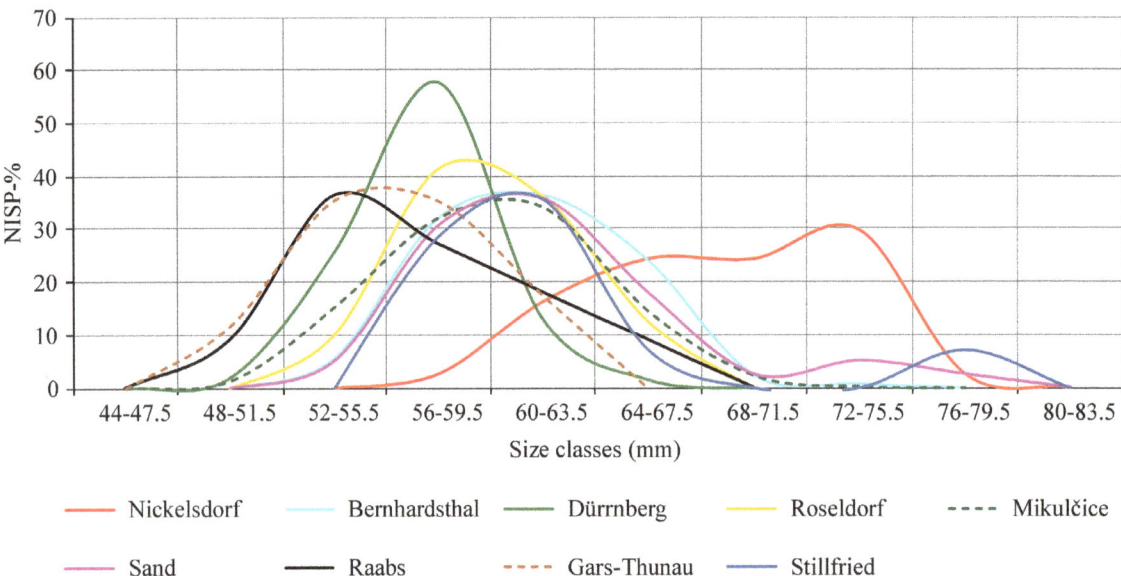

Figure 19. Cattle: size classes for the GLl measurement of talus (in mm) NISP%. Comparative study among different sites. Nickelsdorf: n=37, Roseldorf: n=80, Raabs: n=11, Bernhardsthal: n=129, Mikulčice: n=1210, Gars-Thunau: n=17, Dürrnberg: n=191, Sand: n=39, Stillfried: n=14.

presence of the Iron Age cattle, supported by finds from three medieval sites from the eastern Alps (Pflindsberg, Thierberg, Saaleck).

4.2.7.1.8 Stillfried

Stillfried is one of the most important archaeological sites because it demonstrated a great continuity starting from the Palaeolithic until the medieval period (Felgenhauer et al. 1988). The site is located at the northern eastern part of Lower Austria and yielded many animal bones, offering the unique opportunity to study the evolution of the cattle population during the various periods. Of great interest is the material from the medieval period (12th-13th century AD). During the Middle Ages, domesticated animals dominated (92.5%) and cattle were the dominant species (49.4%).

Morphometric investigation

Figure 19 suggests a great range of variation for the cattle population from Stillfried between 56.0-59.5 and 76.0-79.5 mm. Note, however, that almost all the findings are distributed between the size classes 56.0-59.5 and 64.0-67.5 mm, which indicates a homogeneous population. Only one bone derives from the size class 76.0-79.5 mm, which expands the variation.[17] The most frequent size class is 60.0-63.5 mm, similar to Mikulčice and Bernhardsthal. The talus average is 58.3 mm.

Results

The metric analysis of the Stillfried material suggests noteworthy similarities to the Mikulčice and Bernhardsthal populations. All three sites exhibited many individuals

at the size class 60.0-63.5 mm, pointing to middle-sized individuals. This result is interesting because all three sites are close to each other.

4.2.7.1.9 Sand

The aforementioned analyses provided important information about the existence of different cattle breeds in the past and their geographical distribution. The main aim was to create a framework for evaluating the material from Sand. The task is to study the morphological traits and to analyse the metric data for the cattle bones from Sand to test for similarities with one (or more) of the above populations.

Metric analysis: talus

The first important information derives from talus measurements. Most remains fall in the size class 60.0-63.5 mm, suggesting similarities to Bernhardsthal, Stillfried, and Mikulčice (Figure 19). Figure 20 depicts the GLl (max. length) and Bd (distal breadth) talus measurements for the populations of Stillfried, Mikulčice, Dürrnberg, Gars-Thunau, and Raabs. Previous analyses showed the presence of the small-sized cattle (Dürrnberg, Gars-Thunau, Raabs) and middle-sized cattle (Stillfried, Mikulčice).

Numerically, the two big groups are Dürrnberg and Mikulčice and thus they present a wider variability. Careful analysis shows that although the two breeds overlap, there is a different accumulation centre in which the majority of the animals are concentrated. The Dürrnberg group is mainly concentrated at lower GLl values. Most individuals are between 54.0-60.0 mm (GLl) and 32.0-40.0 (Bd), whereas at Mikulčice they are between 57.0-65.0 (GLl) and 33.0-43.0 mm. The averages for Dürrnberg are 57.4 (GLl) and 35.7 (Bd), whereas the averages for Mikulčice are 60.2 (GLl) and 38.0 (Bd).

---

[17] It remains unclear if this bone is from the Middle Ages or a modern infiltration. There were some findings with unclear dating.

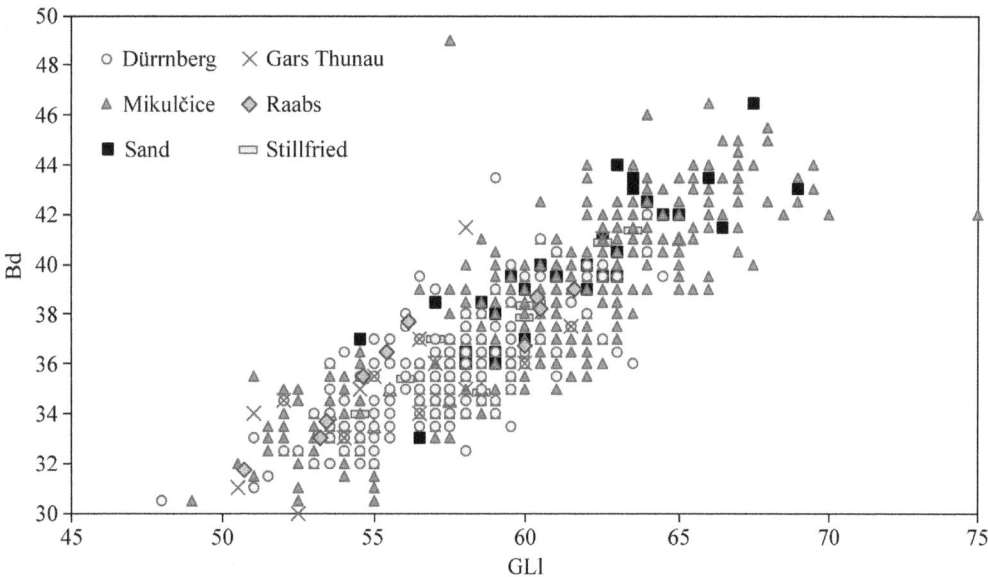

Figure 20. Cattle: comparative study for the GLl/Bd of talus (in mm) (x:GLl/ y:Bd). Raabs: n=10, Mikulčice: n=509, Gars-Thunau: n=17, Dürrnberg: n=187, Sand: n=39, Stillfried: n=9.

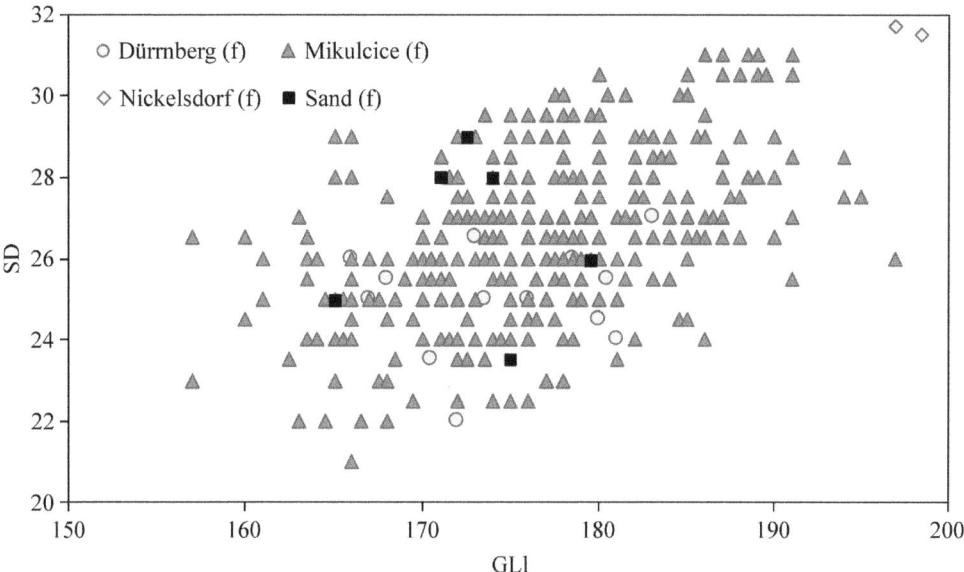

Figure 21. Cattle: comparative study for the GLl/SD of female metacarpals (in mm) (x:GL/y:SD). Nickelsdorf: n=2, Mikulčice: n=361, Dürrnberg: n=13, Sand: n=6.

The other populations provided much fewer samples. Nonetheless, Raabs and Gars-Thunau apparently had a similar variation range as Dürrnberg. The range at Sand is similar to Mikulčice. Although the material is limited, a number of individuals clearly fall out of the variation of the small-sized cattle. The average GL and Bd values for Sand seem to be closer to Mikulčice, which yielded 60.9 (GLl) and 39.1 mm (Bd).

Metric analysis: metapodials

Figure 21 presents the statistical analysis of the metric data from the female metacarpals of Mikulčice,[18] Dürrnberg, and Nickelsdorf. These populations were selected because they have been sexually identified. The diagram is

restricted to complete female metacarpals and depicts two measurements (in mm), the GL (x axis) and SD (y axis). These were chosen because they best represent size and shape.

The diagram shows that Mikulčice and Dürrnberg share a common, overlapping area, whereas the Nickelsdorf material is clearly separated. The alpine cattle of Dürrnberg are mainly concentrated at the lower part of the diagram. Some samples from Sand overlap with the Dürrnberg population, but others fall in the same variation range with Mikulčice. The diagram depicts a tendency similar to that of the two talus diagrams. The limited number of whole female metacarpals from Sand did not enable more detailed investigations of the variation range of the group.

---

[18] According to the sex distribution noted by statistic 2.

Samples from males were not used due to their low numbers in Sand and the other sites. Metacarpals of castrated animals were not statistically assessed even though they constituted most of the material; the number of measurements was very limited due to the high degree of fragmentation.

Interestingly, some values of female metacarpals were unusually low. If the material from Sand is similar to Bernhardsthal and Stillfried, then these low values are unexpected. A similar phenomenon, however, has been observed in Mikulčice. There, single finds raised a new question about the homogeneity of the material. The analysis of Sand 1 already provided indications that some individuals do not fit the expected variation range (Pucher & Schmitzberger 1999a, 355–378).

This observation led to an estimation of the variation coefficient (V value). The very high V value resulting from the long bones of humerus, radius, ulna, femur, and tibia is normal, due to difficulties in sex identification. The most important results were obtained from the metapodials, where the animals are categorised according to their sex (Tables 6 and 7). At this case any high value cannot be interpreted as reflecting dimorphism.

The V value was examined for the measurements GL (maximum length), Bp (proximal breadth), SD (smallest breadth of diaphysis), DD (smallest depth of the diaphysis), and Bd (distal breadth) of the metapodials as defined by Driesch (1976). The V values calculated for the female metacarpals show relatively high values for the Bp and SD measurements (Table 6).

In order to test if the V value of the female metacarpals is higher and thus out of the range of the normal values, that value was estimated for well-studied populations (Dürrnberg, Nickelsdorf, Roseldorf). The analysis suggests that the variation coefficient for the animals from Sand exhibited the highest values. Although SD tends to be higher compared with other measurements because it might significantly differ individually, the reference populations exhibited values between 6.0 and sometimes 7.0; only in Sand was 8.19 reached. DD was also high (8.55).

Figure 22 investigates the metric data of female metatarsals. The differences already noted between Dürrnberg and Mikulčice (Figure 21) are also visible here. The average values of GL in Mikulčice are 205.6 and of SD 22.5 mm, whereas for Dürrnberg the corresponding values are 197.2 and 20.8. The few female metatarsals from Sand fell into the region of overlap between Dürrnberg and Mikulčice. The average values are 196.0 (GL) and 21.0 (SD). Finally, the V value for the metatarsals demonstrated the expected values (Table 7).

Withers height

The withers height estimation for metacarpals of cows is between 99.5 and 108 cm (average 104 cm), for the males between 110 and 117 cm (average 113 cm), and for the oxen between 117 and 124.4 cm (average 121.1 cm). The metatarsals yielded a withers height estimation for the females between 99 and 119 cm (average 107 cm), and for the castrated animals between 113 and 124.7 cm (average 119.2 cm). The withers height estimation is similar to Mikulčice, Bernhardsthal, and Stillfried.

Shape differences

As it has been already demonstrated during the analysis of the Italic and alpine cattle (Pucher 2006a, 253–268; 2013, 9–36), differences among cattle breeds are related not only to size, but also to shape. In this work, the same method was applied to the cattle bones from Sand, Mikulčice, and

Table 6. Cattle: the variation coefficient (V) was calculated for female cattle metacarpals in order to test the homogeneity of the population in Sand

Measurement	N	Min	Max	x	s	V
GL	6	165.0	179.5	172.83	4.80	2.78
Bp	12	43.5	57.5	48.67	3.76	7.72
SD	11	22.5	29.0	26.23	2.15	**8.19**
DD	5	16.0	20.0	18.30	1.57	**8.55**
Bd	8	47.0	56.0	49.94	3.19	6.39

Table 7. Cattle: the variation coefficient (V) for female cattle metatarsals

Measurement	N	Min	Max	x	s	V
GL	5	187.0	207.0	196.00	10.27	5.24
Bp	16	37.0	45.5	41.77	2.38	5.70
SD	11	20.0	24.0	22.20	1.42	6.39
TD	7	20.5	23.0	21.67	1.17	5.40
Bd	10	43.0	54.0	46.56	3.25	6.99

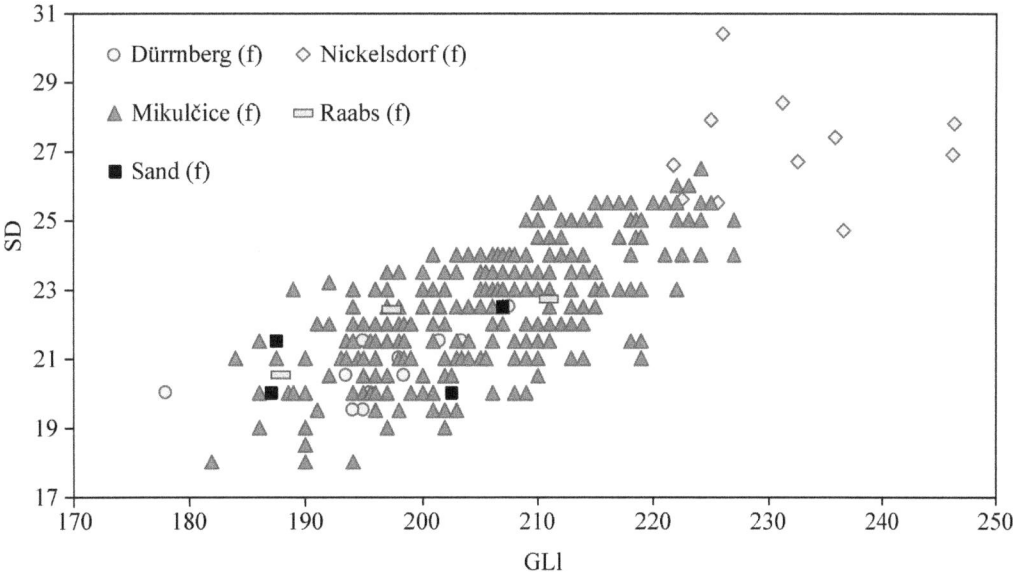

Figure 22. Cattle: comparative study for the GLl/SD of female metatarsals (in mm) (x:GL/y:SD). Nickelsdorf: n=11, Mikulčice: n=305, Dürrnberg: n=13, Sand: n=4, Raabs: n=3.

Roseldorf as for Dürrnberg and Nickelsdorf. The method is based on comparing the average of the height at withers for the metapodials and other long bones (radius and tibia). Humerus and femur produce lower values than radius and tibia, explaining why they were not included in this study. The average of the height at withers has been estimated for each bone separately.

The difference between the average of the height at withers for radius and metacarpal for the alpine cattle is minimal. The Italic cattle from Nickelsdorf showed a much bigger difference, indicating a proportional difference. The material from Mikulčice (middle-sized population) was also considerably different (Table 8).

When applying this method for Sand, the difference in the average height at withers is enormous, also in comparison with Nickelsdorf. Note, however, that Dürrnberg, Mikulčice, and Nickelsdorf exhibit a high frequency of females (between 70% and 60%), whereas in Sand oxen prevail. Studies on sheep bones demonstrate that castration affects the growth rhythm (Davis 2000, 373–390). The epiphyseal ossification of the castrated animals takes place later, and parts of bones, including the proximal part of the radius, apparently continue growing for some time after the fusion of the epiphyses.

In order to test whether the castration effect has an impact on cattle populations as well, the same method was applied to the Roseldorf material, which exhibited a homogeneous cattle population with a high number of oxen. At this case the results were similar to Sand and not to Dürrnberg, as it would have been expected. Roseldorf exhibited an enormous difference between radius and metacarpus. This observation suggests that the sex distribution might significantly affect the results of this methodology. Under a normal sex distribution, which in the case of Sand would mean the dominance of cows, similar results to Mikulčice would have been expected.

Table 8. Cattle: average height at withers based on radius and metacarpus

Site	Withers height (Radius)	Withers height (Metacarpus)
Dürrnberg (Alpine cattle)	106.0	106.5
Nickelsdorf (Italic cattle)	134.0	129.1
Mikulčice	112.2	110.0
Sand	119.4	109.8
Roseldorf (Alpine cattle)	119.8	110.5

Morphological observations on cranium

The morphological investigation of the cranial elements from Sand 1 enabled identifying a mixed cattle population (Pucher & Schmitzberger 1999a, 355–378). The fewer measurements from the female metacarpals, and the high V value, provided important but only broad indications. The morphological analysis however, presented some difficulties, due to the low number of finds – especially of horn cores – and due to the fragmentary state of the cranium. In this study, the focus was on the horn cores, the os frontale, and the os parietale. The following observations are cautiously interpreted, but they provide some preliminary observations and thoughts for future work.

Horn cores

The significant features of horn cores are size, the position in relation to the cranium, the grade of robusticity, and the orientation. Size is one of the most obvious differences. Already in Sand 1, two different cattle groups were distinguished based on the horn cores (Pucher & Schmitzberger 1999a, 355–378).

Table 9. Cattle: cranial measurements from Purgstall, Tulln, Eggendorf, and Sand

Measurements (cattle)	Purgstall		Tulln		Sand		Tulln		Eggendorf	
Side	L	R	L	R	L	R	L	R	L	R
Oro-aboral (greatest diameter)	34.5	33.0	30.5	30.5	34.0	34.0	36.0	36.5	(32.5)	(32.5)
Dorso-basal (least diameter)	28.5	29.0	29.5	29.0	27.0	30.5	-	-	-	-
Length of the outer curvature	-	(12.0)	-	-	-	-	-	-	-	-
Horncore basal circumference	11.5	11.5	11.0	10.0	10.5	11.0	13.0	-	11.5	(11.0)
Distance between the horn core tips	130.0		130.0		130.0		150.0		12.5	
Least occipital breadth	(96.0)		(109.0)		-		(124.0)		-	
Sex	female		female		female		male		castrated	

The first group of horn cores is easy to differentiate because they are robust and elongated. Their orientation starts with a slight nuchal inclination and bends to oral, more or sometimes less intensively, without any specific tendency to dorsal or nuchal (Pucher & Schmitzberger 1999a, 355–378; Riedel & Pucher 2008, 159–194). Similar finds came from Bernhardsthal, Stillfried, and Mikulčice.

The second group of horn cores demonstrated some distinct differences. They are significantly smaller, indicating a very weak and gracile construction. The dimensions and proportions cannot be attributed to sexual dimorphism and they do not seem to be the result of a pathological alteration. The orientation of the horn cores was also different; the identified females in Sand show that the direction of the horn cores is nuchal and then bent to dorsal with a small tendency to oral.

Illustrations of horn cores from Mikulčice (Kratochvíl 1987a) exhibit – for a small number of samples – the same tendency; they are tiny and gracile. In this case, it is useful to recall the talus diagram (Figure 19), which provided evidence for a mixed population at Mikulčice with indications for a small-sized group. This is also suggested by the horn cores. Thus, the individuals exhibiting very low values in Figure 19 could be associated with the group of these small-sized horn cores. The question raised in the previous chapter was whether these small-sized animals indicate the presence of the small-sized Iron Age cattle breed.

The material from Sand helps provide an answer to that question. The very well-preserved horn core number 115/96 was compared with findings from Dürrnberg and a recent Bergschecken population. The comparison shows that the horn cores of the alpine animals are neither very small nor so gracile; they are relatively robust, compact, and their orientation and position on the cranium different.

This indicates that the material from Sand and probably from Mikulčice exhibits another small-sized cattle breed unrelated to the Iron Age population. The question now is which population is represented, when and where this group appears. As both Sand and Mikulčice date to the early medieval period, faunal assemblages from this period

were re-examined. Not all the early medieval sites were re-investigated because for some of them, like Stillfried, it was clear (based on published morphological characteristics and the metric analysis) that they did not exhibit traces of this group.

The only finds that have been detected and could be associated with this group are single specimens from a few early medieval sites: Tulln (cemetery), Purgstall (cemetery), and Eggendorf (settlement). Tulln yielded horn cores from one male and one female. The orientation of the female specimen was similar to that from Sand: nuchal and then bent to dorsal with a small tendency to oral. The female from the early medieval cemetery of Purgstall showed a similar direction. These similarities are also suggested by the metric data in Table 9, especially for females, which constituted the majority.

The male specimen from Tulln exhibits the same orientation but bears the characteristics that typically differentiate males from females. For instance, the distance between the horn core tips and the smallest occipital width indicates that the male is significantly wider than the females and castrated (Figures 23, 24). Still, the Tulln male is relatively gracile (Table 9).

Other cranial elements

Additional observations derive by the study of the *os frontale*. Bones that come from the archaeological comparative material of the early medieval sites (Tulln, Sand, Eggendorf, Purgstall) exhibited sloping sides. A similar tendency has also been detected at the recent blond breed animals from Waldviertel and the animals from the archaeological site of Bernhardsthal.[19] The alpine Bergschecken population is strongly differentiated in bearing a very flat and wider os frontale, particularly the females (Figures 23, 24).

The next observation concerns the *protuberantia intercornualis* at the nuchal part. In the smallest individuals from the early medieval sites (Tulln, Sand, Eggendorf,

---

[19] This was not surprising because they are already identified as an older form of blond breed.

38

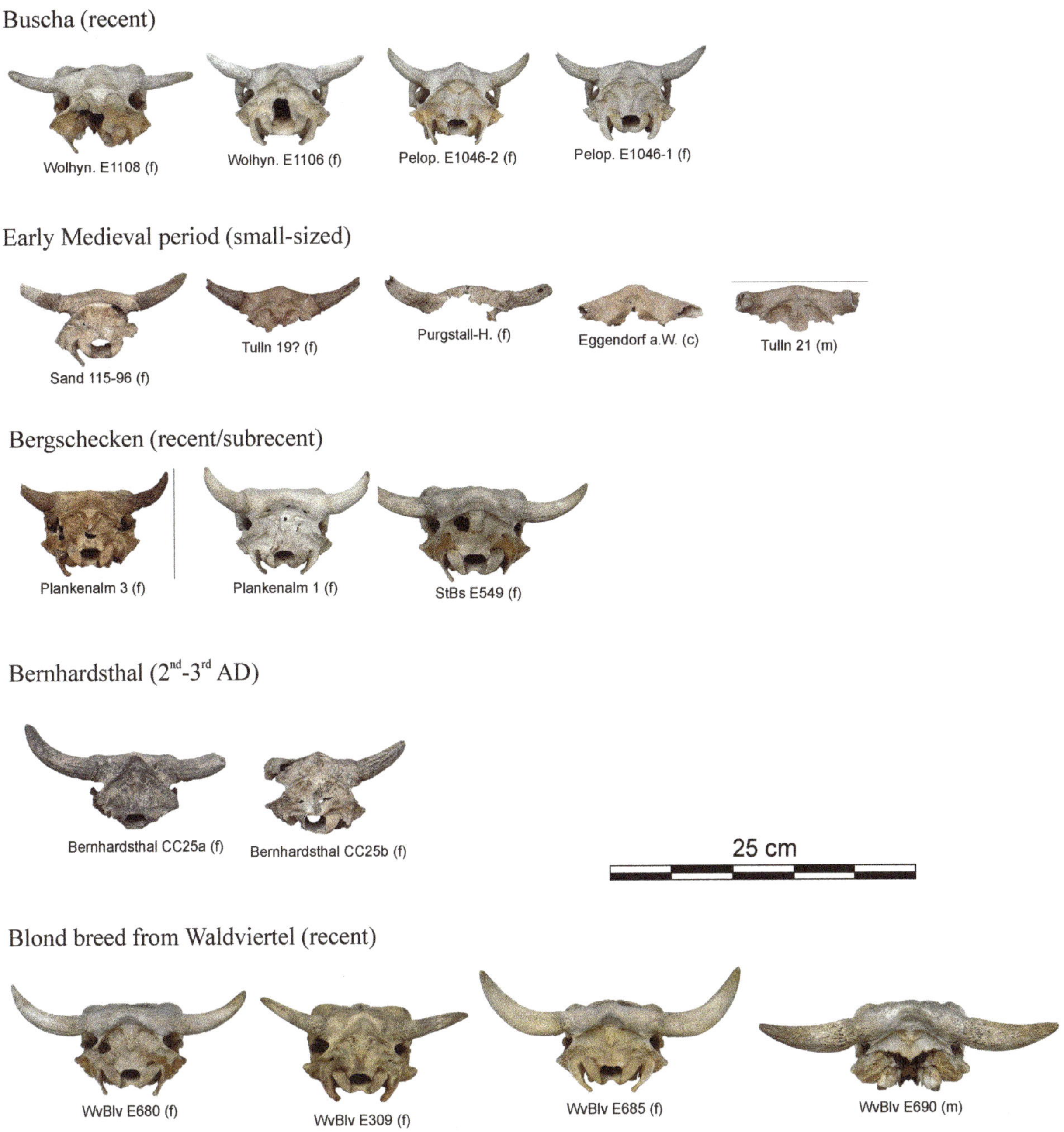

Buscha (recent)

Wolhyn. E1108 (f)   Wolhyn. E1106 (f)   Pelop. E1046-2 (f)   Pelop. E1046-1 (f)

Early Medieval period (small-sized)

Sand 115-96 (f)   Tulln 19? (f)   Purgstall-H. (f)   Eggendorf a.W. (c)   Tulln 21 (m)

Bergschecken (recent/subrecent)

Plankenalm 3 (f)   Plankenalm 1 (f)   StBs E549 (f)

Bernhardsthal (2nd-3rd AD)

Bernhardsthal CC25a (f)   Bernhardsthal CC25b (f)

25 cm

Blond breed from Waldviertel (recent)

WvBlv E680 (f)   WvBlv E309 (f)   WvBlv E685 (f)   WvBlv E690 (m)

Figure 23. Morphological comparative study among recent crania (19th century) from the Adametz Collection and archaeological material: a) archaeological material from Bernhardsthal (2nd-3rd cent AD), b) recent blond/yellow breed from Waldviertel, c) recent Bergschecken from Plankenalm, d) archaeological material from early medieval sites (Tulln, Purgstall, Eggendorf), e) recent Buša group from Volhynia and Peloponnese (Greece). Graphic: Pucher. Abbreviations: f: female, c: castrated, m: male.

Purgstall), this part of the cranium is pointed, almost triangular. The same characteristic has been also detected in the recent blond breed population and the animals from the equivalent archaeological assemblages (Bernhardsthal). In contrast, the Bergschecken population exhibits a rounded and wider protuberantia intercornualis, which is even wider in males and castrated animals.

Although the small-sized early medieval cattle population shares interesting similarities in some cranial elements with the blond breed (both the recent material and the archaeological samples), the strong differences in the horn cores makes clear that they constitute two different populations.

Results

The morphological and metric analysis of the material from Sand indicates that the animals were mainly represented by a middle-sized cattle population, probably an early form of the blond breed. Similar finds derive from Bernhardsthal, Stillfried, Tulln, and Mikulčice, indicating a zone of this early form of blond breed cattle at the north-eastern part of Austria and the south-eastern part of the Czech Republic (Figure 25).[20]

_____
[20] It is interesting to recall that the inhabitants of Raabs imported the small-sized Iron Age cattle. Knowing that this part of Austria belongs to

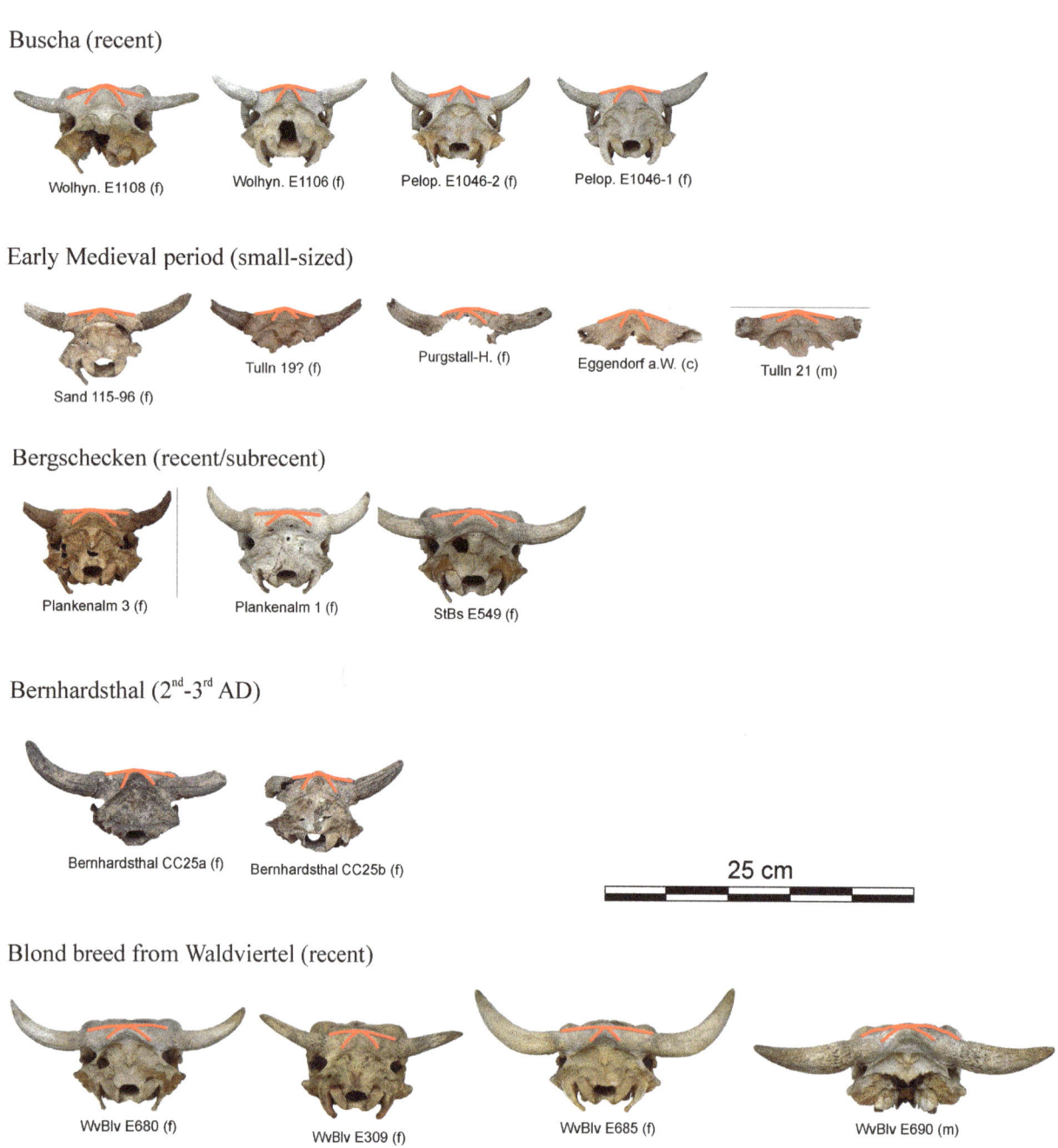

Figure 24. Morphological comparative study among recent crania (19th century) from the Adametz Collection and archaeological material: a) archaeological material from Bernhardsthal (2nd-3rd century AD), b) recent blond/yellow breed from Waldviertel, c) recent Bergschecken from Plankenalm, d) archaeological material from early medieval sites (Tulln, Purgstall, Eggendorf), e) recent Buša group from Volhynia and Peloponnese (Greece). The red line indicates the regions, where the main differences were observed. The fragmented nature of the archaeological material considerably limited the area of investigation. Graphic: Pucher. Abbreviations: f: female, c: castrated, m: male.

Moreover, the morphometric analysis of the material from Sand provides evidence for another small-sized cattle population, which is still not easy to identify. Importantly, all the sites that exhibit similar finds of this population in Austria (Tulln, Eggendord, Purgstall) share two similarities: the dating and the cultural tradition. This is because all of them date to the early medieval period and are related to the Slavic culture. According to the literature, Slavic human populations of the 19th century are connected to a small-sized cattle breed with low milk and low meat

production, the Buša group (Hengeveld 1865, 188–189; Rohde 1876, 120).

This insight prompted the author study the crania of Buša cattle available in the Adametz Collection. The samples come from Volhynia and Peloponnese (Greece). All the characteristics mentioned above and analysed on the horn cores and the other cranial elements during the investigation of the small-sized early medieval cattle population were also found on the crania of the recent Buša group (Figure 24). This could indicate a close relationship to this population. Nevertheless, in order to determine, whether the early medieval small-sized cattle constitute an

the so-called blond breed zone, the import of the alpine cattle from the inhabitants of Raabs points to a deliberate selection.

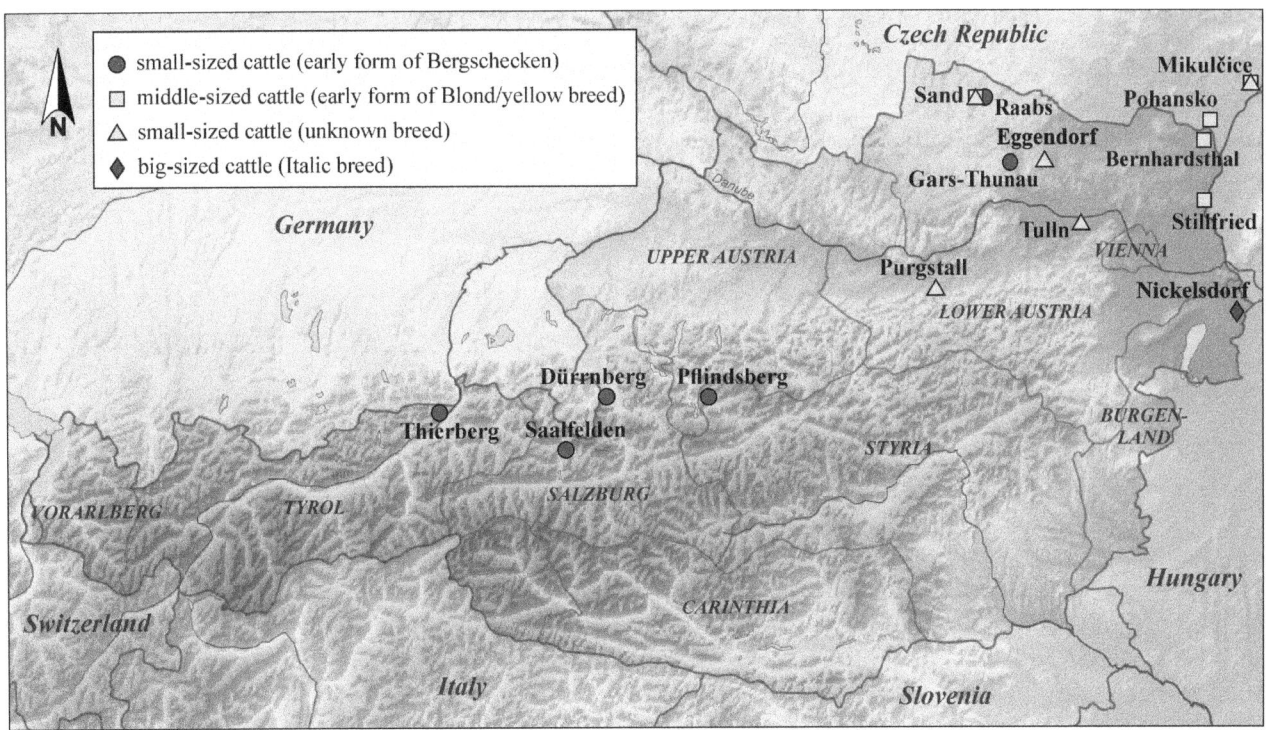

Figure 25. Sites described in the text during the morphometric analysis and possible breeds that were identified. This investigation enabled a better understanding of the distribution of the different cattle populations. Source: https://commons.wikimedia.org/wiki/File:Austria_location_map.svg.

early form of the Buša group more archaeological material is necessary and additional methods such as DNA should be applied.

A final question concerns the expansion of this small-sized medieval group, which has been detected in Austria (Sand, Tulln, Purgstall, Eggendorf) and the Czech Republic (Mikulčice). A very interesting study on the domesticated and wild fauna of the early medieval Baltic Sea countries yielded some very significant results (Makowiecki 2014, 261–437) that are relevant for the Sand material. In early medieval Pomerania, namely between 900 and 1300 AD, similar small-sized animals have been found. The withers height has been estimated between 95.9 and 110.7 cm. In the evolution of cattle in that region from the prehistoric aurochs up to the 18th century, this early medieval form of cattle is the smallest reported (Makowiecki 2014, 261–437). One of the most important illustrations is a photograph of a skeleton of a medieval cow from the Museum of Lębork (Makowiecki 2009, Figure 7); it shows a small-sized animal with the same form of horn cores found in Sand and in Tulln. The studies from Poland have raised new questions that can inspire systematic future work on tracing the origins and understanding the evolution of this population.

4.3 Sheep (*Ovis orientalis* f. *aries*) and Goat (*Capra aegagrus* f. *hircus*)

4.3.1 Quantification

The analysis of the material and the criteria used to separate the small ruminants suggest a high number of goats. There is no evidence for the presence of sheep. A number of fragments, however, could not be identified with certainty due to the poor state of preservation and the lack of characteristic anatomical features. For this reason the category sheep/goat has been added.

The preliminary analysis of the species representation shows that goats played a secondary role in Sand. In total, 552 bones have been identified, corresponding to 5065.1 g. In recording the unidentified specimens, 429 bones were attributed to the category sheep/goat, and 123 could be attributed to goats. This corresponds to 2321.9 g (sheep/goat) and 2702.2 g (goat) (Table 10).

According to the weight analysis, goats represent 3.7% of the domesticated animals and 2.0% including the wild species. In Sand 1, the corresponding values are 2.1% and 1.2%. The weight analysis in Sand 2 showed that small ruminants represented 4.2% (1.3% goats) among the domesticated species and 2.8% (0.8% goats) including the wild taxa. In the Westwall area, the small ruminants represent 5.0% (2.1% goats) among the domesticated taxa and 2.3% with the wild fauna (1% goats).

The faunal assemblages showed a high number of domestic goat. Such a high value has been recorded at only very few places in Austria (see Melk-Winden in Pucher 2004, 363–403 and Ölkam in Schmitzberger 1999 and 2009). The faunal assemblages from contemporaneous early medieval sites suggest a low frequency of goats. Raabs (11th century AD) showed a significantly higher percentage of small ruminants (19%) with a clear prevalence of sheep (n=70), whereas goats were rare (n=3) (Riedel & Pucher

Table 10. Sheep/goat: number of identified specimens (NISP) and weight analysis

| Area | *Ovis orientalis* f. *aries/* *Capra aegagrus* f. *hircus* | | *Capra aegagrus* f. *hircus* | |
	NISP	Weight (g)	NISP	Weight (g)
Upper settlement terrace (S1*)	100	1174.0**	37	-
Lower settlement terrace (S2)	117	700.6	21	302.0
Westwall area (WW)	212	1662.3	65	1226.2
Total	429	2362.9***	123	2702.2****

* In Sand 1 all the identified bones and horn cores point towards goats.
** This number represents mixed material: sheep/goat elements and identified elements of goat.
*** Sand 1 is excluded from this calculation because it has been already estimated for both categories sheep/goats and goats.
**** Sand 1 is included because according to the identification only goats have been recorded.

2008, 159–194). Similar results were obtained from Gaiselberg (12th-16th century AD), where small ruminants represent 17.7%. 90 bones can be definitively attributed to sheep, 6 bones to goats (Spitzenberger 1986, 121–161). Gars-Thunau (8th-11th century AD) yielded similar results. Sheep/goats represent 17.2%, and the prevalent species among the small ruminants is sheep (Kanelutti 1990, 1993, 169–184). 13.3% is the small ruminant value in Stillfried (12th-13th century AD) and the ratio between sheep and goats is 6.8:1 (Pucher 1982). The frequency of small ruminants is low at the medieval site of Möllersdorf (11th-13th century AD) with 7.5% (Pucher 1986b, 47–57); at the site of Hainburg (13th-15th century AD) sheep are found at a higher percentage than goats (Galik 2004, 59–72). In the Czech Republic the faunal assemblages from the early medieval site of Pohansko (5th-11th century AD) yielded 15.2% of sheep/goats, with a clear prevalence of sheep (Kratochvíl 1969b).

It is important to differentiate between sheep and goats because the two species show differences regarding the environment, behaviour, keeping, and economic exploitation. Thus, the dominance of goats (in the identified material) in Sand can be underlined and interpreted as being associated with a favourable ecological background (Saliari et al. 2016, 245–288). The geographic position of Sand would have favoured the small-scale keeping of goats. The ecological background, which is characterized by intensive woodland, offers better fodder opportunities for goats. Goats are generally more flexible and they can adapt to different environments (Clutton-Brock 1987, 57; Benecke 1994, 238); they are browsers and their fodder can vary. Usually they select a more nutritious, variable diet consisting of leaves, weeds, bushes, twigs, and shrubs. In contrast, sheep are grazers; they prefer tender grass and are found in the corresponding habitats. Sheep are more demanding concerning the environment and fodder; they prefer open grasslands and the proximity to water.

As it will be discussed later, the presence of goats might have been favoured by the environment, but they were also intensively exploited. According to the archaeological finds, leather played an important role for the inhabitants of the site and the local economy (Saliari & Felgenhauer-

Schmiedt 2017, 95–114). The skin features of goat differ from those of sheep; the former is more tear resistant and probably more durable (Ewersen 2010, 53–75).

4.3.2 Sex ratio

4.3.2.1 Results and interpretation

The reconstruction of sex distribution is mainly based on the horn cores of goats because the number of pelvis specimens was very limited. The number of horn cores suggests that female animals dominate in Sand 1 with eighteen specimens, and only one male horn core has been identified. Similarly, females prevail in the Westwall area (14 finds); no male horn cores were detected. Only in Sand 2 male horn cores prevail (6 specimens). The very few pelvis fragments indicate one female for Sand 1 and one for the Westwall area.

Figure 26 shows a clear prevalence of female individuals, contributing 82.1% for the entire site. The dominance of female goats is a typical phenomenon in an autarchic peasant economy. This is because, economically, goats present important similarities to cattle. The birth rate must be also regulated by the peasants. Males are usually slaughtered at a young age, whereas female animals survive

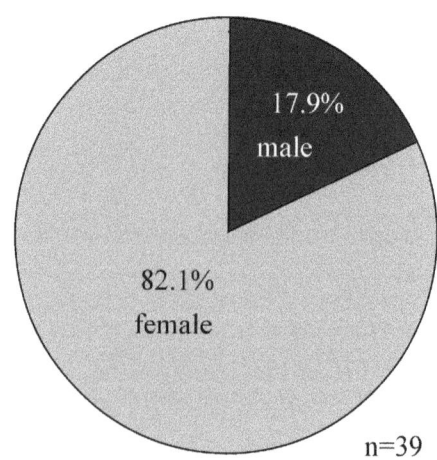

Figure 26. Goat: sex determination based on horn cores – Sand total (NISP%).

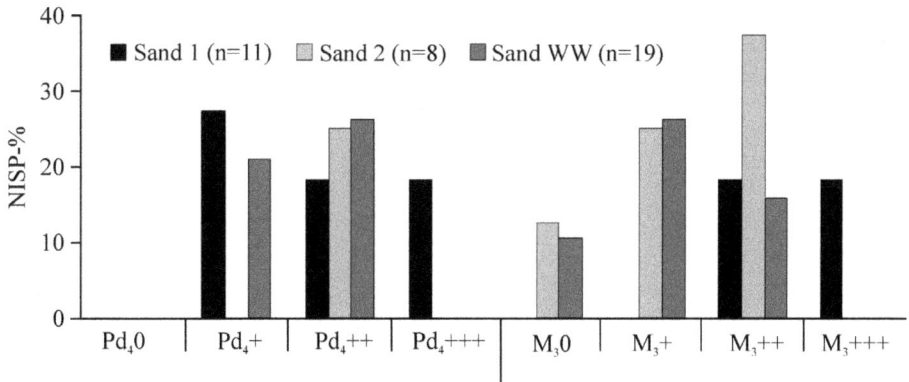

Figure 27. Goat: mortality profiles – per area – mandibular teeth (NISP%).

in order to secure the next generation and to be further exploited. Although cattle are a prevalent species for the local record, sometimes goats provided an alternative source of secondary products such as milk. In order to better understand their role in Sand, the mortality profiles are investigated below.

4.3.3 Age at death

4.3.3.1 Results and interpretation

The diagrams presented in this chapter refer to goats and not to sheep/goat. This is because all the identified cranial elements derive from goats and thus there was no reason to assume that the mandibles come from sheep. Nonetheless, a number of cranial elements and mandibles could not be identified due to lack of the relevant anatomical features. Concerning maxilla and mandible, many teeth could not be categorised as sheep or goat.

To begin with, the age structure of the mandibular teeth is based on 18 temporary and 20 permanent teeth. Due to the fact that the number of finds is sometimes low, the statistical processing should be treated with caution. In Sand 1, immature animals (Pd_4) dominate with 63.6% (Figure 27). Adults make up 36.4% and are mainly older than 7 years. In Sand 2, adult individuals of different stages prevail. The dominant tendency is older adults. Immature individuals make up 25%. Figure 27 indicates a higher number of immature animals for the Westwall area with 47.4%. Concerning adults, animals between 5-7 years dominate.

Figure 28 presents the total profile for the entire site. The prevalent stage is Pd_4++, which indicates a high number of animals between 1-2 years. Immature animals represent 47.3%. The high frequency of immature individuals and the fragmentary mortality profile[21] do not suggest the existence of an autarchic peasant economy. Similarly to cattle, the many young animals indicate provision from outsiders. Immature individuals older than one year (Pd_4++) offer considerably more meat than younger animals. The prevalence of young age stages suggests consumption of

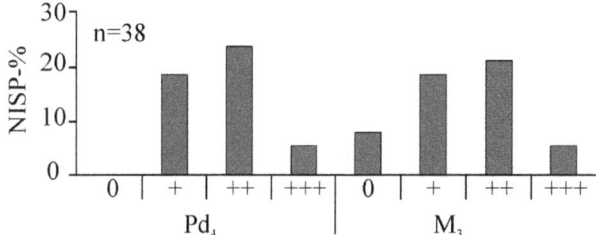

Figure 28. Goat: mortality profile – Sand total – mandibular teeth (NISP%).

good-quality meat because the flesh of young animals is more tender and tasty. Skin exploitation is also possible; especially the hides of young individuals are of very good quality.

4.3.4 Combining sex and age distribution

4.3.4.1 Discussion and interpretation

Combining age and sex distribution sheds light on the daily life of the site's inhabitants. As noted earlier, the prevalence of females in peasant economies is unsurprising. However, the archaeozoological record has shown that female goats might also dominate in cases of provision. Although imported sheep might exhibit a high number of males, in the case of goats, males are rarely imported due to practical considerations. The flesh of adult males has a very strong taste due to the effect of different hormones, often making the meat almost inedible. Since the age profile suggests imports of very young individuals, male animals are expected to be found at the younger stages that cannot be sexed.

Better understanding the role of domestic goats calls for considering the total profile and the combination of the different stages. The overview in Table 11 indicates that 73.7% of the animals were slaughtered at the optimum age for meat consumption. A similar high percentage of young animals is evident in Table 4 for cattle, suggesting that 78% of the individuals served as meat suppliers, providing the inhabitants of Sand with very good-quality meat. Nonetheless, the low percentage of goats points to a small contribution to the diet.

---

[21] $Pd_4$0 is absent.

Table 11. Goat: mortality profile and animal exploitation (NISP and NISP%)

	Meat supply		Secondary exploitation		NISP (total)
	$Pd_4$0 - +++	$M_3$0 - +	M_3++	M_3+++	
Sand 1	7	0	2	2	11
Sand 1 %	63.6	0	18.2	18.2	
	63.6		36.4		
Sand 2	2	3	3	0	8
Sand 2 %	25.0	37.5	37.5	0	
	62.5		37.5		
Sand WW	9	7	3	0	19
Sand WW %	47.4	36.8	15.8	0	
	84.2		15.8		
Sand Total (%)	73.7		26.3		

The number of adult animals could suggest small-scale keeping of some individuals, but the mortality profiles do not support the secondary exploitation of goats (milk) based on the high frequency of immature animals and young adults (Table 11). Figure 28 indicates a relatively high number (n=8) of animals between 7-10 years (M_3++). A number of other sites have exhibited a relatively high frequency of sheep and goats represented mainly by females between 7-10 years (M_3++), such as Hauenstein (Pucher & Schmitzberger 2006, 608–623), Roseldorf (Abd el Karem 2013a) and Salzburg Residenz (Pucher 1991, 71–135); at these sites small ruminants served mainly as meat suppliers and were not further exploited. These sites exhibited a very low percentage of animals older than 10 years (M_3+++), similarly to Sand.

4.3.5 Skeletal element distribution

4.3.5.1 Results and interpretation

The skeletal element representation concerns bones of goats and unidentified bones of sheep/goat. A considerable number of fragments could not be further categorized, especially small parts of the diaphyses that bear no characteristic anatomical details. If the element representation had been analysed solely based on the identified goat material, then the results would not have been realistic because the underrepresentation of some elements would have depicted identification problems rather than true values.

According to the MNI, fifteen individuals were recorded from the Westwall area, seven from Sand 2, and seven from Sand 1. The highest numbers represent the mandibles and humeri, two of the most robust bones. No dramatic fluctuations of MNI were noted. Thus, MNI apparently indicates imports of whole animals.

The total element representation for the site (Figure 30) shows that the cranial region and the mandible together make up 39%, the meaty regions of the fore- and hindlimbs 35.4%, vertebra and ribs 15.9%, and all the other bones with less meat 9.4%. Elements such as mandibles, radii and tibiae are very robust and usually survive in a good state of preservation.

Some slight differences were observed when examining each area at the site separately (Figure 29). The highest frequency of meaty regions derives from the Westwall area, whereas Sand 1 exhibited relatively abundant cranial elements. Sand 2 presents many ribs and vertebrae, but few bones such as metapodials, carpals, tarsals, and phalanges.

Comparing the profiles of domestic sheep/goat and cattle reveals certain similarities that mainly point to taphonomic processes (e.g. more and less robust elements), but also some differences that probably reflect anthropogenic factors (Figure 30). In this case, horn cores are interesting. Goats present a high number of horn cores, whereas in cattle they are underrepresented. Generally their intensive presence (and sometimes even their absence) is related to craft contexts such as leather and horn working (e.g. Bartosiewicz 1995; Albarella 2003, 71–86); the amount of the different elements might vary based on economic interest and the stage of processing. Note here that no artefacts out of horn cores were found in Sand.

4.3.6. Modifications

4.3.6.1 Butchery marks

The butchery techniques are similar to those observed for cattle. Intensive butchery has been recoded, pointing to full exploitation of the carcasses, but without indicating the application of a systematic technique. Cut and chop marks are mainly related to portioning, disarticulation, filleting, and marrow extraction. The study of cut marks from the Westwall area indicates skin removal. These marks were detected at anatomically relevant regions, namely the base of the horn cores and the distal part of the diaphysis of the metapodials. The cranial fragments suggest that both adult and immature goats were skinned. The adult animals

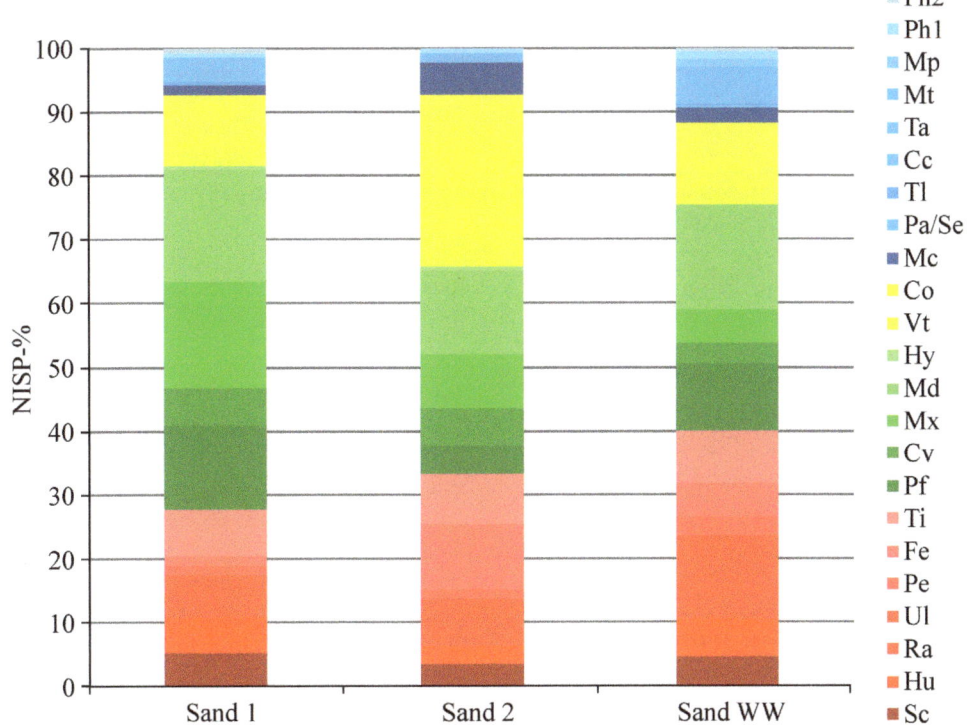

Figure 29. Sheep/Goat: skeletal element representation per area (NISP%). Abbreviations: Pf: processus frontalia, Cv: calvaria, Mx: maxilla, Md: mandible, Hy: hyoid, Vt: vertebrae, Co: costae, Sc: scapula, Hu: humerus, Ra: radius, Ul: ulna, Ca: carpalia, Pa: patella, Se: sesamoidea, Mc: metacarpus, Pe: pelvis, Fe: femur, Ti: tibia, Tl: talus, Cc: calcaneus, Ta: tarsalia, Mt: metatarsus, Mp: metapodia, Ph1: first phalanx, Ph2: second phalanx.

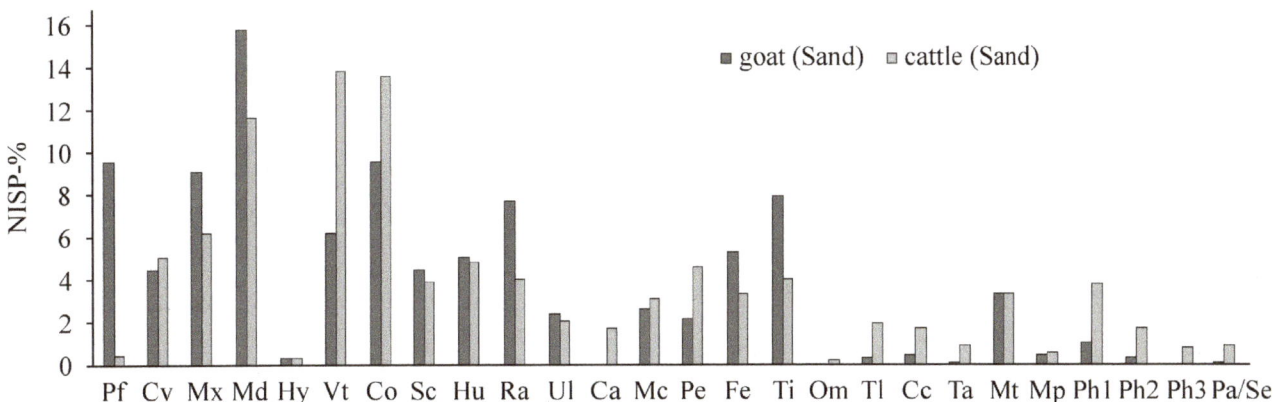

Figure 30. Skeletal element representation (NISP%). Comparative study between goat and cattle. Abbreviations: Pf: processus frontalia, Cv: calvaria, Mx: maxilla, Md: mandible, Hy: hyoid, Vt: vertebrae, Co: costae, Sc: scapula, Hu: humerus, Ra: radius, Ul: ulna, Ca: carpalia, Mc: metacarpus, Pe: pelvis, Fe: femur, Ti: tibia, Om: os malleolare, Tl: talus, Cc: calcaneus, Ta: tarsalia, Mt: metatarsus, Mp: metapodia, Ph1: first phalanx, Ph2: second phalanx, Ph3: third phalanx, Pa: patella, Se: sesamoidea.

represent females. The abundant horn cores found in Sand, and the fact that they are usually connected to hide exploitation, suggests that horn cores in the Westwall area probably reflect waste. Additionally, the author re-examined the material from Sand 1 in order to record cut marks that might indicate skinning activities. No relevant marks were found.

4.3.7 Morphometric analysis of goat

Morphologically, mostly the horn cores of females have been investigated due to their high frequency and very good state of preservation. The differences between male

and female goats vary considerably, as expected. Very few male horn cores were recovered and all were fragmented. Those of the females from Sand are elongated and their axis is arched without spiral twisting. The male finds point towards more robust, compact, and wider horns with thicker walls. Only one horn core from Sand 1 shows a weak twisting (Pucher & Schmitzberger 1999a, 355–378).

Most other sites have yielded much lower percentages of goats. This makes it difficult to find assemblages that have produced a sufficient number of measurements in order to understand the variation of the population and to conduct a comparative analysis. Single goat bones were discovered in Raabs (Riedel & Pucher 2008, 159–194) and Pohansko (Kratochvíl 1969b). Pohansko (5th-11th century AD) is close to the Thaya River and Raabs (11th century AD) is just 1.6 km away from Sand.

Raabs yielded very little material and thus very few measurements.[22] Only two bones could be compared to Sand, one radius and one first phalanx. The Bp and BFp measurements for the radius are 30.5 and 29.0 mm, respectively, falling within the variation of Sand. The material from Sand (n=9) exhibited radius Bp values between 30.0-33.0 and BFp values between 28.0 and 31.5 mm. The GLpe value of the first phalanx from Raabs is 37.5 and the SD value 10 mm. In Sand, only 3 first phalanges produced these measurements. Based on this material the GLpe was between 39.0 and 45.0 and the SD between 9.5 and 13.0 mm.

The material from Pohansko yielded similar results especially for the scapula and humerus, which produced the most measurements (Kratochvíl 1969b). Concerning scapula the variation for the SLC measurement in Pohansko is between 20.5 and 26.0 (n=10) and in Sand between 19.0 and 21.5 mm (n=3). Concerning the humerus, Bd in Pohansko (n=152) varied between 26.0 and 36.0 and in Sand between 28.5 and 32.0 mm (n=9). BT in Pohansko (n=149) is between 24.5 and 34.0 and in Sand (n=10) between 27.0 and 30.5 mm.

Despite the few metric data, the measurements from Sand, Raabs, and Pohansko fall into the same range of variation. According to Kratochvíl (1969b) the goats from Pohansko belong to a primitive small type that was widely distributed at many early medieval sites of Central Europe. This is also suggested by the finds from Sand. The assessment of withers at height, based on the factors defined by Schramm (1967a, 89–105), is estimated based on one metacarpal, which yielded 63.8 cm, and one metatarsal that yielded 65.7 cm.

4.4 Pig (*Sus scrofa* f. *domestica*)

4.4.1 Quantification

A total of 1718 bones were identified, corresponding to 17947.1 g. Based on weight, pig is the second most dominant domesticated species in Sand, making up 13.1% among the domesticated species and 7.1% including the wild species. In Sand 1, pigs contribute 8.7% among the domesticated species and 5.1% including the wild fauna. In Sand 2 the corresponding values are 15.2% and 10.1%, in Westwall 16.4% and 7.8%. Similarly to the small ruminants, pigs were more abundant in Sand 2 and Westwall area (Table 12).

The frequency of pigs would have been expected to be higher because of their abundance at other early medieval

Table 12. Pig: number of identified specimens (NISP) and weight analysis

Sus scrofa f. *domestica*		
Area	NISP	Weight (g)
Upper settlement terrace (S1)	435	4878.0
Lower settlement terrace (S2)	421	3633.0
Westwall area (WW)	862	9436.1
Total	1718	17947.1

assemblages. The faunal material from Raabs (11th century AD) exhibits a clear dominance of pigs with 42.0% (Riedel & Pucher 2008, 159–194). In Pohansko (Burgwall 5th-11th century AD), pigs represent 42.8% of the total material, with more than 8000 animal bones (Kratochvíl 1969b). In Gaiselberg (12th-16th century AD) and Gars-Thunau (8th-11th century AD), pigs are the second most abundant species, with 35.5% (Spitzenberger 1986, 121–161) and 32.9%, respectively (Kanelutti 1990, 1993, 169–184). Pigs were also very abundant in Möllersdorf (11th-13th century AD) with 34.5% (Pucher 1986b, 47–57) and in Stillfried (11th-12th century AD) with 21.0%.

4.4.2 Sex ratio

4.4.2.1 Results and interpretation

The sex determination suggests that female individuals prevail in Sand (65%) and in each separate area of Sand (Figure 31a, b). In a normal peasant economy, females prevail, whereas males are slaughtered at a young stage. Although there is no secondary exploitation – as is the case for the Bovidae – females play an important role in securing the next generation. When animals are imported from outsiders, then the archaeozoological record has shown that the sex distribution can differ significantly (Schülke 1965; Prilloff 2000; Riedel & Pucher 2008, 159–194). In some cases males dominate and in some others females; this is because pigs offer important advantages – they become sexually mature at a very early age and they produce a great number of offspring. However, the prevalence of males/castrated animals usually indicates a well-organised and specialised system (Pucher 2008, 74–77).

4.4.3 Age at death

4.4.3.1 Results and interpretation

The first remarkable observation pertains to the ratio between immature and adult pigs. More than 50% of the mandibular and maxillary teeth derive from immature individuals (Pd^4/Pd_4). Adults are mainly represented by younger stages ($M^3/_3 0$, $M^3/_3 +$), whereas animals older than 7 years constitute less than 10%. Overall, piglets and young adults represent more than 90%, indicating that the vast majority of pigs were slaughtered at the optimal age for meat consumption (Figure 32). The frequency of piglets in all three areas of the site was high (Figures 33-

---

[22] Most remains derive from females, similarly to Sand, which is important to consider when analysing measurements.

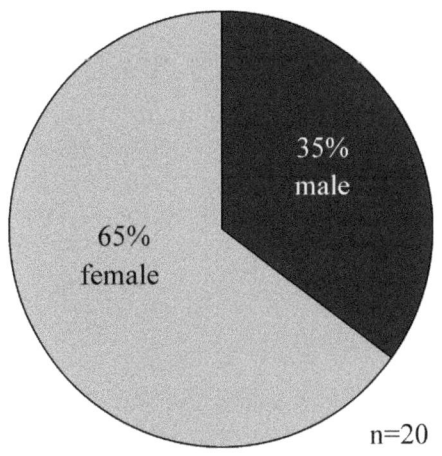

Figure 31a. Pig: sex determination – Sand total – maxillary and mandibular alveoli (NISP%).

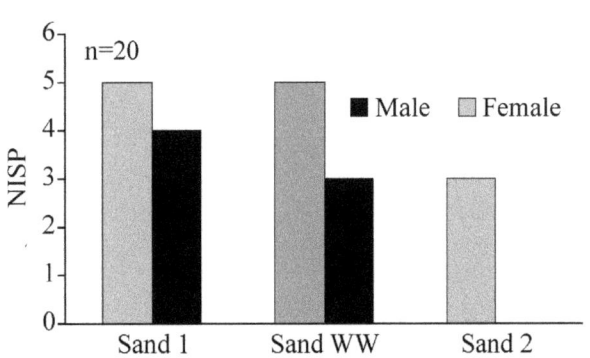

Figure 31b. Pig: sex determination – per area – maxillary and mandibular alveoli (NISP).

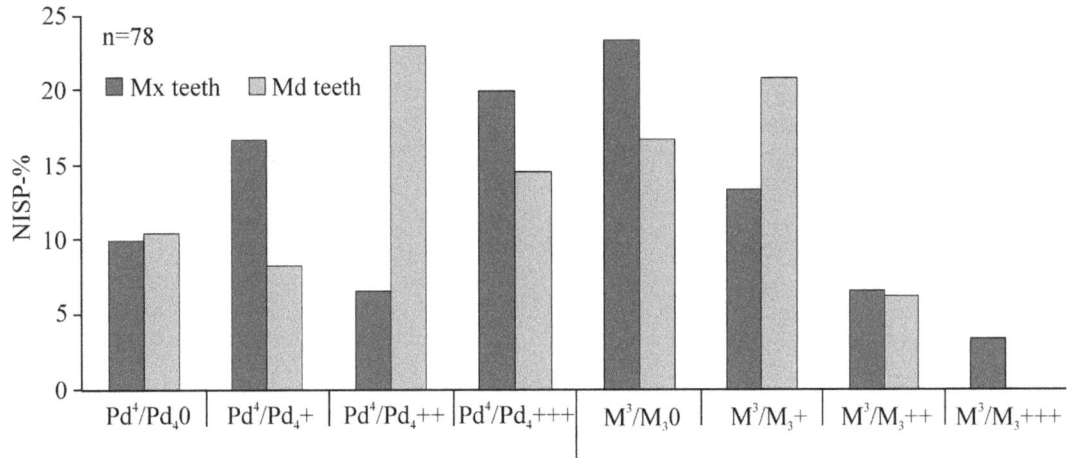

Figure 32. Pig: mortality profile – Sand total – maxillary and mandibular teeth (NISP%).

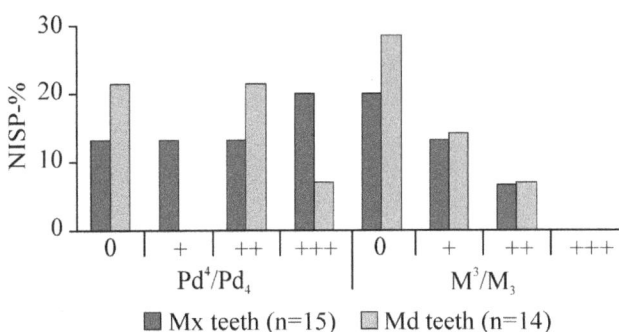

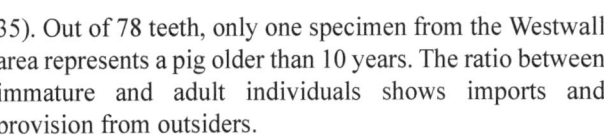

Figure 33. Pig: mortality profile – Sand 1 – maxillary and mandibular teeth (NISP%).

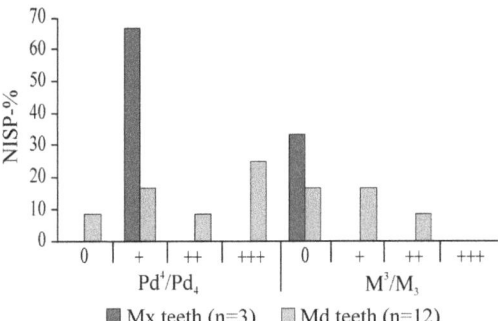

Figure 34. Pig: mortality profile – Sand 2 – maxillary and mandibular teeth (NISP%).

35). Out of 78 teeth, only one specimen from the Westwall area represents a pig older than 10 years. The ratio between immature and adult individuals shows imports and provision from outsiders.

The age distribution is surprising. Although slaughtering pigs at a young age (especially young adults) is a usual phenomenon verified by various assemblages, Sand presents a very strong prevalence of piglets that has been very rarely documented in the local archaeozoological record. Even in Raabs, where pigs dominate, the number

of piglets is significantly lower (Riedel & Pucher 2008, 159–194).

4.4.4 Combining sex and age distribution

4.4.4.1 Discussion and interpretation

The mortality profile shows a very high number of young adults, and the sex ratio indicates the prevalence of females. Although it is expected that most males and castrated animals fall into the younger stages, the few older individuals indicate that many females could represent young adults. The very few older animals (> 7 years) might represent females because older female pigs taste better than older males. Immature animals cannot be sexed, but probably they mainly represent male or castrated pigs. Small-scale keeping of pigs is suggested by the dominance of female animals, the presence of some older individuals, and the fact that they are easy to keep. They do not have any specific space requirements and they could easily find fodder at the forested area of Sand. As expected, pig is an important meat supplier; the slaughtering of such a high number of young animals suggests patterns of behavior by the inhabitants of Sand that are attributable to nobility.

4.4.5 Skeletal element distribution

4.4.5.1 Results and interpretation

The MNI estimates did not fluctuate dramatically, which suggests no specific over- or underrepresentation. According to the MNI, nineteen individuals were recorded for the Westwall area, thirteen for Sand 1, and ten for Sand 2. The fore- and hindlimbs are not overrepresented (Figure 36). This shows that there was no separate delivery

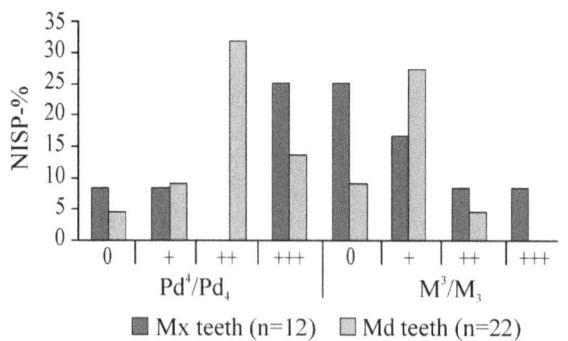

Figure 35. Pig: mortality profile – Westwall area – maxillary and mandibular teeth (NISP%).

of anatomical regions rich in meat. Whole animals were apparently transported to the site. This supports the idea of small-scale keeping of a few individuals. The distribution of the skeletal elements among the three regions of Sand is balanced (Figure 37). Westwall area yielded a slightly higher percentage of the meaty regions, but the difference from the other two areas is minimal.

4.4.6 Modifications

4.4.6.1 Butchery marks

The butchery marks confirm the lack of a systematic technique, as was the case in cattle and small ruminants. Most of the bones have been severely chopped, resulting in a high number of fragments. The long bones bear various chops and cuts at various locations, without any specific pattern and of different frequency. People experienced in animal keeping and slaughtering produce less waste and they employ efficient techniques to save time and energy. The best parallel to compare with derives not from the early medieval period, but from Hallstatt. This is because a significant part of the economic organisation was based on the delivery and transportation of pigs. Cut and chop marks at Hallstatt indicate a professional butchery technique, evidenced by the homogeneity of the location, frequency, and orientation of the marks (Pucher 1997, 26–27; 2009b, 74–77).

4.4.7 Size and shape

In Sand the size estimation and the morphological examination of the pigs are based on only a few specimens; the vast majority of the material derives from immature individuals. The metric information that enables estimating the withers height for pigs is based on the factors defined by Teichert (1969, 237–292). Importantly, the height at withers can significantly vary depending on which skeletal

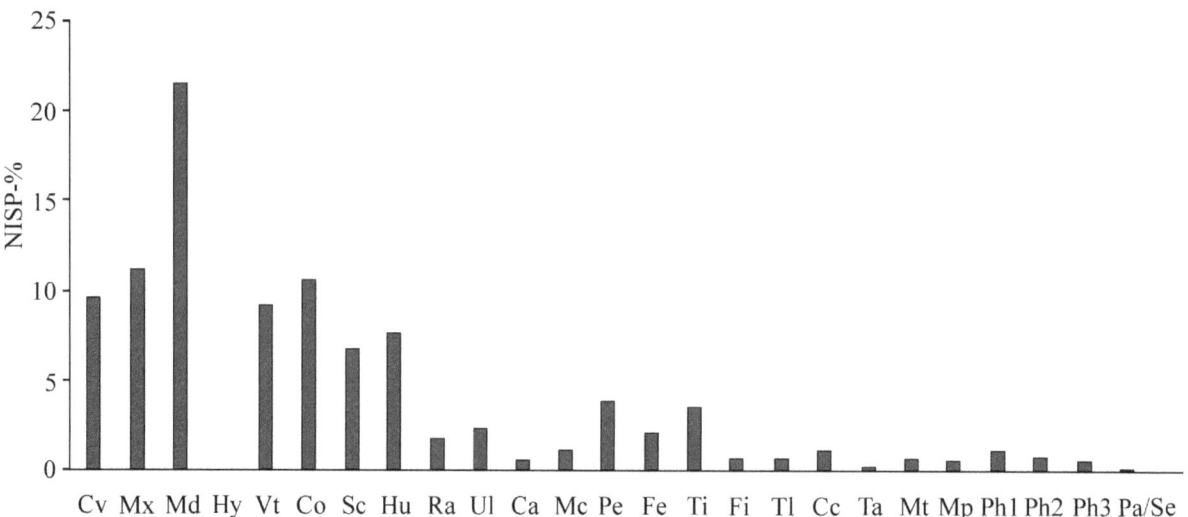

Figure 36. Pig: skeletal element representation (NISP%) – Sand total. Abbreviations: Cv: calvaria, Mx: maxilla, Md: mandible, Hy: hyoid, Vt: vertebrae, Co: costae, Sc: scapula, Hu: humerus, Ra: radius, Ul: ulna, Ca: carpalia, Mc: metacarpus, Pe: pelvis, Fe: femur, Ti: tibia, Fi: fibula, Tl: talus, Cc: calcaneus, Ta: tarsalia, Mt: metatarsus, Mp: metapodia, Ph1: first phalanx, Ph2: second phalanx, Ph3: third phalanx, Pa: patella, Se: sesamoidea.

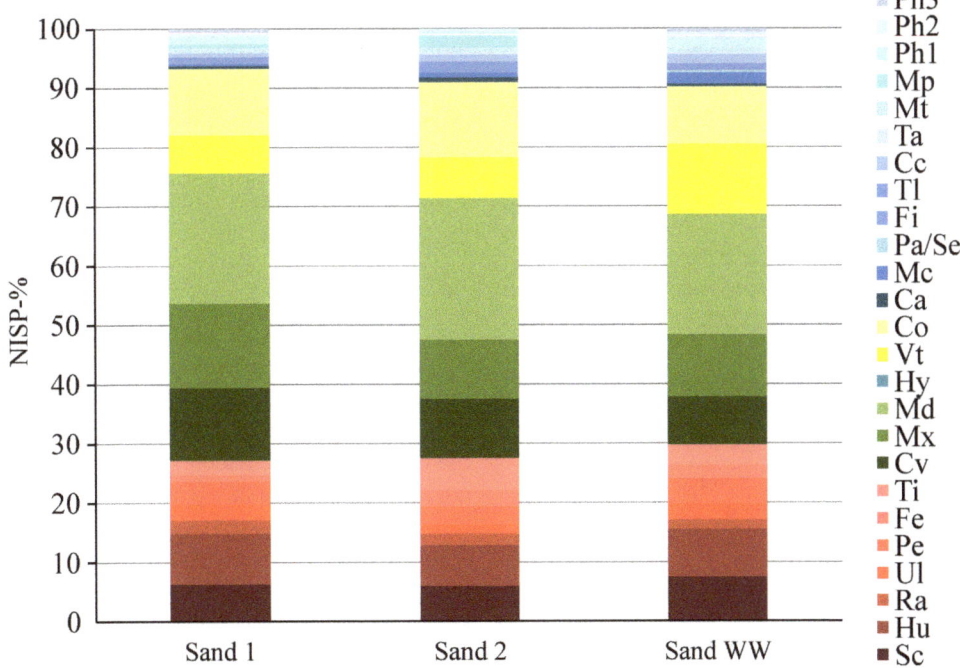

Figure 37. Pig: skeletal element representation per area (NISP%). Abbreviations: Cv: calvaria, Mx: maxilla, Md: mandible, Hy: hyoid, Vt: vertebrae, Co: costae, Sc: scapula, Hu: humerus, Ra: radius, Ul: ulna, Ca: carpalia, Mc: metacarpus, Pe: pelvis, Fe: femur, Pa: patella, Se: sesamoidea, Ti: tibia, Fi: fibula, Tl: talus, Cc: calcaneus, Ta: tarsalia, Mt: metatarsus, Mp: metapodia, Ph1: first phalanx, Ph2: second phalanx, Ph3: third phalanx.

element is used; small bones such as tali tend to yield much higher values than the actual heights. Thus the size reconstruction for pigs remains uncertain.

The analysis of one radius yielded 62.1 cm; two metacarpals IV produced 57 cm and 63.7 cm. A previous study of one metacarpal III from Sand 1 yielded 82 cm, one talus 70 cm. The tali exhibited a variation between 61.7 and 84.1 cm, one calcaneus 69.1 cm. The average based on tali is 73.4 cm. Comparative studies with other pig populations are very interesting, but the results shall be treated with caution. Pigs are morphologically plastic animals and changes in size and shape are influenced by various factors such as fodder variation. Morphometric studies are therefore difficult and demand systematic research.

In Raabs (11th century AD) the height at withers (tali) has been calculated between 68 and 76 cm (average ca. 72 cm) (Riedel & Pucher 2008, 159–194). The population from Stillfried (12th-13th century AD) exhibited an average of 73 cm (Pucher 1986a, 23–116). The tali measurements from Bernhardsthal (2nd-3rd century AD) yielded between 65.5 and 82 cm with an average of 71.8 cm and the metapodials between 71 and 82 cm with an average of 76.7 cm (Riedel 1996, 55-144). At Mikulčice (6th-10th century AD) and Gaiselberg (12th-16th century AD), the animals showed a slightly higher average estimated at 78 cm (Kratochvíl 1981) and 80.9 cm, respectively (Spitzenberger 1986, 121–161).[23]

[23] Gaiselberg has been studied by Spitzenberger (1986, 121–161), but the results have been reviewed and corrected by Pucher.

Table 13. Horse: number of identified specimens (NISP) and weight analysis

Equus ferus **f.** *caballus*		
Area	**NISP**	**Weight (g)**
Upper settlement terrace (S1)	67	5991
Lower settlement terrace (S2)	17	915
Westwall area (WW)	44	2260
Total	128	9166

Although the differences are not dramatic, an important question is whether these values represent different populations or variations of one population. This is difficult to answer due to the lack of sufficient material and for practical reasons. For example, castrated animals cannot be morphologically identified, and this is important because castration can significantly affect the height at withers and consequently the range of the population's variation.

4.5 Horse (*Equus ferus* f. *caballus*)

In total 128 horse bones have been identified corresponding to 9166 gr (Table 13). The weight analysis shows that horses represent 6.7% of the domesticated taxa and 3.6% of the total remains, including the wild species. The highest frequency of horse remains come from Sand 1 with 10.7% among the domesticated and 6.3% with the wild species. At this area horses are the second dominant species after cattle. In Sand 2 and Westwall area horses are found at a lower number, following cattle and pigs. This is an important observation because usually horses are connected to aspects of social status and hierarchy.

Due to lack of findings the sex determination was not possible, and only a limited number of bones contributed to the reconstruction of age at death, which is based on the study of the epiphyses. The mortality profile shows that the vast majority of the remains come from adults. Concerning modifications, the existence of butchery marks indicates that horses constituted part of the diet, similarly to dogs.

The withers height estimation has been calculated by one radius, three tibiae, and two metatarsals based on the factors of May (1985, 368–382). The calculation of GL for radius exhibited 137.1 cm and of Ll 135.1 cm. The GL for tibiae was 133.2, 135.5 and 136.1 and for the metatarsals 136.2 and 144.5.

Similar results have been produced for other contemporaneous archaeozoological assemblages of Central Europe exhibiting an average between 133 and 140 cm.[24] The investigation of the horse population from the Slavic-Avar site Nové Zámsky (Müller 1966, 661–696; Ambros & Müller 1980, 24–30) shows a variation range between 132 and 141 cm (based on Vitt).[25] Many early medieval assemblages indicate an increase in size. One metacarpus from Raabs (11th century AD) exhibited 144 cm and one radius 146 cm. The material from Pohansko (5th-11th century AD) produced an average of 137 cm (133-143 cm), whereas the remains from Gars-Thunau (8th-11th century AD) demonstrated an average value of 143 cm (129-154 cm). Comparable values have been exhibited by the study of the remains from Stillfried (12th-13th century AD), where the variation of the height at wither's has been estimated between 130 and 140 cm (Pucher 1982).

4.6 Dog (*Canis lupus* f. *familiaris*)

Only a limited number of bones has been recovered from Sand 2 and the Westwall area (Table 14). A few bones (n=6) were also recorded in Raabs (Riedel & Pucher 2008, 159–194). Similarly, in Gaiselberg (12th-16th century AD) and Stillfried (12th-13th century AD) dogs are represented with 1.5% (Spitzenberger 1986, 121–161) and 2.7% (Pucher 1982), respectively.

Due to the low frequency of findings it was not possible to assess the sex distribution. This is because the baculum, which is mainly used for sexing, is very fragile and only rarely found (or even recorded) at the excavations. The sacrum presents some useful traits for sexing, but no sacrum was found in Sand. Concerning the age at death, information comes from the Westwall area. The long bones derive mainly from adult individuals, but one mandible with the deciduous premolars 1-4 indicates the existence of an animal younger than 4 months.

Table 14. Dog: number of identified specimens (NISP) and weight analysis

Canis lupus f. *familiaris*		
Area	NISP	Weight (g)
Upper settlement terrace (S1)	-	-
Lower settlement terrace (S2)	1	3
Westwall area (WW)	15	105
Total	16	108

Regarding modifications, cut marks at the distal part of the humerus and chop marks at the distal part of the radius indicate cynophagy.[26] Although dogs were included in the diet, their participation in other daily aspects (hunting companions) cannot be excluded.

Dogs, similarly to wolves, are plastic animals regarding morphology, and many different breeds have been recorded over time. The absence of whole bones and the very small sample precluded reconstructing the height at withers or conducting a morphological analysis. In general, the size of dogs has increased over time. The study of early medieval assemblages illustrates the presence of a middle-sized population that had already been detected back in the La Tène period (Pucher 1999).[27] The material from Raabs suggests that dog size ranged between 50 and 60 cm (Riedel & Pucher 2008, 159–194), whereas the remains from medieval Stillfried exhibit animals between 55 and 67 cm (Pucher 1982). The macroscopic analysis of the remains in Sand yielded nothing unusual. Middle-sized dogs may very well have been represented.

4.7 Domestic fowl (*Gallus gallus* f. *domestica*)

Domestic fowl contributed only minimally to the daily diet of the inhabitants (Table 15). According to the weight analysis, chickens are represented at very low percentages. In Sand 1 they represent 0.08% among the domesticated animals and 0.05% with the wild species. In Sand 2 and the Westwall area they represent 0.1% of the total material. In some castles the number of domesticated fowl is higher than in the settlements; this is because domestic fowl can be easily kept without demanding specific space requirements.

The majority of chicken bones in Sand derive from adult individuals. The absence of the spur on the tarsometatarsus indicates a higher number of females, but due to the low amount of finds the statistical processing of the data was

---

[24] Certainly, the number of samples is important for the average.

[25] Although sometimes the Avar horses seem to be relatively taller (133-144 cm) they share a common region of overlap with other contemporaneous populations. They are differentiated by the cranial features and the robusticity of the bones (Pucher et al. 2015, 71–78). The archaeozoological record shows that Avar horses are found at very small percentages in modern Austria.

[26] These specimens come from Westwall area. This habit was not compatible with Christianity, however.

[27] During the La Tène period there is evidence for the existence of two populations. One population is similar to what is known today as the German shepherd dog, whereas the second group is represented by small-sized individuals (Pucher 1999). Concerning the small-sized group, very little information is available and the question that remains open is whether this population was imported, which of course generates additional questions regarding when and where. During the Roman Period, great differences have been observed between cities and villages regarding dogs. The breeding of different dog populations was intensively encouraged and used as prestige symbols.

Table 15. Domestic fowl: number of identified specimens (NISP) and weight analysis

Gallus gallus f. *domestica*		
Area	NISP	Weight (g)
Upper settlement terrace (S1)	33	47.0
Lower settlement terrace (S2)	12	21.2
Westwall area (WW)	96	142.4
Total	141	210.6

Table 16: Domestic fowl: average humerus GL (various sites)

Site	Average	N
Sand (10th century AD)	62.7	10
Raabs (11th century AD)	65.0	4
Pohansko (5th-11th century AD)	63.0	20
Podersdorf (7th/8th century AD)	63.0	3
Bernhardsthal (2nd/3rd century AD)	64.5	2
Tulln (15th century AD)	63.2	28

not possible. Concerning the element representation, the robust humerus and tibiotarsus are better represented than other fragile elements (e.g. cranium).

Table 16 presents the average value for the maximal length of humerus. The humerus is a preferable element because it is relatively abundant and well preserved. The comparative analysis revealed relatively small-sized individuals. Other early medieval sites have produced similar results and only rarely bigger individuals have been described. The material from the two early medieval Avar cemeteries in Vösendorf (Pucher et al. 2007, 107–115) and Podersdorf (Saliari et al. in press) yielded very small and gracile individuals.

WILD SPECIES

4.8 Aurochs (*Bos primigenius*), Bison (*Bison bonasus*) and wild Bovidae

Prior to the analyses that involve the quantification, the age and sex reconstruction, and the skeletal element representation, a brief introduction is given regarding the process of identification and differentiation between aurochs and European bison.

4.8.1 Identification

One very important issue is the distinction between aurochs (*Bos primigenius*) and European bison (*Bison bonasus*). This is a significant aspect because the two species exhibit certain differences that require consideration during the interpretation. For instance, wild animals are often used as indicators of the environment (see chapter 5.1.1); even if there is an ecological overlap between the two species, there are some significant differences that offer substantial information concerning the landscape and the ecological background. This is very useful in order to understand the space in which people moved and acted. For this reason, the separation between the two wild forms is important.

The remains from Sand 1 exhibited only bones of European bison (*Bison bonasus*). The excavation in Sand 2 and the Westwall area, however, brought to light a very limited number of aurochs (*Bos primigenius*) together with material deriving from the European bison (*Bison bonasus*). Distinguishing the domesticated form (*Bos primigenius* f. *taurus*) from the wild is relatively simple (*Bos primigenius* or *Bison bonasus*) due to major differences in structure and size.[28] The difficulty involved differentiating fragments of *Bos primigenius* (BP) from *Bison bonasus* (BB). This is because the bones of the two wild species, especially of the postcranial skeleton, bear striking similarities, complicating the identification.

4.8.1.1 Previous research

One important step in distinguishing aurochs (*Bos primigenius*) from European bison (*Bison bonasus*) is to find and study publications that describe morphological and metric differences between the two species. During this effort, palaeontological and archaeological publications were used. Some of the most well-known publications were written by Scherz (1936, 37–71) regarding the differences between *Bison priscus* and *Bos primigenius* on metapodials and astragalus, by Lehmann (1949, 163–266) regarding osteological criteria to separate *Bison* from *Bos*, by Olsen (1960) concerning postcranial differences between *Bison* and *Bos*, by Stampfli (1963, 117–169) regarding differences among *Bison bonasus*, *Bos primigenius*, and domesticated cattle, by Empel & Roskosz (1963, 259–300) regarding the analysis of 42 wisent skeletons, and by Martin (1987, 1–124) regarding differences observed on the long bones.

4.8.1.2 Methodology

The identification of the remains from Sand is based on two major steps. The first is the comparison of morphological traits with material from Austrian archaeological assemblages that exhibited abundant aurochs or bison bones and with recent animal remains. This task proved to be quite difficult due to a lack of assemblages with many wild Bovidae, and especially with European bison. The most important site for the present study is the Neolithic site of Friebritz, which produced a very high number of *Bos primigenius* bones.[29] Bones of European bison derive mainly from recent material.[30]

The most significant element for the morphological study and separation of the two species is the cranium. Cranial

---

[28] However, this can be sometimes complicated, depending on the breed of the domesticated cattle. The domesticated Italic cattle exhibited some similarities with the aurochs, and sometimes the size can be quite similar. An overlap is possible between domesticated Italic castrated animals and wild female individuals.
[29] The material from Friebritz is not yet published.
[30] Found at the Museum of Natural History in Vienna.

elements such as horn cores differ distinctly between the two species. In Sand some cranial elements (os petrosum, temporal bone, and horn cores) are in a very good state of preservation and thus helped in identifying the material.

Concerning the mandible, Stampfli (1963, 117–169) published some criteria for the separation of the two species based on the occlusal surface of the adult M_3. These criteria were not applicable here because the mandible (with teeth) from Sand belongs to a young animal.[31] For this reason and after a thorough examination of the teeth, the identification was based on the morphology of the basis of the crown of the molar M_3 and on general mandible shape. The comparison with other mandible fragments from Sand 1 and Friebritz indicates that the aurochs mandibles are more robust and massive than those of bison.

For the long and flat bones as well as the small compact bones (carpalia, tarsalia), the aurochs material from Friebritz differed in shape and proportions compared with recent bison bones; bison have more slender and less robust bones. For the humerus, a new criterion has been published by Pucher & Schmitzberger (1999a, 355–378), which describes a morphological difference at the fossa olecrani.

The second step is to study publications related to the separation of the two species based on morphological and metric criteria. Clearly, the comparison of morphological traits and measurements with the published material has its own problems. For instance when comparing with the work of Stampfli (1963, 117–169), it is important to know that most of his material derives from females. Usually there is considerable sexual dimorphism between males and females. When males are excluded or underrepresented, then the range of variation is limited. Additionally, sexual dimorphism is decisive when studying morphological differences. The form or structure of some morphological traits can significantly vary between males and females.

4.8.1.3 Results

The cranial elements indicate the strong representation of European bison, as is the case in Sand 1. The identified cranial fragments have not confirmed the presence of aurochs.[32] This result has been verified by other long and flat bones, which indicate the prevalence of bison; only very few bones have been attributed to aurochs. One mandible and one humerus fragment were identified as *Bos primigenius*. Additionally, one talus, one calcaneus, and one os centroquartale were attributed to aurochs and they probably came from the same individual.

Abundant bones from Sand 2 and the Westwall area have been generally identified as wild Bovidae because the uncharacteristic fragments did not enable a more concrete identification. Moreover, bones such as ribs were difficult

to separate due to the high number of wild taxa. Some of the ribs are similar not only among the Bovidae, but also the Cervidae and sometimes even the Equidae. Only some pieces were characteristic enough to be identified.

The presence of aurochs in a 10th century assemblage at the northern part of Austria is extremely important. According to the present state of research, Sand is the youngest site where aurochs has been detected in Austria.[33] These finds could enable in the future the opportunity to conduct a systematic study on crucial topics regarding both archaeological and zoological aspects.

4.8.2 Quantification

Bones of aurochs, bison, and unidentified fragments of wild Bovidae are represented with 651 bones corresponding to 40129.9 gr (Table 17).

Table 17. Wild Bovidae: number of identified specimens (NISP) and weight analysis

Bos primigenius		
Area	**NISP**	**Weight (g)**
Upper settlement terrace (S1)	0	0
Lower settlement terrace (S2)	2	857
Westwall area (WW)	4	671
Total	6	1528
Bison bonasus		
Upper settlement terrace (S1)	167	13017
Lower settlement terrace (S2)	25	1287
Westwall area (WW)	59	6168
Total	251	20472
Wild Bovidae		
Upper settlement terrace (S1)	0	0
Lower settlement terrace (S2)	93	3360
Westwall area (WW)	301	14769.9
Total	394	18129.9

4.8.2.1 Aurochs

As described above, the number of aurochs bones is minimal and they come only from Sand 2 and the Westwall area. The weight analysis at Sand 2 indicates a relatively high percentage[34] for aurochs, with 7.1% among the wild species and 2.4% with the domesticated animals, after bison, red deer, and wild boar. In Westwall area, aurochs make up 1.1% of the wild species and 0.6% including the domesticated animals, after Cervidae, wild boar, bison, and brown bear.

---

[31] The premolar 4 is still there (Pd_4+++).
[32] Some fragments are very small or bear no anatomical features that could help in the identification.

[33] The last individuals survived in Poland, dying out in the 17th century.
[34] Due to the very robust and heavy bones of the aurochs. Additionally a heavy piece of mandible, which bears almost the whole dentition, was also identified as aurochs.

4.8.2.2 Bison

According to the weight analysis, bison is represented in Sand with 17.8% among the wild species and 8.1% with the domesticated taxa. In Sand 1 the corresponding values are 33.1% and 13.7% and in Sand 2 10.7% and 3.6%, respectively. In the Westwall area the percentages recorded are 9.7% among the wild species and 5.1% including the domesticated animals. Most bison bones derive from Sand 1. Bison and red deer are almost equally represented in Sand 1 and the Westwall area.

Such an impressively high number of *Bison bonasus* constitutes a very rare case; not many sites have exhibited such an accumulation. The presence of bison in early medieval assemblages is scarce. In Sand, the percentage of bison was expected to be higher, but is somewhat masked by the identification difficulties.

4.8.2.3 Unidentified fragments of wild Bovidae

The number of bison bones is much higher than that of aurochs, but the difficulty in identifying the latter necessitated adding the group wild Bovidae. On a weight basis, wild Bovidae constitute the most numerous group of the wild species in Sand 2 with 27.9% and with 9.4% when the domesticated taxa are included; in the Westwall area, wild Bovidae follow red deer and wild boar with 23.2% of the wild fauna and 12.2% including the domesticated species. In total, the highest frequency of Bovidae (including bison, aurochs and the unidentified fragments) occurred at Sand 2 (45.6% of the wild animals and 15.3% including the domesticated fauna), followed by Westwall area with 33.9% and 17.8%, respectively, and Sand 1 with 33.1% and 13.7%.

4.8.3 Sex ratio

4.8.3.1 Results and interpretation for bison

The pelvis and horn cores were equally distributed among males and females (Table 18). Nonetheless, only few pelvis fragments could be sexed, and thus talus (n=9) and tibia (n=6) were additionally examined. The metric data for the GLl of talus and the Bd of tibia were divided into size classes and compared to the work of Empel & Roskosz (1963, 259–300). They show the variation range for the

GLl tali of females to lie between 67.0 and 79.0 mm[35] and of males between 79.0 and 87.0.[36] Concerning tibia, Empel & Roskosz (1963, 259–300) define the range of variation for the female fragments between 66.0 and 72.0 and for males between 76.0 and 86.0 mm.[37] Accordingly, the Sand material comprises almost equal numbers for females and males. Concerning tali, five individuals fall into the variation of females, three into the variation of males and one individual does not present clear evidence. Concerning tibia, three fragments fall into the variation range of females and three into the range of males.

The internal distribution exhibits some interesting differences. Based on the analysis of pelvis fragments, Sand 1 exhibits an equal number of males and females (n=4), but the statistical analysis of the measurements of the long bones suggests a clear prevalence of males (Pucher & Schmitzberger 1999a, 355–378). In Sand 2 and Westwall area, the metric data indicate a stronger representation of female animals.[38] Estimating the sex distribution for aurochs was not feasible due to the lack of appropriate skeletal elements.

4.8.4 Age at death

4.8.4.1 Results

All the examined bison elements derive from adults at different stages. Most come from young adults (M_3+) and a smaller number involve late-stage individuals (Figure 38). Due to the very few teeth, it was not possible to trace differences among the different areas. The age distribution for aurochs is based on very few specimens. The epiphyses mainly point to adult individuals. One complete mandible from Sand 2 indicates a young animal, since the premolar 4 coexists with molar 3 (Pd_4+++, M_3+).

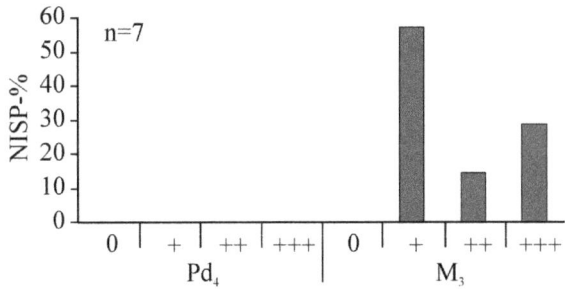

Figure 38. Bison: mortality profile – Sand 2, Sand Westwall – mandibular teeth (NISP%). Sand 1 exhibited no teeth.

Table 18. Bison: sex determination based on horn cores and pelvis (NISP)

Area	Element	Male	Female	Total
Upper settlement terrace (S1)	Pelvis	2	2	4
Lower settlement terrace (S2)	Horn cores	1	0	1
Westwall area (WW)	Pelvis	2	3	5
Total		5	5	10

---

[35] For females between 2 and 18 years.
[36] For males between 4 and 18 years.
[37] Some low values in the Empel & Roskosz publication might be related to younger individuals included in the study.
[38] The limited number of measurements discouraged the statistical processing. Comparing with the tables of Empel & Roskosz (1963, 259–300), however, the frequency of females appears to be higher in these two areas.

4.8.5 Combining sex and age distribution

4.8.5.1 Discussion and interpretation

The sex ratio and age at death profiles reveal important information about the economic strategies and the exploitation of natural resources. Concerning age, there is a slight tendency toward young adults, but the few findings make the statistics fragile. Similarly, the number of elements that contributed to the sex determination is limited and the analysis of different bones indicates a general tendency.

It seems that the inhabitants of Sand hunted both male and female animals, but mainly adults. This is a significant difference from the material from castle Raabs, where robust adult males mostly prevail (Pucher 2009a, 259–272). This tendency has been interpreted as hunting for trophies (Riedel & Pucher 2008, 159–194). Usually a high number of females and of immature animals is interpreted as an indicator of an essential necessity, in which animals play a key role for the acquisition of meat and raw material (Müller 1982, 239–258).

4.8.6 Skeletal element distribution and butchery marks

4.8.6.1 Results

Aurochs is represented by very few findings. Therefore, the results on the skeletal element distribution refer to the European bison and to the many unidentified fragments of wild Bovidae.[39] The NISP data indicate a high number of vertebrae and ribs for both the European bison and the unidentified fragments of Bovidae. As already noted, the identification of these elements is uncertain due to the big variation in the wild species. Thus, this result may reflect the identification difficulties and should be interpreted with caution.

According to the frequency of the anatomical elements, most of the material derives from the fore- (scapula, humerus, radius) and the hindlimbs (pelvis, femur, tibia), namely the meaty regions. Cranial elements, metapodials, tarsals, and carpals are significantly underrepresented. Note that these elements are usually discarded at the killing place due to the very low meat quantity. Wild Bovidae are very heavy animals that are difficult to transport. Interestingly, horn cores are underrepresented too. Although the skull region does not bear much meat and is an additional weight to carry, the horn cores of males would have been a prestige symbol; bison and aurochs belong to the so-called big game hunting. The phalanges, and especially the first phalanx, are better represented than other small bones.

Concerning modifications, the animal bones were severely chopped, similarly to the other species. Cut marks on the very limited number of metapodials (n=2) from Sand 1

reveal skinning activities. Skinning might have taken place at the killing site because the skeletal element representation indicates that only the meaty parts of the animals arrived at the site.

4.9 Red deer (*Cervus elaphus*)

4.9.1 Quantification

Red deer is one of the most important wild species in Sand together with European bison and wild boar. Table 19 presents the NISP and weight data for every area separately. According to the weight analysis, red deer in Sand make up 31.6% of the wild species and 14.5% including the domesticated animals. In Sand 1 the corresponding values are 33.8% and 13.9%, in Sand 2 22.5% and 7.6%. In Westwall area they make up 32.0% and 16.9%, respectively.

4.9.2 Sex ratio and age at death

4.9.2.1 Results

Twenty-five identifiable pelvis fragments were found, of which 14 belong to females and 11 to males (Figure 39). In some cases the long bone measurements also demonstrated the presence of female individuals. The internal distribution shows that males prevail in Sand 1 (63%, n=11) and females in the Westwall area (75%,

Table 19. Red deer: number of identified specimens (NISP) and weight analysis

Cervus elaphus		
Area	**NISP**	**Weight (g)**
Upper settlement terrace (S1)	446 (10*)	13280**
Lower settlement terrace (S2)	124	2713.4
Westwall area (WW)	592 (11*)	20854.9 (20423.4**)
Total	1162	36416.8

*Number of antlers.
**Number excluding antlers.

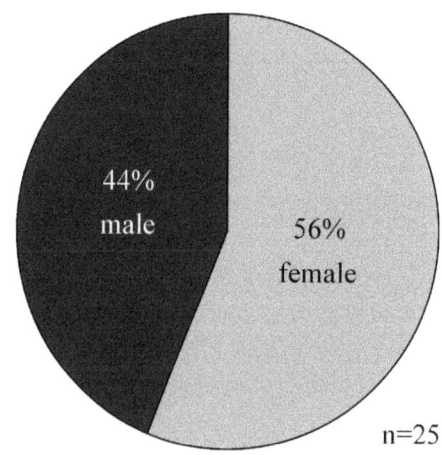

Figure 39. Red deer: sex determination – Sand total – pelvis (NISP%).

---

[39] Due to the high number of unidentified bones, no diagram for the skeletal element distribution is presented.

Table 20. Red deer: mortality profile – mandibular teeth (NISP)

Age at death	Pd_4 0-+++	M_3 0	M_3 +	M_3 ++	M_3 +++
Upper settlement terrace (S1)	2	1	3	1	-
Lower settlement terrace (S2)	-	-	1	-	-
Westwall area (WW)	2	1	-	3	-
Total	4	2	4	4	-

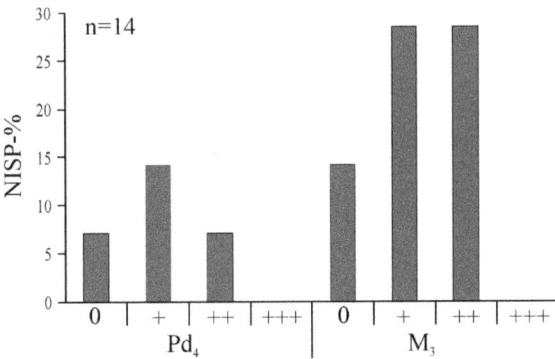

Figure 40. Red deer: mortality profile – Sand total – mandibular teeth (NISP%).

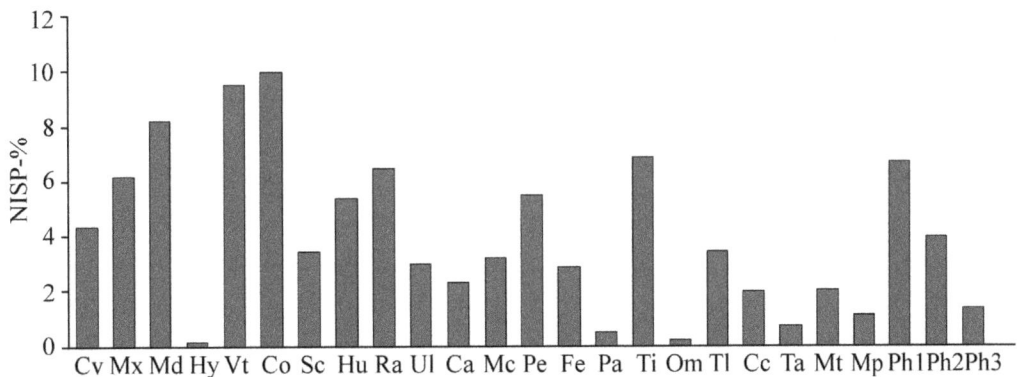

Figure 41. Red deer: skeletal element distribution – Sand total (NISP%). Abbreviations: Cv: calvaria, Mx: maxilla, Md: mandible, Hy: hyoid, Vt: vertebrae, Co: costae, Sc: scapula, Hu: humerus, Ra: radius, Ul: ulna, Ca: carpalia, Mc: metacarpus, Pe: pelvis, Fe: femur, Pa: patella, Ti: tibia, Om: os malleolare, Tl: talus, Cc: calcaneus, Ta: tarsalia, Mt: metatarsus, Mp: metapodia, Ph1: first phalanx, Ph2: second phalanx, Ph3: third phalanx.

n=9 out of 12). The few finds from Sand 2 (n=2) do not provide enough information. Most individuals (71.4%) are adults (Table 20); 42.8% belong to young adults (M_3 0/+). Immature individuals are equally represented in Sand 1 and Westwall area, whereas very old animals (M_3 +++) were not found. As in the wild Bovidae, young adults were slightly more abundant (Figure 40).

4.9.3 Skeletal element distribution

4.9.3.1 Results

The number of anatomical elements shows that the meaty regions – namely the fore- (scapula, humerus, radius) and hindlimbs (pelvis, femur, tibia) – make up almost 34% (Figure 41). Radius and tibia, two of the most robust and compact bones, were the most abundant elements of the long bones. Metapodials and small bones such as carpals, tarsals, and phalanges make up 27.7%. Interestingly, the first phalanx is found at a relatively high

frequency. Cranial elements (including the mandible) and vertebrae/ribs contribute 18.8% and 19.5%, respectively. Antlers were excluded from the analysis because they can reflect both hunting and collecting activities; their presence does not always indicate that the animal itself was present on site. The skeletal elements of red deer are well represented, indicating that whole animals were transported to the site.

The areas differed slightly (Table 21). Sand 1 and Westwall area yielded more fore- and hindlimbs, metapodials, and small bones. Concerning meat-rich elements, Sand 1 yielded more forelimbs and the Westwall area more hindlimbs. Sand 2 exhibited a higher frequency of regions associated with less meat, especially cranial elements (including mandibles); in this area the number of fore- and hindlimbs is equal.

Although antlers were omitted, this element is concentrated mainly in Sand 1 and the Westwall area, the two most

Table 21. Red deer: skeletal element representation (NISP%) – Sand

Area	Meaty parts		Parts with less meat		
	Forelimbs (Sc-Ul)	Hindlimbs (Pe-Ti)	Cv-Md	Vt-Co	Mp-Ph3
Sand 1	23.8	13.8	19.7	21.1	21.6
	37.6			62.4	
Sand 2	14.7	14.7	31.9	16.4	22.4
	29.4			70.7	
Westwall area	17.1	18.9	18.0	21.3	24.6
	36.0			63.9	

Cv: calvaria, Md: mandible, Vt: vertebrae, Co: costae, Sc: scapula, Ul: ulna, Pe: pelvis, Ti: tibia, Mp: metapodium, Ph3: third phalanx.

economically active areas (Felgenhauer-Schmiedt 2006, 253–268; 2011, 551–559; 2012, 57–81). Although in Sand 2 there were many cranial elements, no antlers were retrieved. In Westwall area the accumulation indicates craft contexts, supported by the presence of finished and semi-finished antler artefacts and of production waste. No such artefacts were retrieved from Sand 1. Interestingly, no other bones of red deer were used to manufacture artefacts. Cut marks were limited and mainly observed at the base of the antlers (found in Westwall area), indicating skin removal (Binford 1981, 136).

4.9.4 Morphometric analysis

4.9.4.1 Results

The metric analysis shows that the red deer population from Sand falls within the variation range of the Central European populations (Schmitzberger 2009, 63–69). The withers height estimation based on three metatarsals is between 117 and 128.5 cm. The values in Austria indicate middle-sized animals; still size can vary in the different regions. In Lower Austria, individuals are slightly larger than in Upper Austria.[40] Small-sized animals are found in Western Europe (Bavaria) and bigger-sized in the eastern part (Hungary).

In Sand, talus GLl values range between 53.5 and 62.5 mm (Figure 42). In Lower Austria the values are between 53.0 and 64.0 mm (average 58.5 mm) and in Upper Austria between 50.0 and 63.0 mm (average 57.0 mm) (Schmitzberger 2009, 63–69). Sand is within the range of both populations (average 58.0 mm). Size differences observed on other red deer bones (such as humerus, femur) are due to the sexual dimorphism and they indicate the presence of both males and females in Sand. Finally, another important observation regarding morphology is that one pelvis fragment differs from other fragments. Namely one obtoratum fragment bore a sinus, a feature that is usually present in elk pelves.

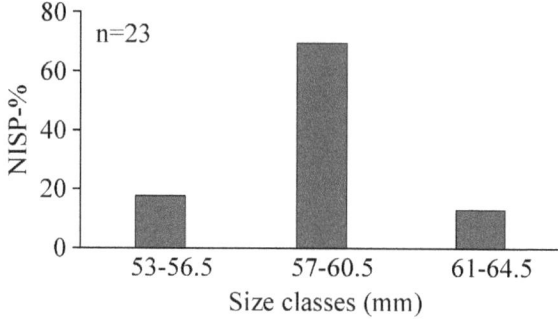

Figure 42. Red deer: size classes (mm) for talus GLl – NISP%.

4.10 Roe deer and Elk (*Capreolus capreolus* and *Alces alces*)

4.10.1 Quantification

Roe deer is rarer in Sand than other wild (Table 22). Based on weight, roe deer makes up 1.4% of the wild fauna species in Sand 1 and 0.6% when domesticated species are included. In Sand 2 the percentage is higher with 3.7% of the wild taxa and 1.3% of the total fauna. In the Westwall area the corresponding values are 2.4% and 1.3%. Elk is also poorly represented in Sand 1 (0.8% of the wild fauna, 0.3% of the total fauna). The values in Sand 2 for elk are higher with 7.1% and 2.4%, respectively, whereas in Westwall area the percentages drop to 3.9% and 2.0%. Interestingly, in Sand 1 elk comes after roe deer and brown bear, whereas in Sand 2 and the Westwall area elk is more abundant than roe deer and brown bear.

4.10.2 Sex ratio and age at death

4.10.2.1 Results

The sex determination for roe deer involves studying the pelvic bone, revealing in total three females and two males; the mortality profile showed a prevalence of young adults (M_3+, n=4 out of 7). Only one immature animal was recorded (Pd_4++). For elk, only one female was identified, with one mandibular molar indicating a young adult ($M_3$0). The intra-site analysis of these profiles was not possible, due to the limited number of the material. The results

---

[40] But the two populations show great overlap.

Table 22. Roe deer and elk: number of identified specimens (NISP) and weight analysis

Area	Capreolus capreolus		Alces alces	
	NISP	Weight (g)	NISP	Weight (g)
Upper settlement terrace (S1)	60 (1*)	573**	11	341
Lower settlement terrace (S2)	53 (3*)	520 (449**)	18	851
Westwall area (WW)	202 (11*)	1734 (1549**)	40	2462
Total	315	2571	69	3654

*Number of antlers.
**Number excluding antlers.

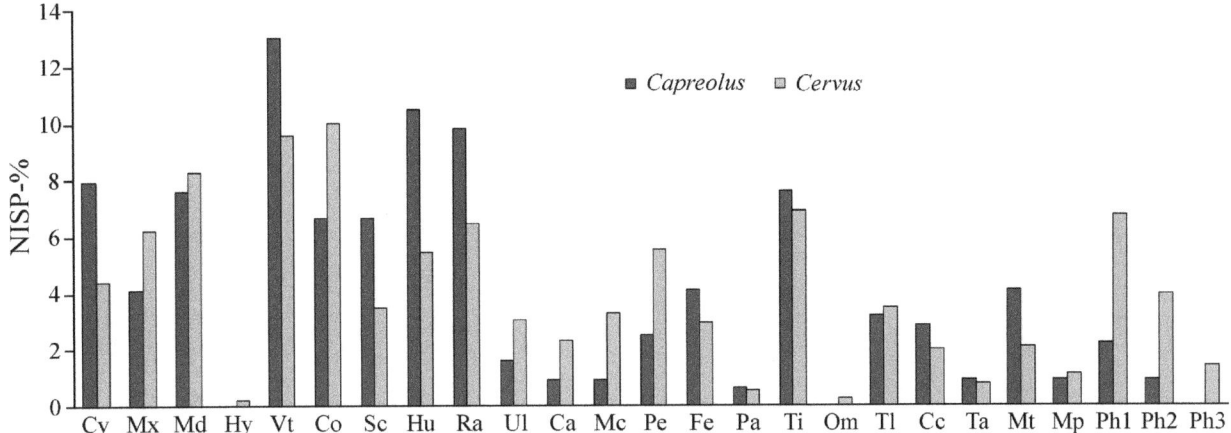

Figure 43. Roe deer and red deer: skeletal element representation – Sand total (NISP%). Abbreviations: Cv: calvaria, Mx: maxilla, Md: mandible, Hy: hyoid, Vt: vertebrae, Co: costae, Sc: scapula, Hu: humerus, Ra: radius, Ul: ulna, Ca: carpalia, Mc: metacarpus, Pe: pelvis, Fe: femur, Pa: patella, Ti: tibia, Om: os malleolare, Tl: talus, Cc: calcaneus, Ta: tarsalia, Mt: metatarsus, Mp: metapodia, Ph1: first phalanx, Ph2: second phalanx, Ph3: third phalanx.

for both species confirm the tendency already observed for other species, namely the presence of young adults, although the number of finds is very small.

4.10.3 Skeletal element representation and butchery marks

4.10.3.1 Results

The skeletal element representation for roe deer is similar to that of red deer (Figure 43). Nonetheless, the number of roe deer bones is significantly lower and thus the statistical evaluation must be interpreted with caution. The meaty regions of roe deer (fore- and hindlimbs) make up 42.9%, higher than the respective regions of red deer with 33.9%. Radius and tibia are the most abundant, similarly to red deer. The forelimbs of roe deer are better represented (28.6%) than the hindlimbs. Metapodials and small bones make up 17.8%. Cranial elements[41] (including mandibles) and vertebrae/ribs (19.7% each) are present at levels similar to red deer. No significant differences among the areas were observed, but this might merely reflect the few bones available. For elk, the limited number of bones does not allow a founded interpretation of the skeletal representation.

Note here that the investigation of the manipulation marks showed skin removal for both species at the area

of Westwall. Cut marks that suggest skinning activities were detected around the base of the antlers (Binford 1981, 136). The relatively high accumulation of antlers (roe deer, red deer) and horn cores (goats) at Westwall area deserves mention and it will be discussed later (chapter 5.2.1).

4.10.4 Morphometric analysis

4.10.4.1 Results

The morphometric analysis focuses mainly on roe deer because the data for elk are very limited. The earlier roe deer populations underwent a considerable size reduction (Schmitzberger 2009). Although only few measurements could be taken, a similar tendency has been observed in Sand too, based on the length of the cheektooth row. The minimum value is 62.5 and the maximal 69.5 mm (average 67.1; n=4). The study on the Neolithic population of roe deer shows a slightly different estimated minimum value: 63.5 mm, which is higher than in Sand (Schmitzberger 2009, 62–69).

4.11 Wild boar (*Sus scrofa*)

4.11.1 Quantification

A total of 1718 bones were identified, corresponding to 17947.1 g. Based on weight, pig is the second most dominant domesticated species in Sand, making up 13.1%

---

[41] Antlers were excluded, similarly to red deer.

Table 23. Wild boar: number of identified specimens (NISP) and weight analysis

Sus scrofa		
Area	**NISP**	**Weight (g)**
Upper settlement terrace (S1)	519	10874.0
Lower settlement terrace (S2)	88	2000.0
Westwall area (WW)	593	14760.2
Total	1200	27634.2

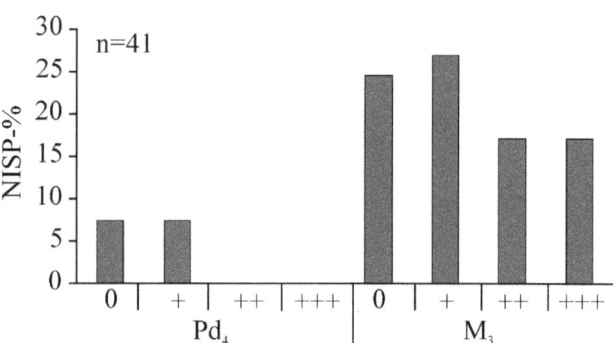

Figure 45. Wild boar: mortality profile – Sand total – mandibular teeth (NISP%).

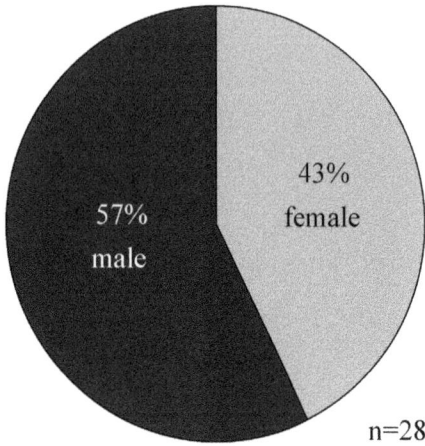

Figure 44. Wild boar: sex determination – Sand total – maxillary and mandibular canini alveoli (NISP%).

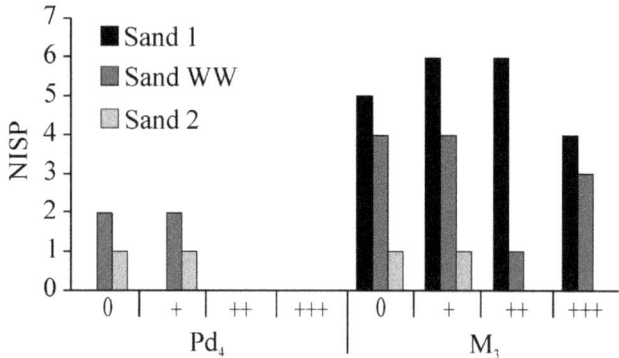

Figure 46. Wild boar: mortality profile – per area – mandibular teeth (NISP).

among the domesticated species and 7.1% including the wild species. In Sand 1, pigs contribute 8.7% among the domesticated species and 5.1% including the wild fauna. In Sand 2 the corresponding values are 15.2% and 10.1%, in Westwall 16.4% and 7.8%. Similarly to the small ruminants, pigs were more abundant in Sand 2 and Westwall area (Table 23).

4.11.2 Sex ratio and age at death

4.11.2.1 Results

The mandibular and maxillary alveoli illustrate the dominance of males (57%) (Figure 44). Although the number of findings per area is limited, females seem to be better represented in the Westwall area (50%) (Table 24).

Concerning the age distribution, the mortality profile shows a high percentage (51.2%) of young adults ($M_3 0/+$)

(Figure 45). Immature individuals are present, but at a low frequency. They were mainly recorded from Sand 2 and Westwall area, whereas the material from Sand 1 indicates a strong presence of adults (Figure 46, Table 25). Similar tendencies were observed for red deer and wild Bovidae; young adults dominate and immature animals are scarce.

4.11.3 Skeletal element distribution

4.11.3.1 Results

The skeletal element distribution is based on NISP data (Figure 47). The number of cranial elements and mandibles is relatively high (27.4%). Ribs and vertebrae represent 15% of the material. Fore- and hindlimbs, the meaty regions, reach 30.3%. Metapodials and small bones make up 27.4%. The body part representation indicates that all the elements are represented; wild boar was probably transported to the

Table 24. Wild boar: sex determination based on maxillary and mandibular canini alveoli (NISP and NISP%)

	Upper settlement (S1)		Lower settlement (S2)		Westwall area (WW)		Total	Total %
	Mx alv	Md alv	Mx alv	Md alv	Mx alv	Md alv		
Female	3	1	0	1	0	7	12	43.0
Female %	36.4		33.3		50.0			
Male	2	5	0	2	2	5	16	57.0
Male %	63.6		66.7		50.0			
Total NISP	5	6	0	3	2	12	28	

Table 25. Wild boar: mortality profile – mandibular teeth (NISP and NISP%)

Age at death	Pd$_4$0-+++	M$_3$0-+	M$_3$++	M$_3$+++	Total
Sand 1	0	11	6	4	21
Sand 2	2	2	0	0	4
Sand WW	4	8	1	3	16
Total NISP	6	21	7	7	41
Total NISP (%)	14.6	51.2	34.1		

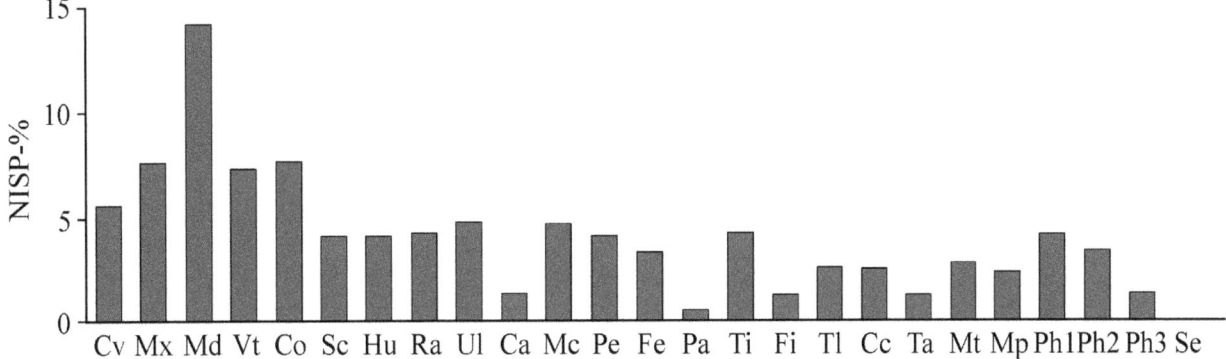

Figure 47. Wild boar: skeletal element representation – Sand total (NISP%). Abbreviations: Cv: calvaria, Mx: maxilla, Md: mandible, Vt: vertebrae, Co: costae, Sc: scapula, Hu: humerus, Ra: radius, Ul: ulna, Ca: carpalia, Mc: metacarpus, Pe: pelvis, Fe: femur, Pa: patella, Ti: tibia, Fi: fibula, Tl: talus, Cc: calcaneus, Ta: tarsalia, Mt: metatarsus, Mp: metapodia, Ph1: first phalanx, Ph2: second phalanx, Ph3: third phalanx, Se: sesamoidea.

Table 26. Wild boar: skeletal element representation (NISP%)

Area	Meaty parts		Parts with less meat		
	Forelimbs (Sc-Ul)	Hindlimbs (Pe-Ti)	Cv-Md	Vt-Co	Mp-Ph3
Sand 1	16.8	7.3	29.7	20.0	26.2
	24.1			75.9	
Sand 2	12.5	26.1	25.0	12.5	23.9
	38.6			61.4	
Westwall area	18.5	16.0	25.6	11.0	28.8
	34.5			65.4	

Cv: calvaria, Md: mandible, Vt: vertebrae, Co: costae, Sc: scapula, Ul: ulna, Pe: pelvis, Ti: tibia, Mp: metapodia, Ph3: third phalanx.

site whole, similarly to red deer. Slight differences among the areas have been observed (Table 26). Cranial elements (including mandibles), vertebrae, and ribs are better represented in Sand 1. Sand 2 and Westwall area exhibit a higher number of elements rich in meat than Sand 1. The Westwall area has more metapodials and small bones.

4.11.4 Morphometric analysis

4.11.4.1 Results

One interesting question involved the metric separation between wild boar and domesticated pig. Both species could be identified without any specific difficulties. When plotting the length/breadth of M^3/$_3$ a variation gap between the two species expresses their clear differences in size and robusticity (Figure 48).

The difference is also clear when estimating the height at withers for wild boars and domesticated pigs. For the former, one metacarpal II yielded the minimum height at withers of 72.1 cm; the maximum value (105.6 cm) was obtained from a metacarpal III. In contrast, two metacarpals IV of domesticated pig produced much lower values, namely 57 and 63.7 cm. Wild boars in the Middle Ages were smaller than at other sites that date to earlier periods. Neolithic finds from Austria have shown higher height at withers, between 85 and 112 cm (Schmitzberger 2009, 56). These values are considerably higher than those calculated for Sand.

Concerning tali, the Sand material exhibited GLl values between 45.0 and 57.5 mm with an average of 52.3 mm (n=23). The analysis of the size classes shows that most individuals (n=10) fall into the size class 49-52.5 mm,

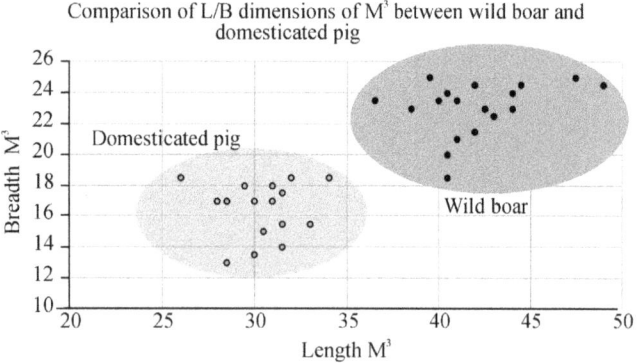

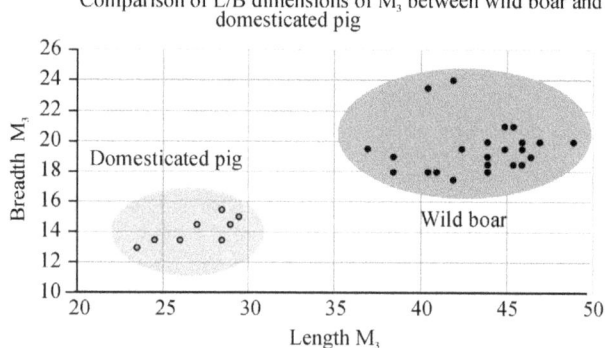

Figure 48. Comparative study between length and breadth of M³/₃ between pig and wild boar.

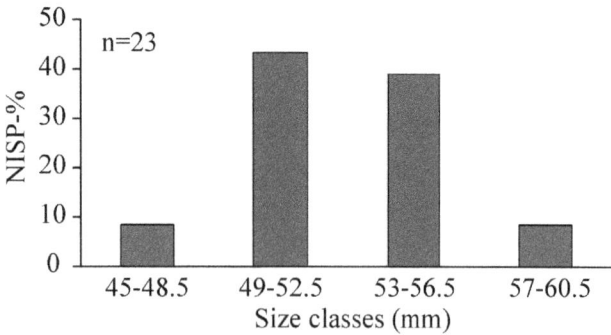

Figure 49. Wild boar: size classes (mm) for talus GLl – Sand total (NISP%).

followed by animals (n=9) between 53.0-56.5 mm (Figure 49).

4.12 European hare (*Lepus europaeus*)

An important observation regarding the wild species is the very low percentage of European hare (*Lepus europaeus*) in comparison to Raabs (Riedel & Pucher 2008, 159–194) (Table 27). This is interesting because hare is connected to woodland clearance, which was much more progressive in Raabs than in Sand. This observation provokes again rethinking the role of goats, despite their low number. The absence of sheep reflects the ability of goats to adapt to different environments and find more easily fodder – in the event that some individuals might have been kept for a longer period in Sand (Pucher 2009a, 259–272).

4.13 Black rat (*Rattus rattus*)

Another significant result is the presence of one femur from *Rattus rattus* (Table 27).[42] Finds from the Middle

Ages are scarce. Some have been recorded at Gaiselberg (12th-16th century AD), Hauenstein (16th century AD), and Salzburg Residenz (16th century AD). The first trustworthy indications originate from Raabs, comprising 28 bones (11th century AD). These bones are not a modern infiltration; it has been stratigraphically proven that they originate from the early phase of the site[43] (Riedel & Pucher 2008, 159–194; Spitzenberger 2001, 521–522). The presence of black rats in Raabs, coupled with the presence of the alpine cattle, demonstrates contacts with the southern Danubian regions and the Alps (Riedel & Pucher 2008, 159–194).

In Sand, it remains unclear whether the find is recent or contemporaneous with the early medieval settlement. Black rats are cultural followers; they are mainly associated with human settlements and indicate an agrarian landscape. Their presence points to origins or contacts with the southern part of Danube, where the species originated. The absence of black rat bones in Sand, which is in great contrast to Raabs (Riedel & Pucher 2008, 159–194), probably indicates that the human inhabitants of the site did not come from the southern Danubian regions.

4.14 Wild cat (*Felis silvestris*)

Another find that deserves discussion is possible bones of wild cat (*Felis silvestris*). Wild or house cats are only rarely found in archaeological records (Table 27). In Austria, during the Roman period, the presence of house cats south of the Danube was intensified (Riedel 2007, 29–72). Numerous publications are devoted to the distinction of the two species based on skeletons or on small numbers of single bones. Kratochvíl (1973) published the criteria for separating crania, but they could not be applied in Sand because cranial fragments are lacking. Later, in 1976, that same author published the differences between the two species based on elements of the postcranial skeleton

---

[42] Black rat already reached Europe in the Neolithic period according to finds from Sardegna and, up by the Late Bronze Age, it has been recorded from Spain and western Switzerland. Bronze Age findings in Crimea indicate a presence in eastern Europe. The expansion of the species in West and Central Europe was abetted by the Roman expansion. The archaeological record allows us to connect the Romans with the expansion of the black rat. Finds from the provinces of Gaul (Gallia) and Britain (Britannia) date to the 1st century AD and from Germania to the 4th century AD. The numbers of black rat were reduced during the post-Roman period, but increased again in Europe during the 8th century AD when the living conditions improved (Spitzenberger 2001, 520).

In Austria the oldest finds derive from the Roman phase (15-45 AD) of Magdalensberg, the main region of Noricum (Celtic Realm). The black rat population vanished when the Romans reached Virunum. The 2nd/3rd (4th) century AD yielded findings from Lauriacum, which are connected to the presence of the Roman legion. Other sites with bones of black rats are the Roman villa at Södingberg/Gem. Attendorf in Graz and Hemmaberg (5th-7th century AD).

[43] In Raabs there may have even been an earlier phase that could overlap with the Sand, but this remains unknown.

Table 27. Other wild species: number of identified specimens (NISP) and weight analysis

Area	Brown bear (*Ursus arctos*)		European otter (*Lutra lutra*)		European polecat (*Mustela putorius*)		European beaver (*Castor fiber*)	
	NISP	Weight (g)	NISP	Weight (g)	NISP	Weight (g)	NISP	Weight (g)
Upper settlement terrace (S1)	16	553	3	17	1	8	46	512
Lower settlement terrace (S2)	10	427	-	-	-	-	17	69
Westwall area (WW)	31	1024	6	19	-	-	177	1774
Total	57	2004	9	36	1	8	240	2355

Area	European pine marten (*Martes martes*)		Red squirell (*Sciurus vulgaris*)		European badger (*Meles meles*)		European hare (*Lepus europaeus*)	
	NISP	Weight (g)	NISP	Weight (g)	NISP	Weight (g)	NISP	Weight (g)
Upper settlement terrace (S1)	9	24	3	3.0	4	37	-	-
Lower settlement terrace (S2)	3	14	2	0.5	-	-	1	0.0
Westwall area (WW)	23	34.7	36	25.8	4	16.9	10	17.1
Total	35	72.7	41	29.3	8	53.9	11	17.1

Area	Wolf (*Canis lupus*)		Wild cat (*Felis silvestris*)		European hedgehog (*Erinaceus europaeus*)	
	NISP	Weight (g)	NISP	Weight (g)	NISP	Weight (g)
Upper settlement terrace (S1)	-	-	-	-	3	3
Lower settlement terrace (S2)	3	25.5	-	-	-	-
Westwall area (WW)	-	-	4	14.3	7	0.3
Total	3	25.5	4	14.3	10	3.3

Area	European hamster (*Cricetus cricetus*)		Black rat (*Rattus rattus*)	
	NISP	Weight (g)	NISP	Weight (g)
Upper settlement terrace (S1)	-	-	-	-
Lower settlement terrace (S2)	-	-	-	-
Westwall area (WW)	1	0.1	1	0.0
Total	1	0.1	1	0.0

(Kratochvíl 1976, 1–43). His measurements and average values have been widely used. Separating populations of wild and domesticated cats based solely on biometric data is known to be difficult, especially in Sand where the findings are so limited, but the comparative study with other archaeological sites helped in identifying the material.

In Sand, only two bones produced measurements, a humerus and a radius. The values agree with those of Kratochvíl for the wild cat. The best criterion is the maximal length, but in our case the bones were only partly preserved. Moreover, the finds from Haithabu show that the measurements from Sand do not fall within the range of variation of domesticated cats (Johansson & Hüster 1987, 1–86). Haithabu produced numerous bones that were compared with the single bones from Sand. Diaphysis breadths (humerus) are between 4.8 and 7 mm, and distal epiphysis breadths are between 14.2 and 19.1 mm. In Sand these values are 8.0 and 20.5 mm, respectively.

Concerning the radius, diaphysis breadth in Haithabu is estimated between 3.5 and 5.4 mm, distal epiphysis breadth between 10.0 and 12.8 mm. The corresponding values in Sand are 7.0 and 15.5 mm. More finds of house cats from the Avar cemetery at Vösendorf (Pucher et al. 2007) and from Gaiselberg (12th-16th century AD, Spitzenberger 1986, 121–161) exhibited lower values than those of Sand. According to Spitzenberger (1986, 121–161), medieval house cats were small and fragile.

Wild cat is a shy and solitary animal, which prefers deciduous and mixed forests, but also riparian forests. It is found close to water sources, such as marshes, but the species is very adaptable and inhabits a variety of habitats

Table 28. Wild birds and fish: number of identified specimens (NISP) and weight analysis

Area	Wild birds		Fish	
	NISP	Weight (g)	NISP	Weight (g)
Upper settlement terrace (S1)	4	7.0	4	2.0
Lower settlement terrace (S2)	3	0.7	2	2.9
Westwall area (WW)	36	31.8	4	5.0
Total	43	39.5	10	9.9

(Spitzenberger 2001, 670–671). The low number of bones indicates rarity, even though hunting activities were very high. The proximity to water sources (Thaya River) no doubt favoured the presence of many different and rare species.

4.15 Carnivora, Lagomorpha, and Rodentia (fur animals)

The remaining wild species are relatively poorly represented at the archaeological assemblages of Sand, but their contribution to understand the social dynamics is important. Many of the species listed below, including the European otter (*Lutra lutra*), the European badger (*Meles meles*), the European polecat (*Mustela putorius*), the European pine marten (*Martes martes*), the European beaver (*Castor fiber*), the European hare (*Lepus europaeus*), the red squirell (*Sciurus vulgaris*), the brown bear (*Ursus arctos*), and the wolf (*Canis lupus*), are important fur animals (Table 27). Some of them were very precious and difficult to find; these species usually symbolize high social status and prestige, such as the European otter.

The inclusion of some taxa in the diet of the inhabitants – and especially of animals that constituted beloved dishes such as beaver – is highly possible, even if they contributed only minimally. Fur animals are found at various other sites as well, but usually at low percentages, similarly to Sand, where in total they represent 2% of the material based on weight and almost 4% based on NISP.

The great variety of fur animals and the fact that textile production has been archaeologically confirmed in Sand supports the idea that fur was exploited. The use and probable processing of skins is also confirmed by cut marks on bones of other species (Saliari & Felgenhauer 2017, 95–114).

4.16 Other wild species

A total of ten bones of European hedgehog (*Erinaceus europaeus*) were recovered from Sand 1 and Westwall area. Bones of the European hamster (*Cricetus cricetus*) from Westwall very probably represent modern infiltration.

Wild birds and fish are poorly represented (Table 28). The Westwall area exhibited the highest frequency of wild birds, even if the value is significantly low compared to the other species. Only some bones from Westwall could be identified at family level: five bones (ulna, carpometacarpus, tarsometatarsus) derive from the family Anatidae, three bones (ulna, carpometacarpus, tarsometatarsus) represent the Columbidae, and one bone (tarsometatarsus) the Corvidae. In Sand 1, two bones come from wood grouse (*Tetrao urogallus*) and two from the ural owl (*Strix uralensis*). Most bird bones were unidentifiable; many of them represent very young individuals, which lack the necessary, well-developed anatomical characteristics. Finally, one fish bone from Sand 2 – that could be identified – belongs to the northern pike (*Esox lucius*). Difficulties with the identification are also related to the preservation of the material.

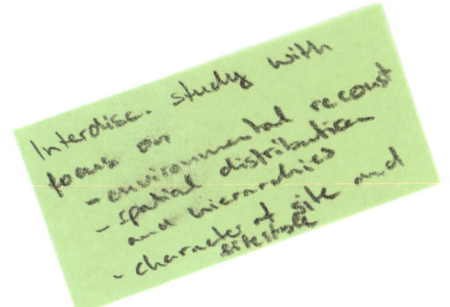

Chapter 5

Discussion

In the chapter of discussion, all the primary data are combined, in order to discuss and interpret the overall archaeological meaning. One of the most important questions concerns the economic strategy and logistic organisation of the human population at the site. The animal bones from Sand brought to light many unique features to approach these issues.

This chapter illustrates how the interdisciplinary study of faunal assemblages can offer key information, which will decisively contribute to the interpretation of the site. The faunal investigation allowed insights into a) the environment and the natural landscape and b) the functional and the socio-economic organisation of the site. The analysis has been divided into two parts (5.1 and 5.2), equivalent to the main topics that will be discussed; the last part (5.3) summarizes and combines the archaeological information with the archaeozoological results.

1. Palaeoenvironmental reconstruction (5.1). This part presents and discusses information gained through the archaeozoological analysis about the environment and the natural context, where human activities took place. Understanding the natural features gives the opportunity to better interpret human choices and decisions.[1] In Sand, the synthetic study of the wild species offers a detailed picture of the local environmental framework; their presence can be associated with specific features including vegetation, soil, climate, seasonality, changes, and even human presence.

2. The second part discusses the distribution of the animal bones at each area separately and for the entire site (5.2.1). The spatial analysis of the faunal material can be connected to aspects of status and hierarchy and can be used as a tool to better interpret the functional organisation of the site. Additionally the profiles of the wild and domesticated species will be examined, in order to gain valuable insights into the economy of the site (5.2.2). In some cases the low number of finds merely indicates tendencies; combining and comparing the different observations is a key step in translating these tendencies into archaeological hypotheses.

3. The last part compiles the faunal analysis with the archaeological information and the historical testimony, in order to interpret the character of the site and the lifestyle of the inhabitants. It discusses the role of the archaeozoological finds as part of the archaeological context and of a specific historical framework (5.3).

5.1 Environment

5.1.1 Wild species as environmental indicators and markers of human activities

There are many ways to obtain information on the natural framework and the environmental setting. Animal bones can provide significant information about the surroundings, landscape, and ecology of a site. Wild animals offer a strong potential as environmental indicators, especially those species whose habits, behaviour, and interaction with other species are well known. Accordingly, not all the species are appropriate for addressing questions regarding environmental reconstructions; some species might be better ecological indicators than others and, of course, different species deliver different information. Sand features a wide variety of wild mammals at high frequencies. Fish and bird bones are rare and the young age of some wild birds precluded identifications.

The wild species that prevail in Sand are wild Bovidae (mainly European bison), red deer, and wild boar. Each of these species offers important information about the local landscape and therefore an accurate identification is necessary, in order to have a detailed picture of the surroundings; this highlights the importance of identifying wild Bovidae since they are crucial in the environmental reconstruction. Bison and aurochs exhibit certain key differences. Bison inhabit high altitudes and mainly wooded areas, whereas aurochs prefer forested steppes, riparian zones, swamps, and wet lowlands (Spitzenberger 2001, 730–735). The physiological and morphological traits show that evolutionary selection enabled bison to better handle cold stress and extreme winter conditions (Spitzenberger 2001, 736–743). Bison have been recorded from the montane zone (400-1200/1400 m), subalpine forests (1200-2100 m), as well as in deciduous and mixed forests with grassy spots of light and boggy places. The habitat differences involve different topography, soil characteristics, and diet. Aurochs is a grazer, whereas bison consume leaves, twigs, and bark (Spitzenberger 2001, 742).

The abundant bison in Sand is unsurprising considering the modern environmental setting (chapter 2.1.2). Nonetheless, an overlap in the biotopes of both species might have existed, especially during the seasonal migrations, when the animals move in search of favourable environmental conditions, fodder, etc.[2]

---

[1] There is plenty of literature about the landscape and its significance in Archaeology. See Doneus 2013.

[2] It remains difficult to understand the habitat preferences of the aurochs, due to its early extinction. The archaeological assemblages from Austria,

Red deer mainly characterize woodlands with thickets and open areas; regionally they can be found close to moorlands and swamps (Görner & Hackethal 1988, 315–319; Corbet & Ovenden 1982, 209–210). Other species from the family Cervidae recorded in Sand are elk and roe deer. Elk is a forest animal that prefers deciduous forests and water bodies. Roe deer seeks deciduous and mixed forests with low vegetation and swamps.

Wild boar prefers deciduous and mixed forests, especially of oak and beech, with marshes and meadows nearby (Görner & Hackethal 1988, 312–313).Wild cat inhabits deciduous, mixed, and riparian forests. They are often found close to water sources, such as marshes, but this very adaptable species is at home in a variety of habitats (Spitzenberger 2001, 670–671), similarly to wolf and brown bear. The few wild cat bones indicate rarity, even though hunting activities were of very intensive character in Sand.

The proximity to water sources (Thaya River) certainly favoured the presence of many different (and sometimes rare) species, including beavers and otters. Beaver prefers flowing *[Environment similar to today]* side vegetation, where *[...]* vide variety of aquatic *[...]* s, lakes, rivers, marsh *[...]* t factor for the occur *[...]*. The European polec*[...]* nes, whereas the European badger prefers deciduous woods with clearings or small patches of woodland. The European pine marten occurs in deciduous, mixed and coniferous woodland.

The investigation of the wild species shows that almost all the animals point to woodland with openings, slow-moving or stagnant water bodies and moors. This corresponds to the landscape of Waldviertel. Beyond indicating the ecological background, wild species provide clues on the intensity of the human presence. The recovery of animals that avoid human presence (European bison,[3] elk, otters), that are solitary and shy (wild cat) suggests no large-scale human activities in the immediate region.

This profile is in strong contrast to the castle of Raabs; the major difference being the frequency of European hare and black rat, which are both cultural followers (Riedel & Pucher 2008, 159–194). Hare is represented in Raabs with 19% and black rat with 17.2%, whereas in Sand the values are 0.3% and 0.1%, respectively.[4] Hare is usually connected to agrarian landscapes and woodland clearance, which seem to have been much more progressive in Raabs, indicating a long-lasting plan (Riedel & Pucher 2008, 159–

194). Black rats are associated with human settlements and indicate contacts with the southern Danubian regions.[5] One bone of black rat found in Sand is probably a modern infiltration.

5.2 Interpreting the faunal assemblages from Sand

5.2.1 S*[...]*

[Analysis focusses on weight rather than NISP]

Conce*[...]*al assemblages some *[...]* recalled. The materia*[...]* d of the Early Middle Ages and it mainly represents primary waste. Archaeological finds and animal bones were found on the surface inside the architectural features excavated at the different areas (Figure 3); finds outside of these features have not been unearthed – with some small exceptions. Animal bones are mainly related to food waste, providing information about the dietary habits, taste, and status of the consumers, but also to production waste, revealing information about activities that probably took place in the site.

5.2.1.1 Archaeological observations and animal bones from Sand 1

Archeologically, the structures of Sand 1 yielded abundant finds suggesting intensive economic activity. The material mainly consists of pottery, metals, and equipment related to textiles, such as spindles, which reveal additional details about the character of the activities. Hearths, furnaces, and grinding stones reveal daily activities such as cooking and processing of those raw materials found in situ. Most spindle whorls stem from Object 5; finds from Objects 4, 5, 6 and 7 also indicate textile (spindle whorls) production together with metal processing (slags). Finds from Objects 3, 4, 5, and 7 suggest pottery production. Object 6 at the western part of the terrace differs from the other architectural features of this terrace due to its careful construction; it has therefore been interpreted as the residence of a possible administrator.

At Sand 1, 3172 animal bones have been retrieved. Although domesticated animals prevail, the upper settlement terrace shows a high percentage of wild species (41.3% of the total weight) (Figure 53). The prevalent wild species are red deer, European bison, and wild boar. The age and sex profiles of the three dominant wild species show that Sand 1 is characterized mostly by strong male adult animals; females and young individuals are rare (Pucher & Schmitzberger 1999a, 355–378). This points to a selective strategy concerning the wild species, which could be associated with the social status of the inhabitants (see chapter 5.2.2.1).

---

especiall*[...]* in aurochs bones, indicate *[...]* e of domesticated cattle (S*[...]*

[Absence of cultural followers]

[3] Almo*[...]* vild Bovidae have been ide*[...]* suggested by the environm*[...]* presence of bison than of a*[...]*

[4] Based on NISP.

---

[5] Intensive contacts of the people of Raabs with the southern regions are also indicated by the alpine cattle population. Although Sand and Raabs are very close the fact that the two sites exhibit different cattle breeds could be connected to different contacts and suppliers (Riedel & Pucher 2008, 159–194).

The investigation of the domesticated fauna showed that cattle are the dominant species (45.9% by weight), followed by horse, pig, and goats; domestic fowl is rare and no dog remains were found. Cattle are mainly represented by young castrated animals. Very old individuals (stage M₃+++) were not detected. Young oxen offer the best and most tasteful meat quality. Pigs also derive mainly from immature individuals and young adults; the profile of goats also suggests a high frequency of very young animals. To conclude, the majority of the domesticated species were slaughtered at the optimum age for meat consumption.

Another significant characteristic of the domesticated fauna in Sand 1 is more horses and fewer pigs and goats than at Sand 2 or the Westwall area (Figure 50). This is an important observation because horses were prestigious animals whose presence is usually related to an elite group. As it has been already mentioned, horses constituted part of the diet.

5.2.1.2 Archaeological observations and animal bones from Sand 2

The lower settlement terrace (Sand 2) presents some similar features to Sand 1. This terrace has a strong fortification, and a number of architectural features were built at the interior side of the fortification wall. Object 13 located at the western part has been interpreted as the residence of an administrator. Overall, this yields a type of symmetry in the way the two terraces were constructed; nonetheless there are some differences in the construction techniques and the archaeological finds (Felgenhauer-Schmiedt forthcoming).

Concerning the material culture, the first noteworthy difference is the smaller number of finds; the suggestion has been that the economic activities in this area are less intensive than those at Sand 1. The activities at this part of the site were probably different. One of the structures (Object 10) has been interpreted as "tradesman's house" (Felgenhauer-Schmiedt pers. comm.). This terrace apparently had rooms that functioned as guestrooms and storage rooms, pointing to a significantly different character and function of Sand 2 versus Sand 1. Finally, precious finds such as non-ferrous metals were found only at the central structure (*Burghügel*) and Sand 1.

Archaeozoologically, 1778 animal bones have been retrieved from this area. The material exhibits similarities as well as important differences to Sand 1 and the Westwall area. Firstly, the frequency of wild species is high (33.6%) similarly to Sand 1, but the number of domesticated animals in Sand 2 is higher (66.4% of the total weight) (Figure 53). The three most dominant wild species are wild Bovidae (mainly European bison), red deer, and wild boar; the total percentage of these species in Sand 1 is 39.2% (on a weight basis) and 28.5% in Sand 2. The profiles of wild Bovidae and red deer cannot be determined because there were insufficient bone and teeth for sexing. Concerning wild boar, males prevail (> 65%). As opposed to Sand 1, the age profile of wild boar showed the presence of some immature animals (n=2).

Among the domesticated species, the dominant animal is cattle (50.8%) followed by pigs, sheep/goats (mainly goats), and horses; only few remains of domestic fowl and dog were found. Cattle are mainly represented by castrated individuals and most of the animals were slaughtered at a young age, as in Sand 1. Only few teeth were found, but this conclusion is also supported by the epiphyses. The age profiles of pigs and small ruminants are similar to Sand 1. The domesticated animals at this terrace were slaughtered at a very good age for meat consumption. Figure 50 shows a noteworthy difference to Sand 1, namely the lower frequency of horse remains, as also recorded in the Westwall area.

5.2.1.3 Archaeological observations and animal bones from Westwall area

This area has a strong fortification, and the wooden structures were constructed along the fortification wall. The archaeological information from this area is limited and little is known about the activities that took place here. Nonetheless, intensive economic activities clearly took place; the material culture indicates iron processing along with the processing of bones and antlers.

This area exhibited the highest number of animal bones; 4880 faunal remains have been unearthed and analysed. An interesting aspect is that according to the weight analysis wild species dominate (52.6%). Domesticated species are

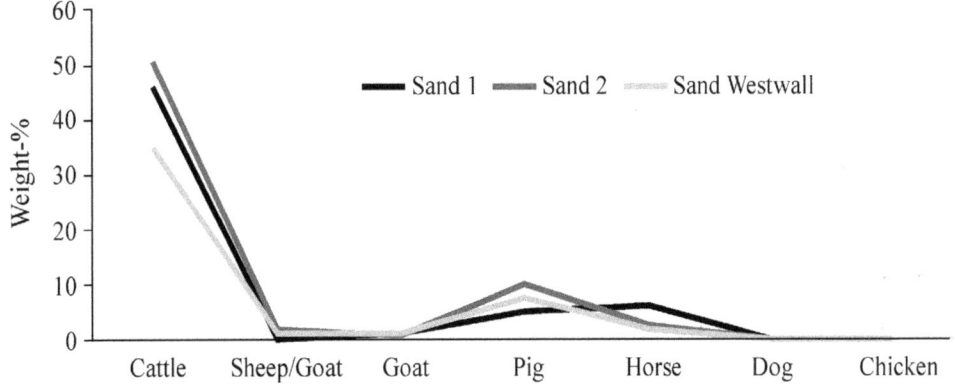

Figure 50. Distribution of domesticated animals in Sand per area (weight% including the wild species).

represented with 47.4% (Figure 53). Among the wild fauna, wild Bovidae (mainly European bison), red deer, and wild boar dominate (> 45% of the wild fauna). The age and sex profiles of wild Bovidae indicate only a tendency due to the low number of finds. Both males and females were recorded, as in the case of wild boar (Figure 44). Similarly to Sand 2, immature individuals of wild boar were present (n=4). Concerning red deer premolars indicating immature animals have been found in both Sand 1 (n=2) and Westwall area (n=2). However, in contrast to Sand 1, most red deer in the Westwall area were female individuals.

Another important information is the variety and number of pelt animals; the species that have been identified include the European otter (*Lutra lutra*), European badger (*Meles meles*), European polecat (*Mustela putorius*), European pine marten (*Martes martes*), red squirrel (*Sciurus vulgaris*), European beaver (*Castor fiber*), European hare (*Lepus europaeus*), wolf (*Canis lupus*), wild cat (*Felis silvestris*) and brown bear (*Ursus arctos*). Even if their presence is limited,[6] most of these animals derive from the Westwall area (Figure 51). Some of these species bear very precious pelts, which served as a symbol of prestige and social status.

Among the domesticated animals, cattle prevail (35.2% weight), followed by pig, sheep/goats (mainly goats), and horse, similarly to Sand 2; domestic fowl and dogs are rare. An important difference to Sand 1 and Sand 2 is the ratio between bulls and cows. Here, female animals are more common, even if bulls and oxen in total prevail. Another important characteristic is the strong presence of immature animals (especially Pd_4+). Although the other two areas exhibited a high number of immature animals as well, the prevalent age stage was represented by molar 3, which indicates older animals. Abundant very young individuals usually reflect a noble diet (Pasda 2004; Küchelmann 2012, 87–97). Animals older than 10 years (M_3+++) were also recorded in this area. As in Sand 1 and Sand 2, the number of young sheep/goats (mainly goats) and pigs was high. Combined, these observations indicate that the inhabitants of the Westwall area also enjoyed luxurious meals.

The analysis of the animal bones revealed further valuable evidence about the activities that took place here; it seems that they were apparently related to the exploitation of materials and products coming from animals (Saliari & Felgenhauer 2017, 95–114). In particular, important characteristics are:

a) The vast majority of the semi-finished and finished artefacts out of bone were found in the Westwall area (63%), including those out of antlers (together with production waste). Most osseous objects derive from cattle metapodials, but their interpretation remains difficult. One sheep/goat metacarpus has been

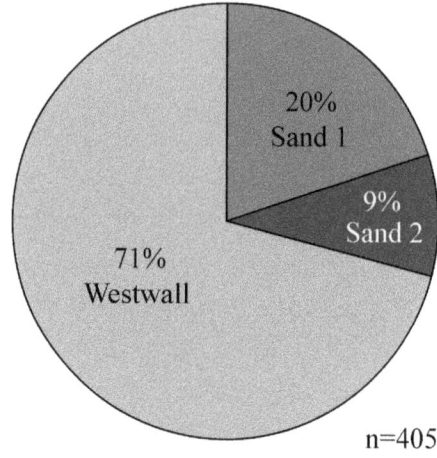

n=405

Figure 51. Distribution of fur animals per area – Sand total (NISP%). Source: Saliari & Felgenhauer-Schmiedt 2017, 95–114.

interpreted as a punch[7] and one sheep/goat metatarsal as an awl or point.[8] Interestingly, bones of wild species were not used; artefacts out of red deer antlers have been only recorded including tines of various sizes (4.0-6.5 mm and 11.0-20.0 mm). No interpretation of the antler artefacts was possible because most are semi-finished objects and their role could be multiple. They might have been used as parts of weapons or of other equipment, as autonomous tools, and some as handles. These objects were present in many different rooms in the Westwall area, including area 21 and 28, were the archaeological findings indicate economically intensive structures (Felgenhauer-Schmiedt pers. comm.). Most of the bigger sized tines (11.0-20.0 mm) were found inside structure 28.

b) Many young animals, especially cattle and goat, which provide very good skin quality (Ruß-Popa pers. comm.).[9]

c) Most of the fur-bearing animals come from the Westwall area (71% based on NISP).

d) A high frequency of goat horn cores (Figure 52); such a phenomenon has often been connected to craft contexts, including horn exploitation and tanning (Prummel 1978, 399–422; Noddle 1994, 117–128; Bartosiewicz 1995, 72–73; 2006, 457-478; Deschler-Erb 2012, 113–137; Rehazek & Nussbaumer 2012, 65–69).

e) Cut marks indicating skinning activities. In general, interpreting cut marks can be problematic, but in the present case they have been detected at all the anatomically relevant areas – such as the base of

---

[6] Which might also be related to taphonomic factors and the excavation techniques, especially for the small-sized animals.

[7] The sheep/goat metacarpus (48/03) was longitudinally split and bears a pointed end. Almost half of the corpus of the bone has been used, and the processed side is the lateral one. Traces of knife cuts around the pointed end indicate processing. No further modifications are visible. Use wear has been detected on the top of the proximal epiphysis. The spongiosa at this part is exposed giving the impression that pressure from above was applied.

[8] It has also been longitudinally chopped and part of the dorsal diaphysis was used as a tool. The original form of the artefact is not known because an old breakage has occurred at the diaphysis, which might have been caused during the manufacture of the artefact or its use.

[9] Also confirmed by cut marks at the cranium of a young female goat.

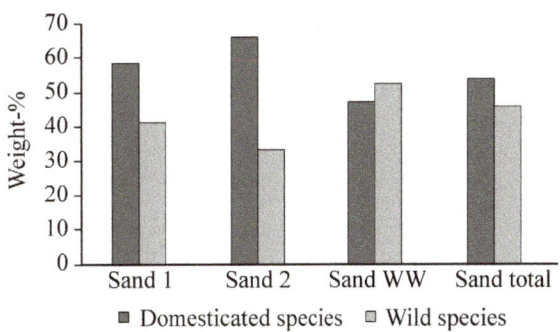

Figure 53. Distribution of wild and domesticated species – Sand per area and total (weight%).

Figure 52. Horn cores of female goats from the Westwall area.

antlers (Binford 1981, 136). It is also known that many activities do not leave marks, but their presence is a significant indication.

These observations provide evidence for the exploitation of skin and fur at the Westwall area, but similar activities for the other areas cannot be excluded, especially when there is no direct evidence for the whole production process. Leather seems to have been a very important material for the inhabitants of Sand, although it remains unclear how skinning and the processing of skin and fur were organised (Grömer et al. 2017, 69–93; Saliari & Felgenhauer 2017, 95–114).

The excavation at the upper and lower settlement terraces yielded metal implements (awls) used exclusively for manufacturing objects out of leather and fur (Walcher 2004). Even if their number is low (n=2), these finds indicate that the processing steps of the raw materials might have taken place elsewhere. Other tools could have been also used for skin processing, but many of them are multifunctional. Logically, however, a part of the processing took place in Sand. This is additionally supported by the fact that the raw hide can be very rapidly destroyed by insects and bacteria unless it undergoes further processing as soon as possible (Ruß-Popa & Grömer pers. comm.).

5.2.1.4 Summary

A total of 9830 animal bones have been examined. The material from all three areas indicates patterns of high social status, prosperity, and consumers who enjoyed luxurious meals. These features are: a) the wide variety of species, b) intensive hunting activities of big-sized game and, in the case of wild Bovidae, the presence of nutritionally rich elements, c) a high number of domesticated taxa slaughtered at the best age for meat consumption, d) the relatively abundant horses. These observations are in accordance with the archaeological results, since the faunal assemblages indicate inhabitants of high status, but they also reveal internal social hierarchies.

There are some noteworthy differences (potentially related to many factors such as economic interest) among the areas.

The material culture from Sand 1 seems to be different from that at Sand 2 and the Westwall area; it suggests intensive and multiple economic activities of noble character. In addition, certain nobility markers are stronger at the faunal assemblages of Sand 1 than at the other two areas; these features are:

a) The more abundant horses (Figure 50). The archaeozoological record shows that horses are rare in rural households, indicating that simple people could not afford many animals. The cattle of Raabs has a higher proportion than the oxen or horses (0.7%) (Riede... ... Interestingly, the *Lex Saxonum* ... ... medieval Saxony, horse thieves were ... ... (Schwerin 1918). At the history of Widukind and Corvey Strabon[11] paragraph 6 book II states that Eberhard, who burned down the stronghold of Helmern and killed the people,[12] had to pay as compensation to the king horses valued at one hundred talents.[13] Horses were expensive animals and their breeding was sometimes a specialized occupation (Leyser 1982, 21). The equipment that was necessary for equestrian service should also be included in the costs. Until today, horses in many different cultures are symbols of economic status and social prestige.

b) The presence of big-sized wild adult males. The following chapter deals with the great difference between male and female wild animals as well as between adult and immature individuals.

In conclusion, Sand 1 was an economically intensive area where textiles and metals were processed and pottery produced. The animal bones from this area come mainly from kitchen waste, which indicate luxurious meals and patterns of noble behaviour (e.g. horses) and from production waste (a very small number of bone artefacts). Sand 2 has been mainly interpreted as an area with resting and storage rooms. Economic activities are limited, but the animal bones indicate luxurious meals. The Westwall area was economically very active, similarly to Sand

---

[10] *Lex Saxonum* consists of laws issued by Charlemagne from 782 to 803. It constitutes one of the most fascinating sources concerning laws and matters of justice in the early medieval period.
[11] Written in the 10th century.
[12] Regarding the civil wars of Saxons.
[13] English translation by Bachrach & Bachrach (2014).

1. The faunal material derives from food waste, which suggest privileged dietary habits and production waste related to the processing of bones, antlers, and skinning activities.

5.2.2 The socio-economic organisation of Sand

The main aim of this chapter is to understand the socio-economic character of the site and how the inhabitants of Sand tried to meet their daily needs. In short, the animal bones will be used as a tool to understand the logistic organisation of the site and to trace behavioural patterns that will shed light on the lifestyle of the inhabitants.

For this reason important features of the wild and domesticated fauna will be investigated. A major question regarding the wild species is to understand the reason(s) that lead to their intensive exploitation and their role in the economic organisation of the site. Concerning the domesticated animals, of key importance is to combine and interpret the most important aspects that have been already analysed – age and sex distribution, skeletal element distribution, morphometric analysis – in order to gain a full picture of the logistic organisation, which will allow insights into the interaction of the inhabitants as consumers with their providers.

5.2.2.1 The role of the wild species in the economic organisation of Sand

The quantification of the material is an essential criterion to understand the significance of the different species or of a group of animals in the economic organisation of a site. In Sand, intensive hunting activities, indicated by the high percentage of wild species, suggest that the wild fauna played a key role in the organisation of the site. The question that now raises is to understand how the wild fauna contributed to the economy and to the general lifestyle of the inhabitants.

According to the literature (Müller 1962, 81–97; 1982, 239–258; Becker 1989; Schmitzberger 2009) an increasing percentage of wild fauna can be related to hunting as sport (trophies acquisition), as a method to serve daily needs (acquisition of meat and raw materials), or in some cases can express both tendencies.

Hunting for trophies is usually synonymous with a selective process concentrated on a particular species, or on a specific age and sex spectrum. A case in point is castle Raabs (Riedel & Pucher 2008, 159–194). The wild animals from Raabs (11th century AD) show a clear selection for adult males (...*die Raabser dekorierten sich noch mit den Trophäen mächtiger Wisentbullen*[14]...), which suggests hunting as a noble activity for trophy acquirement. A similar example comes from castle Meißen (10th-11th century AD). Hunting activities have been interpreted as

a noble sport for the lords of the castle (*Beschäftigung der Burgherren*) based on the low frequency of females and immature animals, which are easier to catch (Müller 1982, 239–258).

Hunting for the acquisition of meat and raw materials is usually not concentrated on particular characteristics, such as species, size, age, and sex. The site of Köpenick (11th-12th cent AD) in Germany exhibited an abundant number of wild remains with 45%. (Müller 1962, 81–97). Part of the material has been interpreted as indicating trophy hunting, but the general high frequency of animals together with the presence of young individuals and females show that the people were also interested in the acquisition of other products and materials.[15] Similar results were obtained from the faunal remains in the castle Glienke (eastern Mecklenburg 9th-10th century AD). The presence of immature individuals of red deer and wild boar (almost 5% and 9%, respectively) shows that hunting activities went beyond trophy acquisition (Prilloff 2015, 224–233).

When all these observations are taken into consideration, then it is possible to assume the role of the faunal remains also in Sand. In particular, key characteristics are:

a) The high percentage of wild fauna indicates a level of effort, time, and energy that possibly goes beyond mere sports. Of course, the proximity to water (Thaya River) would have promoted the presence and the wide variety of the wild species. Hunting activities, however, go beyond reflecting the ecological background to also expressing cultural and economic aspects. The castle Raabs is a good example, because although the site is just 1.6 km away from Sand, it has a completely different character. Game in Raabs is represented by just 5% (Pucher 2009a, 259–272). This situation clearly points to cultural factors and matters of logistic organisation rather than environmental considerations.

b) In Sand females and males are usually found in almost equal percentages, and in some cases immature individuals represent 20%.

c) The skeletal element representation shows that some animals have been delivered as whole individuals (red deer, wild boar), but for some species there is a relatively high number of meaty regions (European bison).

d) Cut and chop marks suggest that the people tried to use all the materials obtainable from the wild fauna (meat, skin, fur). Raw materials, such as antlers, have been used for the manufacture of artefacts.

e) Lack of trophies. Horn cores, antlers, or other cranial elements are lacking, or they were further processed into simple artefacts or even discarded as waste.

These observations point to a strong interest in the economic exploitation of the wild animals. Overall, the hunting activities indicate the efforts of the people to serve

---

[14] The inhabitants of Raabs were decorated with trophies of strong bison males.

[15] Generally, intensive hunting activities cannot be connected to the Slavic culture because other Slavic castles presented a completely different character with less than 5% hunting (Müller 1984, 161–188).

their own needs and perhaps use some of the products as trading goods. However, due to the presence of animals that represent *Hochwild*, hunting for trophies cannot be excluded, but it seems that the trophies did not constitute the first priority. It can be suggested that in Sand the wild fauna had a mixed role, as it has been already observed in other (early) medieval sites (Köpenick, Glienke).

5.2.2.2 Domesticated species as markers of provision - comparison with other representative sites

The age and sex structure of the animals shows that in Sand the economically most important domesticated species (cattle, pig, and goat) have been imported to the site, indicating a system of provision. Therefore, the material offers a great opportunity to shed additional light on the economic organisation, the system of provision, and the relationship between consumers and producers.

In this part the comparative study with other sites plays a major role. The main aim of the comparative study is to understand how different systems (settlements, castles, etc.) were organised regarding keeping, maintaining, and delivery of domestic stock based on the animal bones. All the cases that will be investigated and are presented in Table 29 exhibited traces, which suggest provision from outsiders, and thus they offer important information about the mechanism(s) of provision, how it functioned, and how provision could vary. This comparison will help to better understand the character of Sand, to find parallels/analogues, and to better appreciate the range of cultural variation, testified by the archaeozoological finds.

Important features that will be examined are mainly related to age and sex distribution. As it has been already mentioned in the chapter of methodology age at death and sex estimation contributes to better understand the economic exploitation of the animals. Tables 30-32 show the age structure and the sex estimation for all the case studies. Most sites that will be examined derive from the Middle Ages, except Roseldorf and Traismauer Augustiniana. These sites have been additionally added because the material indicates very specific economic strategies that have been thoroughly analysed and published. The case studies will be chronologically presented, starting from the oldest faunal assemblages. The profiles of all the three main species will be combined for each case separately.

To begin with, in *Roseldorf* both cattle and sheep/goats present in total a high number of immature animals and young adults, suggesting meat supply of very good quality. Concerning cattle not all the age stages of immature animals are present ($Pd_40/+$), indicating a selective strategy. They are older than 1 year, when the animal is old enough to offer a respectable meat quantity. Older cattle individuals between 7-10 years (M_3++) are also present. Animals older than 10 years have been recorded in the case of sheep/goats. These older animals might have been probably further exploited by the producers, before delivered to Roseldorf. Pigs are mainly represented by young adults (M_30); the number of piglets is relatively low.

In *Traismauer Augustiniana* cattle are represented by young adults (M_3+), but older age stages are also well represented, indicating that oxen and cows have been exploited (labour animals and secondary products, such as milk) before being slaughtered. Calves are found at a much lower frequency. Small ruminants are also represented by young adults (M_3+). In comparison to these species, pigs have been slaughtered at younger stages (M_30) and they exhibit a higher frequency of piglets.

In castle *Glienke* more than 50% of the pigs are younger than 2 years, but small ruminants and cattle are mainly represented by adults. In Glienke, the percentage of calves is relatively high in the castle, but the frequency of

Table 29. Archaeological sites mentioned in the text

Sites	Location	Date	Interpretation	Literature
Roseldorf	Austria	4th century BC	Celtic settlement	Abd el Karem 2013a
Traismauer/ Augustiniana	Austria	1st century AD	Roman city with military camp	Riedel 1993,179–294
Glienke	Germany	9th-10th century AD	Castle	Prilloff 2015, 224–233
Raabs	Austria	10th-12th century AD	Castle	Riedel & Pucher 2008, 159–164
Neu-Schellenberg	Liechtenstein	12th-16th (material from 13th-14th century AD)	Castle	Schülke 1965
Hummertsried	Germany	13th-17th century AD	Castle	Wiedemann 1974, 61–67
Salzburg Residenz	Germany	16th century AD	Luxurious restaurant	Pucher 1991, 71–135
Prösels	Italy	16th-17th century AD	Castle	Boschin 2012, 283–290
Hauenstein	Austria	16th century AD	Military camp	Pucher & Schmitzberger 2006, 608–623

Table 30. Cattle: age at death, sex distribution, and animal exploitation – a comparative study

	Cattle								
	Meat supply						**Secondary exploitation**		
	Immature				**Young adults**		**Older adults**		
Sites	$Pd_4 0$	$Pd_4 +$	$Pd_4 ++$	$Pd_4 +++$	$M_3 0$	$M_3 +$	$M_3 ++$	$M_3 +++$	**Sex estimation**
Roseldorf	0	0	2	3	2	2	4	0	Males prevail
				9				4	
Traismauer/ Augustiniana	1	2	5	1	12	28	21	17	Males prevail
				49				38	
Salzburg R.	2	25	0	0	0	1	5	2	Males prevail
				28				7	
Raabs	0	0	0	0	2	1	1	2	Females prevail
				3				3	
Prösels	0	7	0	2	0	3	3	0	Not enough data
				12				3	
Hummertsried	1	0	0	0	3	2	1	0	Not enough data
				6				1	
Neu-Schellenberg	3	3	2	0	3	7	9	9	Females prevail
				18				18	
Hauenstein	5	4	2	1	1	10	3	0	Females prevail
				23				3	
Sand	3	9	6	4	4	13	9	2	Males prevail
				39				11	

immature sheep/goats is higher in the settlement. *Raabs* demonstrates a high number of adult cattle and sheep/ goat, whereas pigs were slaughtered at younger stages. *Neu-Schellenberg* exhibits a very low number of calves, in contrast to goats, which shows a much higher percentage of immature individuals. Pigs are mainly represented by young adults ($M_3 +$) and exhibit a lower number of piglets. In *Hummertsried* cattle have been slaughtered as young adults, but the percentage of calves is minimal.

Salzburg Residenz exhibited a high number of cattle younger than one year ($Pd_4 +$). All the other age stages are represented at very low numbers, or not at all, showing a selective strategy. The vast majority of pigs derives from young adults, whereas sheep/goats are mainly represented by immature animals. Similar results come from *Prösels*. Only one age stage for cattle is well-represented, indicating luxurious meals ($Pd_4 +$). Pigs are mainly represented by young adults ($M_3 0/+$) and sheep/goats by slightly older individuals ($M_3 ++$).

In all these cases the age and sex profiles and their combination shows that systems based on supply from outsiders are characterized by mutual compromise, reflecting a logistical balance. This balance is suggested by a selective strategy. The strategy followed is different for each species, depending on its special characteristics (size, reproduction, birth rate etc.) and is related with various factors, such as the number of suppliers. For instance, Salzburg Residenz had many different suppliers from distant areas. Its economy was not based merely on local producers.

The present case studies show that not all the species can be slaughtered at the same age stage, because they are connected to a different economic exploitation and thus different compromises should be made. According to the archaeozoological analysis, the noble people at the castle of Raabs seem to have enjoyed tender piglet meat, whereas the noble inhabitants of Glienke preferred calves. Similar results derive from various studies in and outside Europe, long before the early medieval period (e.g. Zeder 1985).

According to Tables 30-32 the only exception in this kind of system seems to be *Hauenstein*. The ruins of the former castle Hauenstein have been later used as a military camp. The faunal material exhibited the profile of consumers. A high number of immature animals and young adults for all the main three species (Tables 30-32) has been recorded (Figure 54). Hauenstein does not present the logistic compromise that has been observed on all the other case

Table 31. Pig: age at death, sex distribution, and animal exploitation – a comparative study

Sites	Immature				Young adults		Older adults		Sex estimation
	Pd_40	Pd_4+	Pd_4++	Pd_4+++	M_30	M_3+	M_3++	M_3+++	
Roseldorf	4	2	7	2	21	8	7	0	Females prevail
			15			29		7	
Traismauer/ Augustiniana	0	4	20	5	29	20	5	2	Males prevail
			29			49		7	
Salzburg R.	4	0	0	0	7	6	6	0	Males prevail
			4			13		6	
Raabs	1	3	0	0	6	7	2	0	Females prevail
			4			13		2	
Prösels	0	1	0	0	6	1	1	0	Not enough data
			1			7		1	
Neu-Schellenberg	1	7	4	1	12	15	0	6	Males prevail
			13			27		6	
Hauenstein	10	14	6	1	8	5	2	0	Males prevail
			31			13		2	
Sand	5	4	11	7	8	10	3	0	Females prevail
			27			18		3	

Table 32. (Sheep) Goats: age at death, sex distribution, and animal exploitation – a comparative study

Sites	Immature				Young adults		Older adults		Sex estimation
	Pd_40	Pd_4+	Pd_4++	Pd_4+++	M_30	M_3+	M_3++	M_3+++	
Roseldorf	1	5	12	6	5	11	15	8	Females prevail
			24			16		23	
Traismauer/ Augustiniana	0	9	3	0	6	23	11	6	Females prevail
			12			29		17	
Salzburg R.	4	20	23	23	9	9	21	5	Females prevail
			70			18		26	
Raabs	0	0	0	0	1	3	2	2	Not enough data
			0			4		4	
Prösels	4	0	1	1	1	1	6	0	Not enough data
			6			2		6	
Neu-Schellenberg	2	1	5	9	3	3	2	0	Females prevail
			17			6		2	
Hauenstein	0	5	4	2	4	2	2	0	Females prevail
			11			6		2	
Sand	0	7	9	2	3	7	8	2	Females prevail
			18			10		10	

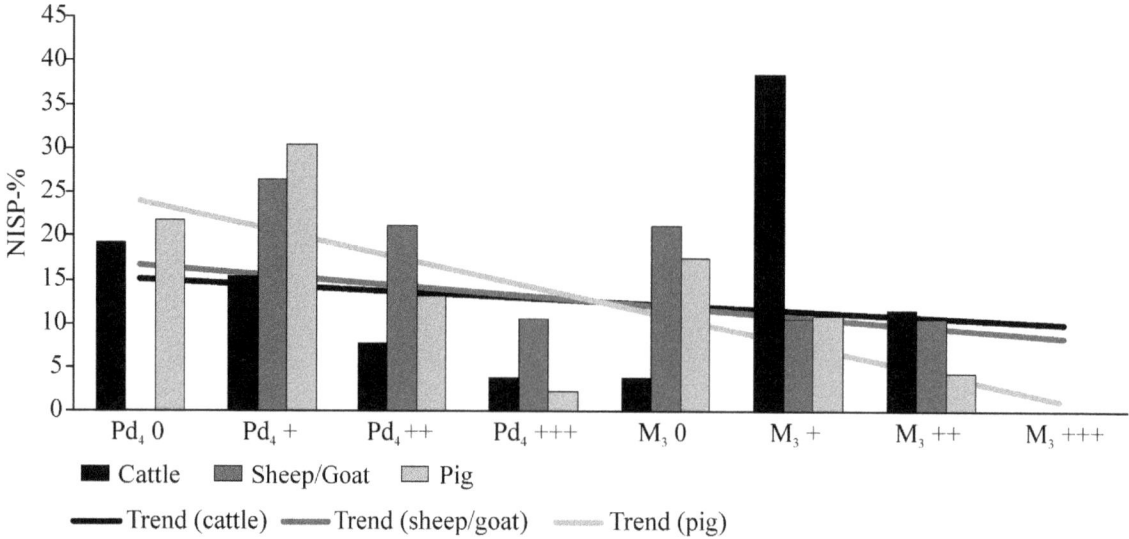

Figure 54. Age at death for the main domesticated species in Hauenstein (NISP%). The ratio among the different age stages suggests that the inhabitants of Hauenstein acted carelessly against the local peasants.

studies. Taking into consideration that especially cattle was mainly represented by young cows, it has been suggested that such a provision would have had dramatic consequences on the peasants.

5.2.2.2.1 The system of provision and the economic organisation of Sand

The question that now raises is to understand the system of provision in Sand, which requires the composition of all the profiles from the three main species. Concerning *cattle* two significant characteristics are the high frequency of immature individuals and the high number of young oxen (Table 4). The abundant immature individuals can have several explanations, including high mortality rate, socially-privileged meals, socio-economic alterations, acquisition of hide, logistic reasons (winter fodder limitations), rituals, feasts, or other unknown reasons (Müller 1978, 101–170; 1984, 161–188; Teichert 1988, 143–220). It is always difficult to understand the reason(s) for each case and it becomes even more complicated when written sources are absent. Certainly, even if the causes are not always clear, young animals are usually connected to tender and tasty meat, and thus noble meals.

In Sand, the luxurious character of the dietary habits is also confirmed by the consumption of young oxen. The age profile of adults indicates that the vast majority was slaughtered at a young stage, indicating that the animals were important meat suppliers. This suggests that oxen (and probably some female animals) were slaughtered, without being further exploited (as labour animals – for oxen and cows, or for their milk – for cows). Breeding castrated individuals is a very demanding task, when taking into consideration the low birth rate of cows and the abundant (and good quality) fodder and space that castrated animals require (see chapter 4.2.2.2).

Another consideration is the number of animals that would have been available per supplier at a normal local rural

economy.[16] At this part, it should be remembered that the morphometric investigation confirmed the involvement of local animal populations, which excluded provision from many different and distant regions (e.g. as was the case for Roseldorf and Salzburg Residenz). Therefore, it is suggested that the systematic loss of calves and young oxen might have had a significant impact on the economy of the local peasants.

Concerning *pigs*, they are usually slaughtered at a young age; their role is connected to meat production and consumption. Pigs are ideal meat suppliers. They are sexually active at a very young age and they produce a high number of piglets. They pose less demand on fodder and do not compete other species. They can find fodder in the woods and even from human kitchen wastes. Additionally, pig meat is much easier to conserve than cattle meat (Pucher 2014b, 65–93). Thus, slaughtering at a young stage is common. In all the cases studied above (Table 31) pigs were usually slaughtered at an age between 2 and 3 years ($M_3 0/+$). Young adults usually dominate. During that period the meat of females and castrated pigs is tasteful and the animals big enough to secure a sufficient quantity. In Sand, most bones derive from animals between 1-2 years (Pd_4++), and, in general, immature animals ($Pd_4 0-+++$) are more abundant than young adults ($M_3 0-+$). In Sand, pigs also confirm privileged dietary habits.

Sex ratio and mortality profiles suggest that *goats* served in Sand mainly as meat suppliers, even if their percentage was quite low. Although the prevalent stage is M_3++ (7-10 years), the high number of immature animals and young adults (Table 11) fits to the profile of consumers, who enjoyed luxurious meals. Economies focusing on

---

[16] Each peasant had a limited number of animals. This is the case until the 19th century, before industrialization. Each peasant had around 4-5 cattle. These numbers are based on the literature of the 19th century and on realistic paintings that depict scenes of daily life, such as by Alfred Steinacker and Friedrich Gauermann.

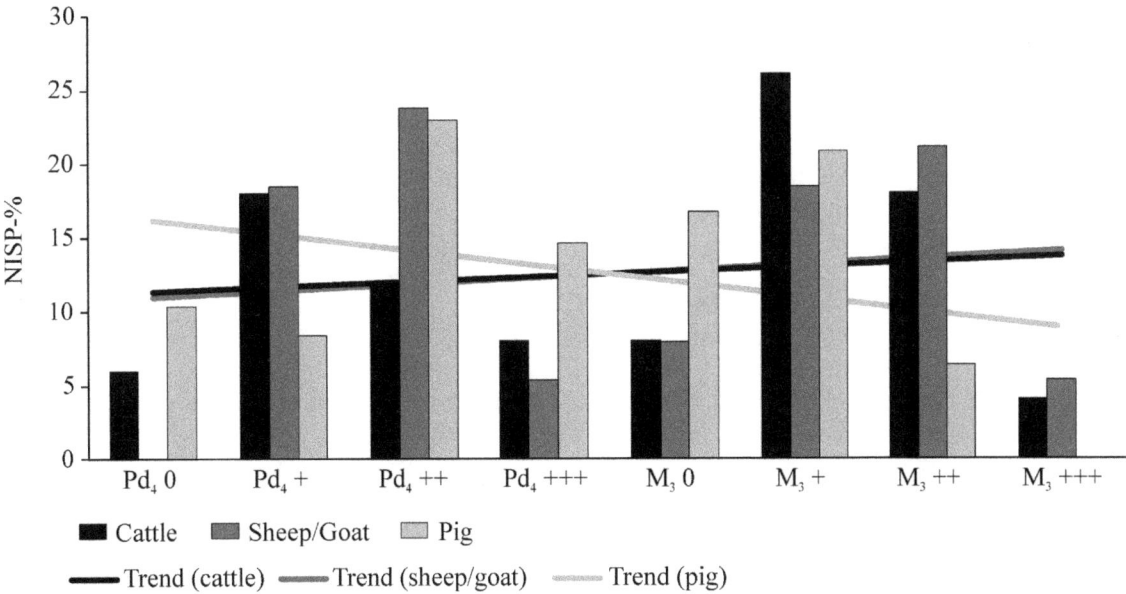

Figure 55. Age at death for the main domesticated species in Sand (NISP%). The ratio among the age stages is critical to understand the economic organisation of the site.

secondary products present a different profile, with more older (M_3++/+++) and fewer young individuals. The predominance of females is because male goats do not taste well. When comparing Tables 31 and 32 it is possible to observe that the majority of the examples mentioned, indicate that small ruminants derive from younger stages than pigs (e.g. Roseldorf, Salzburg R., Prösels, and Neu-Schellenberg).

The profiles of the main domesticated species from Sand suggest a clear tendency to very young animals, both immature and young adults (Figure 55). This result was unexpected; it gives to Sand a unique character and it shows a different system of provision, than the ones already examined, suggesting that between the inhabitants of Sand (consumers) and the producers there was no mutual compromise. The only parallel that could be found in the local archaeozoological record comes from Hauenstein. Such a system can be characterized as opportunistic, with a negative effect on the local economy.

5.3 Bridging archaeozoology and archaeology: unravelling the unique character of Sand

The on-site processing of materials such as clay, metals, skin/fur, and animal bones shows that the inhabitants of Sand tried to serve their own daily needs, to the extent possible (Felgenhauer-Schmiedt 2011, 551–559).[17] Archaeological findings, such as chain armour, bridles, and horseshoe, point towards the existence of a group of mounted warriors (Felgenhauer-Schmiedt 2012, 57-81). Precious objects such as rings and precious material (metals) indicate patterns of nobility. Additionally, the faunal remains yielded important data to understand the daily life of the inhabitants and to interpret the socio-economic organisation of the site. In summary:

a) The wealthy character of the site is demonstrated by the dietary habits of the inhabitants (high frequency of young animals, high number and variety of big-sized game).

b) The analysis of the faunal assemblages suggests little experience with handicraft. The butchery marks and the produced artefacts out of bones and antlers are important in this respect. First, the animal bones were intensively butchered and the techniques practised would have cost a lot of time, effort, and energy. Second, the bone and antler artefacts indicate that simple and fast techniques were employed, especially when compared with material from other medieval sites such as Berlin-Spandau (7th-12th century AD) (Becker 1989). Finally, the low frequency of artefacts found in Sand was very unusual.

c) As far as the domesticated animals are concerned, the inhabitants of Sand might have kept a very small number of mainly goats and pigs, but the many immature animals indicate imports. This is also confirmed by the analysis of cattle. The morphometric investigation indicates that the vast majority of the animals derives from local populations.

d) The domesticated fauna suggests that the people occupying Sand paid little attention to the future economy of the providers (peasants). The system of animal acquisition was careless, indicating an opportunistic requisition of animals with hard economic consequences for the peasants, who during the early medieval period had to survive with few animals.

e) Hunting activities indicate a mixed character, suggesting acquisition of meat/ raw materials and trophies. Even if hunting was favoured by the ecological backdrop, such a high frequency of wild species suggests the expenditure of precious time and energy.

f) The residents of Sand apparently needed a major supply of meat. Oxen grow larger and produce much more meat as a result of the castration. The meat of one ox is

---

[17] Agricultural products and animals were imported.

equivalent to that of eight pigs weighing 50 kg each. One male cattle weighed 400 to 450 kg, a cow about 350 kg. Horses are also close to the oxen category with 450-500 kg. Bison weigh the same as two oxen (up to 1000 kg). Other wild animals such as red deer weigh less (ca. 200 kg). These considerations provide an indication for the high density of people settled at Sand, also confirmed by the archaeological record (Felgenhauer-Schmiedt pers. comm.).

g) The intra-site analysis of the animal bones suggests internal social hierarchies. Sand 1 exhibited stronger markers of nobility, expressed by the high number of horses and the high frequency of wild male and robust animals. Additionally, the study of the faunal remains provided evidence to better understand the functions of some areas. Semi-finished artefacts out of bones and antlers together with production waste indicate craft contexts at the area of Westwall. It is also suggested that in the same area some of the major steps for the skin and pelt exploitation took place.

The above observations indicate that the residents of Sand exhibit more similarities to a military group than to simple farmers[18] and traders,[19] or to an elite group settled in a castle.[20] These people seem to have been acquainted with warfare and a special way of life; this different lifestyle is reflected in the archaeozoological analysis.

5.4 Historical testimony: *Res gestae Saxonicae* by Widukind of Corvey

The unexpected archaeozoological results addressed a new question and namely if the hypothesis that has been expressed by the investigation of the animal bones could be also historically supported. According to written sources, the idea of a military group acting carelessly and conducting raids against settlers (providers) during this period is highly plausible. Crucial information in this case is presented by the monk Widukind in his work *Res gestae Saxonicae* (Deeds of the Saxons).

Based on documents bearing the name Widukind twice (Bachrach & Bachrach 2014), he was born at around 920-925 AD. Widukind was a monk at the Saxon monastery of Corvey and it has been assumed that he came from a noble family. This is because the monastery of Corvey was under the royal favour of Otto I, suggesting that the monastery and its residents enjoyed many privileges. Admission to such a prominent monastery would have been given to selected people. Widukind's interest in Saxony has been taken to suggest that his family was probably Saxon. He died after 973 when he completed his history (*Res gestae Saxonicae*).

Res gestae Saxonicae (Deeds of the Saxons) consists of three books; the first book provides an overview of the history of the Saxons, the end of the Carolingian dynasty, and the career of Henry I (919-936 AD). The second and third books focus mainly on the political and military affairs of the German kingdom, but from different perspectives.

Interesting for the present work is book I, paragraph 35 *"how King Henry used his nine years of peace"*. According to Widukind, during the nine-year-peace Henry I tried to protect the fatherland and he selected men to live in fortifications. This sentence suggests that Henry, in order to defend his land, picked people to live in fortresses (Leyser 1982: 15). As discussed earlier, Sand was erected during a period when the peace-contract between Henry I "the Fowler" and the Magyars was in place. Although historically it is unclear who was responsible for the erection of Sand and under which circumstances the decision has been taken, it is suggested that the peace-contract probably favoured the existence of the stronghold. In this point, it should be recalled that Sand was located in the middle of the woods, relatively isolated, at the later border between Germans and Slavs.

Another interesting part of *Res gestae Saxonicae* is book II, paragraph 3 "regarding the war undertaken against Boleslav". According to the English translation of Bachrach & Bachrach (2014) Widukind writes: "King Henry was quite severe with foreigners, but showed mercy to his countrymen in all cases. When he saw that a thief or highwayman was strong and suited to war, Henry spared the man from the punishment that was due, and settled him in a suburb of Merseburg. He gave them fields and arms, and ordered them to spare their countrymen. However, they were to exercise their thievery against the barbarians as much as they dared. When a large number of men of this type had been gathered, Henry created a legion that was fully prepared to go on campaign."[21]

The historian Leyser (1982) comments that the story of outlaw-warriors[22] is more plausible than it may sound. Henry I had highly probably established these people (thieves and robbers) and given them arms to live on a permanent war-footing, since they could be useful at the frontier district. These people conducted predatory raids on the Slavs even when no hostile activities took place and it appears that some of them even had horses. This kind of military element seems to have played a role in the Ottonian military establishment (Lesyer 1982, 22).[23]

Of course the association of this text with Sand shall be done with great caution. This narration provides only an

---

[18] Whose economic organisation has been already discussed

[19] See (as an example) the interesting work of Schmölke (2004) about Groß Strömkendorf. The site is characterized by intensive trading activities and handicraft. In his discussion, Schmölke comments on the characterization of the site based on faunal remains.

[20] Compare the cases studies presented in this work.

[21] The Latin text: *Rex quippe Heinricus cum esset satis severus extraneis, in omnibus causis erat clemens civibus; unde quemcumque videbat furum aut latronum manu fortem et bellis aptum, a debita poena ei parcebat, collocans in suburbano Mesaburiorum, datis agris atque armis, iussit civibus quidem parcere, in barbaros autem in quantum auderent latrocinia exercerent. Huiuscemodi ergo hominum collecta multitudo plenam in expeditionem produxit legionem.*

[22] The so-called Merseburg Legion.

[23] See Bachrach & Bachrach 2014 comment nr. 27.

analogue to show that such a way of life – exactly in the same period when Sand existed – was possible.

5.5 Animal bones and history

To conclude, the analysis of the faunal assemblages from Sand significantly contributed to the archaeological interpretation of the site, offering a new alternative interpretation. Their study required interdisciplinarity, since the combination of Archaeology and Natural Sciences was almost imperative. Animal bones cannot be viewed outside of their archaeological context or even the historical framework. They represent a specific assemblage, which was created in a particular space and time under special conditions. The composition of the animal bones indicates the choices that people made and the effect their actions and decisions had on other human populations or even on the environment. In Sand the faunal remains provides us with valuable information about aspects of hierarchy and social status, economic organisation, and possible economic activities that took place in the site. In short, animal bones became a great source to better approach different lifeways and lifestyles, proving that they can give answers to archaeological and historical questions.

Bibliography

Abd el Karem, Mona. "Die spätlatènezeitlichen Tierknochenfunde des Simonbauerfeldes auf dem Dürrnberg, Salzburg." *Annalen des Naturhistorischen Museums in Wien*, Serie A, 110 (2009): 133–154.

Abd el Karem, Mona. *Keltische Festmähler und italische Rinder. Die tierischen Überreste aus dem „Großen Heiligtum" der latenezeitlichen Siedlung Roseldof*, Archäologische Forschungen in Niederösterreich Band 13. St. Pölten: Selbstverlag des NÖ Instituts für Landeskunde, 2013a.

Abd el Karem, Mona. "Von der Weide im sonnigen Süden in den Graben eines boischen Heiligtums – Funde von italischen Rindern im nordwestlichen Weinviertel am Beginn der Latènezeit." In *Beiträge zur Archäozoologie und Prähistorischen Anthropologie* Band 9, edited by Stephan Flohr, 97–104. Langenweißbach: Beier & Beran, 2013b.

Albarella, Umberto. "Shape variation of cattle metapodials: age, sex, or breed? Some examples from Medieval and postmedieval sites." *Anthropozoologica* 25-26 (1997): 37–47.

Albarella, Umberto. Tanners, tawyers, horn working and the mystery of the missing goat. In *The Environmental Archaeology of Industry. Symposia of the Association of Environmental Archaeology* 20, edited by Peter Murphy and Patricia E.J. Wiltshire, 71–86. Oxford: Oxbow books, 2003.

Ambros, Cyril and Müller, Hanns Hermann. *Frühgeschichtliche Pferdeskelettfunde aus dem Gebiet der Tschechoslowakei*. Bratislava: Veda Verlag, Vydavateľstvo Slovenskej Akadémie Vied, 1980.

Bachrach, Bernard S. and Bachrach, David S. *Widukund of Corvey. Deeds of the Saxons. Translated with an introduction and notes*. Washington: The Catholic University of America Press, 2014.

Bartosiewicz, László. *Animals in the urban landscape in the wake of the Middle Ages*, BAR S609. Oxford: BAR Publishing, 1995.

Bartosiewicz, László. "Hungarian Grey Cattle: in search of origins." *Hungarian Agricultural Research* 5/3 (1996): 13–20.

Bartosiewicz, László. "Animal bones from the medieval settlement Otok (Gutenwerth) near Dobrava pri Škocjanu, Slovenia." *Arheološki vestnik* 37 (2006): 457–478.

Becker, Cornelia. "Die Geweihfunde vom Spandauer Burgwall." In *Ausgrabungen, Funde und naturwissenschaftliche Untersuchungen auf dem Burgwall Berlin-Spandau: Beiträge zur Vor- u. Frühgeschichte 6, Archäologisch-historische Forschungen in Spandau 3 Sonderdruck*, edited by Adriaan von Müller and Klara von Müller, 101–142. Berlin: Wissenschaftsverlag Volker Spiess, 1989.

Benda Kalman, Hanák Peter, Makkai László, Nagy Zsuzsa L., Niederhauser Emil, Spira György and Vörös Karoly. *Die Geschichte Ungarns. Von den Anfängen bis zur Gegenwart*. Budapest: Reimar Hobbing Verlag, 1988.

Benecke, Norbert. *Archäozoologische Studien zur Entwicklung der Haustierhaltung in mitteleuropa und Südskandinavien von den Anfängen bis zum ausgehenden Mittelalter*, Schriften zur Ur- und Frühgeschichte 46. Berlin: Akademie Verlag, 1994.

Berke, Hubert. "Knochenreste aus einer römischen Räucherei in der Colonia Ulpia Traiana bei Xanten am Niederrhein." In *Xantener Berichte* 6 edited by Gundol Precht, 343–369. Köln: Rheinland Verlag, 1995.

Binford, Lewis Roberts. *Bones. Ancient myths and modern men*. London: Academic Press, 1981.

Boessneck Joachim, Müller Hanns-Hermann and Teichert Manfred. *Osteologische Unterscheidungsmerkmale zwischen Schaf (Ovis aries* Linné*) und Ziege (Capra hircus* Linné*)*, Kühn-Archiv 78/1-2. Berlin: Akademie Verlag, 1964.

Bökönyi, Sándor. *History of Domestic Mammals in Central and Eastern Europe*. Budapest: Akadémiai Kiadó, 1974.

Bors, Kurt and Felgenhauer-Schmiedt, Sabine. *Geschichte aus dem Raabser Boden. 900 Jahre Raabs*. Raabs: Eigenverlag der Stadtgemeinde Raabs an der Thaya, 2000

Boschin, Francesco. "La fauna protostorica del sito di Bressanone-Elvas." In *Studi di archeozoologia in onore di Alfredo Riedel/ Archäozoologische Studien zu Ehren von Alfredo Riedel*, edited by Umberto Tecchiati and Benedetto Sala, 131–142. Bozen: Autonome Provinz Bozen, Südtirol, 2006.

Boschin, Francesco. "Animal remains from Schloss Prösels (Bozen/ Bolzano, Italy, 16th-17th century)." In *Atti del 6o Convegno Nazionale di Archeozoologia. Centro visitatori del Parco dell' Orecchiella. 21-24 maggio 2009 San Romano in Garfagnana-Luccae*, edited by Jacopo De Grossi Mazzorin, Daniela Saccà and Carlo Tozzi, 283–290 Lecce: Associazione Italiana di Archeozoologia, 2012.

Brunner, Karl. "Herzogtümer und Marken vom Ungarnsturm bis ins 12. Jahrhundert." In *Österreichische Geschichte*, edited by Herwig Wolfram, 907–1156. Wien: Ueberreuter Carl Verlag, 2003.

Büntgen, Ulf and Tegel, Willy. "European tree-ring data and the Medieval Climate Anomaly." *Pages* 19 (2011): 14–15.

Cartledge, Bryan. *The Will to Survive. A History of Hungary*. London: Hurst and Company, 2011.

Clutton-Brock Juliet. *A Natural History of Domesticated Mammals*. London: Cambridge University Press, 1987.

Corbet, Gordon and Ovenden, Denys. *Pareys Buch der Säugetiere. Alle wildlebenden Säugetiere Europas.* Hanmburg. Berlin: Verlag Paul Parey, 1982.

Daim, Falko. "Auf den Spuren eines toten Kriegers: Das altungarische Reitergrab von Gnadendorf." In *Heldengrab im Niemandsland. Ein frühugarischer Reiter aus Niederösterreich. Begleitbuch zur gleichnamigen Ausstellung des RGZM 14. September bis 19. November 2006*, edited by Falko Daim, 21–40. Mainz: Verlag des Römisch-Germanischen Zentralmuseums, 2007.

Davis, Simon J.M. "The Effect of Castration and Age on the Development of the Shetland Sheep Skeleton and a Metric Comparison Between Bones of Males, Females and Castrates." *Journal of Archaeological Science* 27 (2000): 373–390.

Davis Simon, Svensson Emma, Albarella Umberto, Detry Cleia, Götherström Anders, Pires Ana Elisabete and Ginja Catarina. "Molecular and osteometric sexing of cattle metacarpals: a case study from 15th century AD Beja, Portugal." *Journal of Archaeological Science* 39, 5 (2012): 1445–1454.

Degerbol, Magnus and Fredskild, Bent. "The Urus (*Bos primigenius* Bojanus) and neolithic domesticated cattle (*Bos taurus domesticus* Linné) in Denmark." *Det Kongelige Danske Videnskabernes Selskab Biologiske Skifter* 17, 1 (1970).

Deschler-Erb, Sabine. "Beiträge zur Verarbeitung von organischen Rohstoffen." In *Das römerzeitliche Handwerk in der Schweiz: Bestandaufnahme und erste Synthesen*, edited by Heidi Amrein, Eva Carlevaro, Sabine Dreschler-Erb, Anika Duvauchelle and Lionel Pernet, 113–137. Montagnac: Editions Monique Mergoil, 2012.

Dingley, John. "On the Origin of Czech Rakousko, Slovak Rakúsko." *Harvard Ukranian Studies* 28, 1-4 (2006): 95–104.

Doll, Monika. *Haustierhaltung und Schlachtsitten des Mittelalters und der Neuzeit. Eine Synthese aus archäozoologischen, bildlichen und schriftlichen Quellen Mitteleuropas*, Internationale Archäologie 78. Rahden/Westfalen: Verlag Marie Leidorf, 2003.

Doneus, Michael. *Die hinterlassene landschaft – Prospektion und Interpretation in der Landschaftsarchäologie,* Mitteilungen der Prähistorischen Kommission. Österreichische Akademie der Wissenschaften Band 78. Wien: Verlag der Österreichischen Akademie der Wissenschaften, 2013.

Driesch, Angela von den. *Das Vermessen von Tierknochen aus vor- und frühgeschichtlichen Siedlungen*. München: Institut für Paläoanatomie, Domestikationsforschung und Geschichte der Tiermedizin der Universität München, 1976.

Empel, Wojciech and Roskosz, Tadeusz. "Das Skelett der Gliedmassen des Wisents, Bison bonasus (Linnaeus, 1758)." *Acta Theriologica* 7 (1963): 259–300.

Ewersen, Jörg. "Hundehaltung auf der kaiserzeitlichen Wurt Feddersen Wierde – ein Rekonstruktionsversuch." *Siedlungs und Küstenforschung im südlichen Nordseegebiet (Settlement and Coastal Research in the Southern North Sea Region)* Band 33, 53–75. Rahden/Westf: Verlag Marie Leidorf, 2010.

Fairnell, Eva. *The utilization of fur-bearing animals in the British Isles. A zooarchaeological hunt for data.* MSc in Zooarchaeology. University of York, https://www.york.ac.uk/media/archaeology/images/people/faces-gradstudents/publicationpdfs/complete%20msc.pdf, 2003.

Fairnell, Eva. "101 ways to skin a fur-bearing animal: the implications for zooarchaeological interpretation." In *Experiencing Archaeology by Expirement. Proceedings of the Experimental Archaeology Conference, Exeter 2007*, edited by Penny Cunningham, Julia Heeb and Roeland Paardekooper, 47–60. Oxford: Oxbow books, 2008.

Felgenhauer Fritz, Szilvássy Johann, Kritscher Herbert and Hauser Gertrud. *Stillfried-Archäologie-Anthropologie*, Veröffentlichungen des Museums für Ur- und Frühgeschichte Stillfried, Sonderband 3. Stillfried: Museum für Ur- und Frühgeschichte Stillfried, 1988.

Felgenhauer-Schmiedt, Sabine. "Die Burg auf der Flur Sand bei Raabs an der Thaya." In *Velká Morava mezi východem a západem. Großmähren zwischen Ost und West*, Spisy archeologického ústavu av Cr Brno 17 (2001): 85–106.

Felgenhauer-Schmiedt, Sabine. "Niederösterreich im 10. Jahrhunder-Der archäologische Befund." In *Das frühhungarische Reitergrab von Gnadendorf (Niederösterreich)*, edited by Falko Daim and Ernst Lauermann, 253–268. Mainz: Schnell & Steiner, 2006.

Felgenhauer-Schmiedt, Sabine. "Frühe Herrschaftsbildung im Nordwald. Die Burganlage auf der Flur Sand bei Raabs an der Thaya und die Burg Raabs." In: *Im Schnittpunkt frühmittelalterlicher Kulturen: Niederösterreich an der Wende vom 9. zum 10. Jahrhundert; die Vorträge des 27. Symposiums des Niederösterreichischen Instituts für Landeskunde, Hainburg 3.bis 6. Juli 2007*, Mitteilungen aus dem Niederösterreichischen Landesarchiv 13, edited by Roman Zehetmayer, 298–321. St. Pölten: Niederösterreichisches Institut für Landeskunde, 2008.

Felgenhauer-Schmiedt, Sabine. "Die Burg auf der Flur „Sand" bei Raabs an der Thaya, Niederösterreich- ein Zentralort, aber noch kein Zentrum?" In *Frühgeschichtliche Zentralorte in Mitteleuropa, Internationale Konferenz und Kolleg der Alexander von Humboldt-Stifzung zum 50. Jahrestag des Beginns archäologischer Ausgrabungen in Pohansko bei Břeclav, 5.-9.10.2009, Břeclav, Tschechische Republik*, Studien zur Archäologie Europas Band 14, edited by Jiři Machàcek and Šimon Ungermann, 551–559. Bonn: Rudolf Habelt Verlag, 2011.

Felgenhauer-Schmiedt, Sabine. "Herrschaftszentren und Adelssitze des 10.-13. Jahrhunderts im nördlichen Waldviertel- der Beitrag der Archäologie." In *Adel, Burg und Herrschaft an der „Grenze": Österreich und Böhmen, Studien zur Kulturgeschichte von Oberösterreich Folge* 34, edited by Klaus Birngruber and Christina Schmid, 57–81. Linz: Oberösterreichisches Landesmuseum, 2012.

Felgenhauer-Schmiedt, Sabine. "Burg „Sand" bei Raabs an der Thaya- Fragen von Funktion und Herrschaft im Raum." In *50 Jahre Archäologie in Thunau* (forthcoming).

Fischer, Toni Gayle. "Faunal Analysis: Zooarchaeology in Syro-Palestinian/ Israeli Archaeology." In *Bethsaida in Archaeology. History and Ancient Culture. A Festschrift in Honor of John T. Green*, edited by Harold Ellens, 84–121. Newcastle upon Tyne: Cambridge Scholars Publishing, 2014.

Fock, Jonni. *Metrische Untersuchungen an Metapodien einiger europäischer Rinderrassen*. Inaugural-Dissertation zur Erlagung der veterinär-medizinischen Doktorwürde der Tierärztlichen Fakultät der Ludwig-Maximilians-Universität München. Institut für Palaeoanatomie, Domestikationsforschung und Geschichte der Tiermedizin der Universität München, 1966.

Galik, Alfred. "Mittelalterliche Tierknochen und Nachweise von Knochenverarbeitung und Gerberei aus Hainburg, Niederösterreich." *Beiträge zur Mittelalterarchäologie* 20 (2004): 59–72.

Giuliani, R. "Rinderrassen in Italien und Spanien." In *Handbuch der Tierzüchtung, Rassenkunde*, edited by John Hammond, Ivar Johansson and Fritz Haring. Hamburg-Berlin: Parey Verlag, 1961.

Glaser, Rüdiger. *Klimageschichte Mitteleuropas: 1000 Jahre Wetter, Klima, Katastrophen*. Darmstadt: Primus Verlag GmbH, 2001.

Görner, Martin and Hackethal, Hans. *Säugetiere Europas. Beobachten und bestimmen*. Stuttgart: Ferdinand Enke Verlag, 1988.

Grabner, Michael. "Dendrochronologische Datierung der Holzfunde aus der Wehranlage Sand." *Arbeitsberichte des Kultur- und Museumsvereines Thaya* (2002): 975–976.

Gringmuth- Dallmer, Eike. "Zentren unterschiedlichen Ranges im nordwestslawischen Gebiet." In *Frühgeschichtliche Zentralorte in Mitteleuropa, Internationale Konferenz und Kolleg der Alexander von Humboldt-Stifzung zum 50. Jahrestag des Beginns archäologischer Ausgrabungen in Pohansko bei Břeclav, 5.-9.10.2009, Břeclav, Tschechische Republik*, Studien zur Archäologie Europas Band 14, edited by Jiři Machàcek and Šimon Ungermann, 431–440. Bonn: Rudolf Habelt Verlag, 2011.

Grove, Jean M. *Little Ice Ages: Ancient and Modern*. London: Routledge, 2004.

Grömer Karina, Ruß-Popa Gabriela and Saliari Konstantina. (2017): "Products of animal skin from Antiquity to the Medieval Period." *Annalen des Naturhistorischen Museums in Wien*, Serie A, 119 (2017): 69–93.

Groenman-van Waateringe, Willy. "Haut- und Fellreste vom Dürrnberg." In *Dürrnberg und Manching. Wirtschaftsarchäologie im ostkeltischen Raum. Akten des Internationalen Kolloquiums in Hallein/ Bad Dürrnberg 7. –11. Oktober 1998*, Kolloquien zur Vor- und Frühgeschichte Band 7, edited by Claus Dobiat, Susanne Sievers and Thomas Stöllner, 117–122. Bonn: Dr. Rudolf Habelt, 2002.

Habermehl, Karl-Heinz. *Die Altersbestimmung bei Haus- und Labortieren*, Veterinär-Anatomisches Institut der Justus-Liebig Universität Gießen. 2. Aufl. Berlin und Hamburg: Parey Verlag, 1975.

Habermehl, Karl-Heinz. *Altersbestimmung bei Wild- und Pelztieren*, Veterinär-Anatomisches Institut der Justus-Liebig Universität Gießen. Berlin und Hamburg: Parey Verlag, 1985.

Halstead Paul, Collins P. and Isaakidou Valassia. "Sorting sheep from the goats: morphological distinction between the mandibles and mandibular teeth between of adult *Ovis* and *Capra*." *Journal of Archaeological Science* 29 (2002): 545–553.

Heaton Kevin, Zobell Dare and Cornforth Daren. "Effects of delayed castration of British crossbred cattle on weight gain, carcass traits, and consumer acceptability." *Proceedings, Western Section, American Society of Animal Science* 55 (2004): 130–133.

Helmer, Daniel. "Discrimination des genres *Ovis* et *Capra* à l'aide des prémolaires inférieures 3 et 4 et interpretation des ages d'abbatage: l'example de Dikili Tash (Grèce)." *Anthropozoologica* 31 (2000): 29–38.

Hengeveld, Gerardus Johannes. *Het Rundvee zijne Verschillende soorten, rassen en Veredeling*. Haarlem: De Erven Loosjes, 1865.

Herold, Hajnalka. "Die Besiedlung Niederösterreichs im Frühmittelalter." In *Schicksalsjahr 907. Die Schlacht bei Pressburg und das frühmittelalterliche Niederösterreich*,

Katalog zur Ausstellung des Niederösterreichischen Landesarchiv, edited by Roman Zehetmayer, 77–92. St. Pölten: Niederösterreichisches Institut für Landeskunde, 2007.

Herold, Hajnalka. "The Natural Environment, Anthropogenic Influences and Supra-Regional Contacts at 9th - to 10th - Century Fortified Elite Settlements in Central Europe." In *Fortified Settlements in Early Medieval Europe. Defended Communities of the 8th-10th Centuries*, edited by Neil Christie and Hajnalka Herold, 107–120. Oxford & Philadelphia: Oxbow books, 2016.

Hillson Simon. *Teeth*. Cambridge: Cambridge University Press, 2005.

Jaritz, Günter. S*eltene Nutztiere der Alpen. 7000 Jahre geprägte Kulturlandschaft*. Salzburg: Verlag Anton Pustet, 2014.

Jenček Vladimir, Matějovská Olga and Thiele Otto. *Groß-Siegharts*, Blatt 7. Geologische Karte der Republik Österreich, 1:50,000. Wien: Geologische Bundesanstalt, 1987.

Johansson, Friederike and Hüster, Heidemarie. "Untersuchungen an Skelettresten von Katzen aus Haithabu (Ausgrabung 1966-1969)." *Berichte über die Ausgrabungen in Haithabu* Bericht 24, 1–86. Neumünster: Karl Wachholtz Verlag, 1987.

Kanelutti, Erika. *Slawen- und urnenfeldrzeitliche Säugetiere von Thunau bei Gars am kamp (Niederösterreich)*. Unpubl. Diss. Univ. Wien, 1990.

Kanelutti, Erika. "Archäozoologische Untersuchung am Schanzberg von Gars/ Thunau." In *Bioarchäologie und Frühgeschichtsforschung*, Archaeologia Austriaca Monographien 2, edited by Herwig Friesinger, Falko Daim, Erika Kanelutti and Otto Cichocki, 169–184. Wien: Verlag der Österreichischen Akademie der Wissenschaften, 1993.

Kilian Walter, Müller Ferdinand and Starlinger Franz. *Die forstlichen Wuchsgebiete Österreichs. Eine Naturraumgliederung nach waldökologischen Gesichtspunkten*. Wien: Forstliche Bundesversuchsanstalt, 1993 http://bfw.ac.at/300/pdf/1027.pdf.

Knight, Stephanie Claire. *Butchery and intra-site spatial analysis of animal bone: a case study from Danebury Hillfort, Hampshire, England*. Dissertation Thesis, University of Leicester, 2002.

Kohler-Schneider, Marianne and Vitalos, Melinda. "Verkohlte frühmittelalterliche Pflanzenreste aus der Burg „Sand" bei Raabs a.d. Thaya, NÖ (10Jhd.)", *Amt der Niederösterreichischen Landesregierung, St. Pölten* (2009): 1258–1262.

Kontler, László. *A History of Hungary. Millenium in Central Europe*. New York: Palgrave Mackmillan, 2002.

Kratochvíl, Zdeněk. "Species Criteria on the Distal Section of the Tibia in *Ovis ammon* F. *aries* I. and *Capra aegagrus* F. *hircus* I." *Acta Veterinaria* 38 (1969a). Brno: 483–490.

Kratochvíl, Zdeněk. *Die Tiere des Burgwalles Pohansko*, Přirodevědné práce ústavů Československé akademie věd v Brně. Acta Scientiarum Naturalium Academiae Scientarum Bohemoslovacae Brno III, 1. Praha: Academia, 1969b.

Kratochvíl, Zdeněk. "Schädelkriterien der Wild- und Hauskatze (*Felis silvestris silvestris* Schreb. 1777 und F. lybica f. catus L. 1758)." *Acta Scientarium Naturalium. Academiae Scientarium Bohemoslovacae Brno* 7, 10 (1973): 1–50.

Kratochvíl, Zdeněk. "Das Postkranialskelett der Wild- und Hauskatze (Felis silvestris und F. lybica f. catus)." *Acta Scientarium Naturalium. Academiae Scientarium Bohemoslovacae Brno* 10, 6 (1976): 1–43.

Kratochvíl, Zdeněk. *Tierknochenfunde aus der grossmährischen Siedlung Mikulčice I. Das Hausschwein*, Studie Archeologického Ústavu Československé Akademie věd V Brně. Ročník IX. 3. Zum siebzigsten Geburtstag von Univ. Prof. Ph Dr. Josef Poulík, DrSc., o. Mitglied der Tschechoslowakischen Akademie der Wissenschaft gewidmet. Praha: Academia, 1981.

Kratochvíl, Zdeněk. *Tierknochenfunde aus der Siedlung Mikulčice II (Das Hausrind)*, Přirodevědné práce ústavů Československé akademie věd v Brně. Acta Scientiarum Naturalium Academiae Scientarum Bohemoslovacae Brno XXI, 8-9. Praha: Academia, 1987a.

Kratochvíl, Zdeněk. *Tierknochenfunde aus der Siedlung Mikulčice III (Das Hausrind)*, Přirodevědné práce ústavů Československé akademie věd v Brně. Acta Scientiarum Naturalium Academiae Scientarum Bohemoslovacae Brno XXI, 11. Praha: Academia, 1987b.

Kratochvíl, Zdeněk. *Tierknochenfunde aus der Siedlung Mikulčice II., III., IV. Das Hausrind Maßtabellen*, Archeologický ústev Československá akademie věd sady Osvobení 19, 662 03, Brno. Praha: Academia, 1988a.

Kratochvíl, Zdeněk. *Das Hausrind aus Mikulčice und seine Bedeutung (IV)*, Přirodevědné práce ústavů Československé akademie věd v Brně. Acta Scientiarum Naturalium Academiae Scientarum Bohemoslovacae Brno. XXII, 9, Brno. Praha: Academia, 1988b.

Krämer, Hermann. *Die Haustierfunde von Vindonissa mit Ausblicken in die Rassezucht des klassischen Altertums*. Diss. Zürich. Kündig, Genève, 1899.

Kunst, Günther Karl and Fitzgerald, Sinéad Teresa. "Fleisch am Knochen – Spätmittelalterliche und frühneuzeitliche Arbeitsspuren an Tierresten aus Stockerau (Niederösterreich) und Wien." In *Beiträge zur Archäozoologie und Prähistorischen Anthropologie* 8, edited by Norbert Benecke and Stephan Flohr, 155–164. Langenweißbach: Beier & Beran, 2011.

Küchelmann, Hans Christian. "Noble meals instead of Abstinence? A Faunal Assemblage from the Dominican Monastery of Norden, Northern Germany." In *Proceedings of the General Session of the 11th International Council for Archaeozoology Conference, 23-28 August 2010*, BAR S2354, edited by Christine Lefèvre, 87–97. Oxford: BAR Publishing, 2012.

Kühtreiber, Karin and Obenaus, Martin. *Burgen des 9. bis zur Mitte des 11. Jahrhunderts in Niederösterreich – eine Bestandsaufnahme*, Monographie des Römisch Germanischen Zentralmuseums, Band 132. Mainz: Schnell & Steiner, 2017.

Lehmann, Ulrich. "Der Ur im Diluvium Deutschlands und seine Verbreitung." *Neues Jahrbuch für Mineralogie, Geologie, u. Paläontologie* 90 (1949): 163–266.

Lemppenau, Ute. *Geschlechts- und Gattungsunterschiede am Becken mitteleuropäischer Wiederkäuer*. Inaugural-Dissertation zur Erlangung der veterinärmedizinischen Doktorwürde der Tierärztlichen Fakultät der Ludwig-Maximilians Universität München, Tieranatomisches Institut der Universität München, 1964.

Leyser, Karl. *Medieval Germany and its Neighbours 900-1250*. London: Bloomsbury, 1982.

Luetscher Marc, Borreguero Miguel, Moseley Gina, Spötl Christof and Edwards, R. Lawrence. "Alpine permafrost thawing during the Medieval Warm Period identified from cryogenic cave carbonates." *The Cryosphere* 7 (2013): 1073–1081.

Lyublyanovics, Kyra. "Animal Keeping and Roman Colonization in the Province of Panonia Inferior, Western Hungary." In *Anthropological Approaches to Zooarchaeology: Colonialism, Complexity and Animal Transformations*, edited by Douglas V. Campana, Pamela Crabtree, Susan D. de France, Justin Lev-Tov and Alice Mathea Choyke, 182–193. Oxford: Oxbow books, 2010.

Majoros, Ferenc. *Geschichte Ungarns. Nation unter der Stephanskrone*. Budapest: Caismir Katz Verlag, 2008.

Makkai, László. "The foundation of the Hungarian Christian State 950-1196." In *A history of Hungary*, edited by Peter F. Sugar, Peter Hanák and Tibor Frank. Bloomington, Indianapolis: Indiana University Press, 1990.

Makowiecki, Daniel. "Animals in the landscape of the medieval countryside and urban agglomerations of the Baltic Sea countries." In *Città e Campagna Nei Secoli Altomedievali. 27 marzo- 1 aprile. Settimane di Studio della Fondazione Centro Italiano di Studi Sull' Alto Medioevo*, edited by Andreas Castagnetti, 427–457. Spoleto: BPR Publishes, 2009.

Makowiecki, Daniel. "Studia archeozoologiczne nad znaczeniem wczesnośredniowiecznej i średniowiecznej fauny łęczyckiego grodu." In *Początki Łęczycy. Tom I. Archeologia środowiskowa średniowiecznej Łęczycy. Przyroda-Gospodarka-Społeczeństwo*, edited by Ryszarda Grygiel and Tomasza Jurka, 261–437. Łódź: Muzeum Archeologiczne i Etnograficzne, 2014.

Mangini Augusto, Spötl Christof and Verdes Pablo Fabian. "Reconstruction of temperature in the Central Alps during the past 2000 yr from a _180 stalagmite record." *Earth and Planetary Science Letters* 235 (2005): 741–751.

Mann, Michael E. "Medieval Climatic Optimum." In *Encyclopedia of Global Environmental Change. Volume 1, The Earth system: physical and chemical dimensions of global environmental change*, edited by Michael C. MacCracken and John S. Perry, 514–516. Chichester: John Wiley, 2002.

Mann Michael E., Zhang Zhihua, Rutherford Scott, Bradley Raymond S, Hughes Malcolm K., Shindell Drew, Ammann Caspar, Faluvegi Greg and Ni Fenbiao. "Global Signatures and Dynamical Origins of the Little Ice Age and Medieval Climate Anomaly." *Science* 326 (2009): 1256–1260.

Marciniak, Arkadiusz. "The Secondary Products Revolution, mortality profiles, and practice of zooarchaeology." In *Animal Secondary Products. Domestic Animal Exploitation in Prehistoric Europe, the Near East and the Far East*, edited by Haskel J. Greenfield, 186–205. Oxford: Oxbow books, 2014.

Markonis Yannis, Kossieris Panayiotis, Lykou Archontia and Koutsoyiannis Demetris. "Effects of Medieval Warm Period and Little Ice Age on the hydrology of the Mediterranean Region." *European Geosciences Union Assembly, Vienna, Austria, 22-27 April 2012*. Poster presentation.

Marshall, Larry. "Bone Modification and the Laws of Burials." In *Proceedings of the First International Conference on Bone Modification*, edited by Robson Bonnichsen and Marcella H. Sorg, 7–26. Orono, Maine: Center for the Study of the First Americans, 1989.

Martin, Thomas. *Artunterschiede an den Langknochen großer Artiodactyla des Jungpleistozäns Mitteleuropas*, Courier Forschungsinstitut Senckenberg 96. Frankfurt a.M.: Senckenbergische Naturforschende Gesellschaft, 1987.

Matolcsi, János. "Historische Erforschung der Körpergröße des Rindes auf Grund von ungarischem Knochenmaterial." *Zeitschrift für Tierzüchtung und Züchtungsbiologie* 63 (1970): 155–194.

May, Eberhard. "Widerristhöhe und Langknochenmaße bei Pferden – ein immer noch aktuelles Problem." *Zeitschrift für Säugetierkunde* 50, 6 (1985): 368–382.

Molnár, Miklós. *A Concise History of Hungary*. Cambridge: Cambridge University Press, 2001.

Müller, Hanns-Hermann. "Die Säugetierreste aus der Burg Berlin-Köpenick nach den Grabungen von 1955 bic 1958." In *Köpenick. Ergebnisse der Archäologischen Stadtkernforschung in Berlin. Teil I. Ein Beitrag zur*

Frühgeschichte Gross-Berlins, Deutsche Akademie der Wissenschaften zu Berlin Schriften der Sektion für Vor- und Frühgeschichte, edited by Joachim Herrmann, 81–97. Berlin: Akademie Verlag, 1962.

Müller, Hanns-Hermann. "Die Tierreste der slawischen Burg Behren-Lübchin." In *Eine spätslawische Burganlage in Mecklenburg, Deutsche Akademie der Wissenschaften zu Berlin, Schriften der Sektion für Vor- und Frühgeschichte* Band 19, edited by Ewald Schuldt, 144–153. Berlin: Akademie Verlag, 1965.

Müller, Hanns-Hermann. "Die Pferdeskelettfunde des slawisch-awarischen Gräberfeldes von Nové Zámsky." *Slov. Archaeol.* 14 (1966): 661–696.

Müller, Hanns-Hermann. "Die Tierreste aus der Wiprechtsburg bei Groitzsch, Kr. Borna." In *Arbeits- und Forschungsberichte zur sächsischen Bodendenkmalpflege*, edited by Werner Coblemz, 101–170. Berlin: VEB Deutscher Verlag der Wissenschaften, 1978.

Müller, Hanns-Hermann. "Jagdwild aus mittelalterlichen Burgen Sachsens." *Beiträge zur Ur- und Frühgeschichte* Teil II, 239–258. Berlin: VEB Deutscher Verlag der Wissenschaften, 1982.

Müller, Hanns-Hermann. "Die Tierreste aus der Mecklenburg, Kr. Wismar." In *Die Mecklenburg – eine Hauptburg der Obodriten, Schriften zur Ur- und Frühgeschichte, Akademie der Wissenschaften der DDR Zentralinstitut für alte Geschichte und Archäologie*, edited by Peter Donat, 161–188. Berlin: Akademie Verlag Berlin, 1984.

Noddle, Barbara. "The under-rated goat." In *Urban-rural connexions: perspectives from environmental archaeology. Symposia of the Association of Environmental Archaeology*, edited by Allan Richard Hall and Harry K. Kenward, 117–128. Oxford: Oxbow books, 1994.

O' Connor, Terry. "Vertebrate Demography by Numbers: Age, Sex, and Zooarchaeological Practice." In *Proceedings of the 9th ICAZ Conference, Duhram 2002. Recent Advances in Ageing and Sexing Animal Bones*, edited by Deborah Ruscillo, 1–8. Oxford: Oxbow books, 2006.

Olsen, Stanley John. "Post-cranial skeletal characters of *Bison* and *Bos*." *Papers of the Peabody Museum of Archaeology and Ethnology, Harvard University* 35 (4). Cambridge, Massachusets: Peabody Museum, 1960.

Pasda, Kerstin. *Tierknochen als Spiegel sozialer Verhältnisse im 8.-15. Jh. in Bayern*, Praehistorica Monographien 1. Erlangen: Praehistoricaverlag, 2004.

Payne, Sebastian. "A metrical distinction between sheep and goat metacarpals." In *The Domestication and Exploitation of Plants and Animals*, edited by Peter J. Ucko, and Geoffrey Dimbleby, 295–306. London: Duckworth, 1969.

Peters, Joris. *Römische Tierhaltung und Tierzucht*, Passauer Universitätsschriften Arch. 5. Rahden/ Westf: Marie Leidorf Verlag, 1998.

Popovtschak, Michaela. "Archäobotanische Makroreste aus „Sand" – Vorbericht." *Arbeitsberichte des Kultur- und Museumsvereins Thaya* 2 (1998): 758–762.

Prilloff, Ralf-Jürgen. *Tierknochen aus dem mittelalterlichen Konstanz. Eine archäozoologische Studie zur Ernährungswirtschaft und zum Handwerk im Hoch- und Spätmittelalter, Landesdenkmalamt Baden-Württemberg*. Stuttgart: Konrad Theiss Verlag, 2000.

Prilloff, Ralf-Jürgen. "Archäozoologische Untersuchung der frühmittelalterlichen Tierknochen aus Burg und Vorburg Glienke." In *Glienke. Eine slawische Burg des 9. Und 10. Jahrhunderts im östlichen Mecklenburg. Frühmittelalterliche Archäologie zwischen Ostsee und Mittelmeer, Römisch-Germanische Kommission des Deutschen Archäologischen Instituts*, Band 5, edited by Sebastian Brather, Claus von Carnap-Bornheim, Hauke Jöns, Christian Lübke, Friedrich Lüth, Michael Müller-Wille and Karl-heinz Willroth, 224–233. Frankfurt a.M.: Verlag Reichert, 2015.

Prummel, Wietske. "Animal bones from tannery pits of 's-Hertogenbosch." *Berichten van de Rijksdienst voor het Oudheidkundig Bondemonderzoek* 28 (1978): 399–422.

Prummel, Wietske and Frisch, Hans-Jorg. "A guide for the distinction of species, sex, and body size of sheep and goat." *Journal of Archaeological Science* 13 (1986): 567–577.

Pucher, Erich. *Tierknochenfunde aus Stillfried an der March (Niederösterreich)*. Dissertation zur Erlangung des Doktorgrades an der Naturwissenschaftlichen Fakultät der Universität Wien. Universität Wien, 1982.

Pucher, Erich. "Untersuchungen an Tierskeletten aus der Urnenfelderkultur von Stillfried an der March (Niederösterreich)." In *Forschungen in Stillfried* 7, edited by Fritz Felgenhauer. 23–116 Wien: Verein zu Förderung der Forschungen Stillfried, 1986a.

Pucher, Erich. "Mittelalterliche Tierknochen aus Möllersdorf (Niederösterreich)." In *Beiträge zur Mittelalterarchäologie in Österreich* 2, edited by Fritz Felgenhauer, 47–57. Wien: Österreichische Gesellschaft für Mittelalterarchäologie, 1986b.

Pucher, Erich. "Der frühneuzeitliche Knochenabfall eines Wirtshauses neben der Salzburger Residenz." *Jahresschrift des Salzburger Mus. Carolino Augusteum* 35/36, 1989/90 (1991): 71–135.

Pucher, Erich. "Rätsel und Experimente im Salzberghochtal. Ein Tranchierversuch klärt rätselhafte Knochenfunde in Hallstatt." *Salz aktuell - Nachrichten des Unternehmensverbandes der Salinen Austria* 3/4 (1997): 26–27.

Pucher, Erich. *Archäozoologische Untersuchungen am Tierknochenmaterial der keltischen Gewerbesiedlung im Ramsautal auf dem Dürrnberg (Salzburg).* Mit Beiträgen von Thomas Stöllner und Karin Wiltschke-Schtotta, Dürrnberg-Forschungen 2, Abteilung Naturwissenschaft. Rahden/Westf: Marie Leidorf, 1999.

Pucher, Erich. "Archäozoologische Ergebnisse vom Dürrnberg." In *Dürrnberg und Manching. Wirtschaftsarchäologie im ostkeltischen Raum. Akten des Internationalen Kolloquiums in Hallein/ Bad Dürrnberg 7. –11. Oktober 1998, Kolloquien zur Vor- und Frühgeschichte* Band 7, edited by Claus Dobiat, Susanne Sievers and Thomas Stöllner, 133–146. Bonn: Dr. Rudolf Habelt, 2002.

Pucher, Erich. "Der mittelneolithische Tierknochenkomplex von Melk-Winden (Niederösterreich)." *Annalen des Naturhistorischen Museums in Wien*, Serie A, 105 (2004): 363–403.

Pucher, Erich. "Zwei römische Ochsenskelette aus der Villa rustica von Nickelsdorf (Österreich)." In *Studi di archeozoologia in onore di Alfredo Riedel/ Archäozoologische Studien zu Ehren von Alfredo Riedel*, edited by Umberto Tecchiati and Benedetto Sala, 253–268. Bozen: Autonome Provinz Bozen, Südtirol, 2006a.

Pucher, Erich. "Die Tierknochen aus einem keltischen Bauernhof in Göttlesbrunn (Niederösterreich)." *Annalen des Naturhistorischen Museums in Wien*, Serie A, 107 (2006b): 197–220.

Pucher, Erich. "Steirische Bergschecken und die vergessene Frage nach der Geschichte der Rinderrassen." *Alpen - Festschrift: 25 Jahre ANISA*, Mitteilungen der ANISA 25/26 (2006c): 263–292.

Pucher, Erich. Knochen verraten prähistorische Schinkenproduktion. In *Salz-Reich. 7000 Jahre Hallstatt, Veröffentlichungen der Prähistorischen Abteilung* 2, edited by Anton Kern, Kerstin Kowarik, Andreas Rausch and Hans Reschreiter, 74–77. Wien: Naturhistorisches Museum Wien, 2008.

Pucher, Erich. "Mehr Fragen als Antworten: Archäozoologische Befunde aus den Burgen Sand und Raabs im nördlichen Niederösterreich." *Beiträge zur Mittelalterarchäologie in Österreich* 25 (2009a): 259–272.

Pucher, Erich. "The remains of prehistoric ham production." In *Kingdom of Salt. 7000 years of Hallstatt, Veröffentlichungen der Prähistorischen Abteilung* 2, edited by Anton Kern, Kerstin Kowarik, Andreas Rausch and Hans Reschreiter, 74–77. Wien: Naturhistorisches Museum Wien, 2009b.

Pucher, Erich. "Milchkühe versus Arbeitsochsen: Osteologische Unterscheidungsmerkmale zwischen alpin-donauländischen und italischen Rindern zur Römischen Kaiserzeit." In *Beiträge zur Archäozoologie und Prähistorischen Anthropologie* Band 9, edited by Stephan Flohr, 9–36. Langenweißbach: Beier & Beran, 2013.

Pucher, Erich. "Sechs Jahrtausende alpine Viehwirtschaft." *Forschungsberichte der ANISA* 5 (2014a): 73–100.

Pucher, Erich. "Neue Aspekte zur Versorgungslogistik Hallstatts: Tierknochenfundkomplexe aus Pichl, Steiermark." *Fundberichte aus Österreich* 52/2013 (2014b): 65–93.

Pucher, Erich. "Der Tierknochenfundkomplex eines germanischen Dorfs im römischen Machtbereich: Bruckneudorf." *Fundberichte aus Österreich* (in press).

Pucher, Erich. *Die Tierknochen der mittelbronzezeitlichen Fundstelle Saalfelden-Katzentauern im Salzburger Pinzgau.* Naturhistorisches Museum, Wien (Manuscript).

Pucher, Erich and Engl, Kurt. *Studien zur Pfahlbauforschung in Österreich.* Materialen I Die Pfahlbaustationen des Mondsees Tierknochenfunde, Österreichische Akademie der Wissenschaften. Philosophisch-Historische Klasse. Wien: Verlag der Österreichischen Akademie der Wissenschaften, 1997.

Pucher, Erich and Schmitzberger, Manfred. "Ein mittelalterlicher Fundkomplex aus Niederösterreich mit hohem Wildanteil: Die Flur Sand bei Raabs a. d. Thaya." In *Historia animalium ex ossibus. Beiträge zur Paläoanatomie, Archäologie, Ägyptologie, Ethnologie und Geschichte der Tiermedizin. Festschrift für Angela von den Driesch*, edited by Cornelia Becker, Henriette Manhart, Joris Peters, and Jörg Schibler, 355–378. Rahden/Westf: Marie Leidorf, 1999a.

Pucher, Erich and Schmitzberger, Manfred. "Archäozoologische Ergebnisse von der Burg auf der Flur Sand bei Raabs an der Thaya, NÖ." *Beiträge zur Mittelalterarchäologie in Österreich* 15, (1999b): 111–121.

Pucher, Erich and Schmitzberger, Manfred. "Die Tierknochen aus einer frühneuzeitlichen Kulturschicht der Burgruine Hauenstein (Steiermark)." In *Das obere Kainachtal, Aus der Geschichte der Gemeinden Kainach, Gallmannsegg und Kohlschwarz*, edited by Ernst Lasnik, 608–623. Kainach: Gallmannsegg und Kohlschwarz, 2006.

Pucher Erich, Bruckner Tanja, Baar Anna, Distelberger Gerda, Öhlinger Barbara and Zheden Vanessa. *Tierskelette und Tierknochen aus dem awarischen Gräberfeld von Vösendorf-Laxenburgerstraße*, Sonderdruck aus Fundberichte aus Österreich Band 45/2006. Wien, 2007.

Pucher Erich, Saliari Konstantina and Ramsl Peter. "Römische Haustiere eines Latènezeitlichen Hausherrn in Vindobona (Wien)?" In *Beiträge zur Archäozoologie und Prähistorische Anthropologie* Band 10, edited by Stephan Flohr, 71–78. Langenweißbach: Beier & Beran, 2015.

Rehazek, André and Nussbaumer, Marc. "Speise- und Gerbereiabfall. Tierknochen aus zwei mittelalterlichen Kellern in der Löwengasse 6 und 8 in Solothurn." *Archäologie und Denkmal im Kanton Solothurn* 17 (2012): 65–69.

Reitz, Elisabeth J. and Wing, Elisabeth S. *Zooarchaeology*. Cambridge Manuals in Archaeology. 2nd Edition. Cambridge: Cambridge University Press, 2008.

Reichstein, Hans. "Die Fauna des germanischen Dorfes Feddersen Wierde." In *Feddersen Wierde. Die Ergebnisse der Ausgrabung der vorgeschichtlichen Wurt Feddersen Wierde bei Bremerhaven in den Jahren 1955 bis 1963, IV/1*, edited by Peter Schmid, 1–346. Stuttgart: Verlag Steiner, 1991.

Riedel, Alfredo. "Die Fauna einer bronzezeitlichen Siedlung bei Eppan (Südtirol)." *Rivista di Archeologia* IX (1985): 9–25.

Riedel, Alfredo. "Die Tierknochenfunde des römerzeitlichen Lagervicus von Traismauer/Augustiana in Niederösterreich." *Annalen des Naturhistorischen Museums in Wien*, Serie A, 95 (1993): 179–294.

Riedel, Alfredo. "Die Tierknochenfunde einer germanischen Siedlung an der Thaya bei Bernhardsthal im nordöstlichen Niederösterreich." *Annalen des Naturhistorischen Museums in Wien*, Serie A, 97 (1996): 55–144.

Riedel, Alfredo. "Tierknochen aus der römischen Villa rustica von Nickelsdorf in Burgenland (Österreich)." *Annalen des Naturhistorischen Museums in Wien*, Serie A, 106 (2004): 449–539.

Riedel, Alfredo. "Ein spätantiker Tierknochenfundkomplex aus Drösing an der March (Nederösterreich)." *Annalen des Naturhistorischen Museums in Wien*, Serie A, 109 (2007): 29–72.

Riedel, Alfredo and Pucher, Erich. "Mittelaterliche Tierknochenfunde aus der Burg Raabs an der Thaya (Niederösterreich)." *Beiträge zur Mittelalterarchäologie in Österreich* 24 (2008): 159–194.

Rohde, Ottomar. *Rindviehzucht nach ihrem jetzigen rationellen Standpunkt. Zweiter Band: Racen, Milchwirtschaft, Züchtung und Fütterung*. Berlin: Verlag von Wiegandt, Hempel und Parey, 1876.

Saliari, Konstantina and Kunst, Günther Karl. Fragments of daily life from a closed find: archaeozoological analysis at the 15th century Dominican Monastery in Tulln (Austria). In *Beiträge zur Archäozoologie und Prähistorische Anthropologie* Band 10, edited by Stephan Flohr, 123–134. Langenweißbach: Beier & Beran, 2015.

Saliari Konstantina Pucher Erich and Kucera Matthias. "Archaeozoological investigations of the La Tène A-C1 salt-mining complex and the surrounding graves of Putzenkopf Nord (Bad Dürrnberg, Austria)." *Annalen des Naturhistorischen Museums in Wien*, Serie A, 118 (2016): 245–288.

Saliari, Konstantina and Felgenhauer-Schmiedt, Sabine. "Skin, leather and fur may have disappeared, but bones remain…The case study of the 10th century AD fortified settlement "Sand" in Lower Austria." *Annalen des Naturhistorischen Museums in Wien*, Serie A, 119 (2017): 95–114.

Saliari Konstantina, Tobias Bendeguz, Draganits Erich and Wiltschke-Schrotta Karin (in press). "Animal bones in the burial customs of the Middle Avar Period graves in Podersdorf am See (Burgenland, Austria)." In *Beiträge zur Archäozoologie und Prähistorische Anthropologie* Band 11, edited by Peggy Morgenstern.

Salvagno, Lenny and Albarella, Umberto. "A morphometric system to distinguish sheep and goat postcranial bones." *PLOS One* 12, 6 (2017). http://journals.plos.org/plosone/article?id=10.1371/journal.pone.0178543

Salvagno, Lenny and Tecchiati, Umberto. *I resti faunistici del villaggio dell'età del Bronzo di Sotćiastel. Economia e vita di una communità protostorica alpine (ca. XVII-XIV sec. a.C.)*, Ladinia Monographica 03. San Martin de Tor: Institut Ladin Micurà de Rü, 2011.

Scherz, Eduard. "Zur Unterscheidung von *Bison priscus* Boj. und *Bos primigenius* Boj. an Metapodien und Astragalus, nebst Bemerkungen über einige diluviale Fundstellen." *Seckenbergiana* 18 (1936): 37–71.

Schmitzberger, Manfred. *Die Tierknochen aus der mittelneolithischen Kreisgrabenanlage Ölkam/OÖ*. Diplomarbeit. Universität Wien (unpublished), 1999.

Schmitzberger, Manfred. *Haus- und Jagdtiere im Neolithikum des österreichischen Donauraumes*. PhD Dissertation University of Vienna, Vienna, 2009.

Schmitzberger, Manfred. "Die Tierknochen vom Ramsaukopf, Putzenkopf und Putzenfeld – neue Funde vom keltischen Dürrnberg bei Hallein." *Annalen des Naturhistorischen Museums in Wien*, Serie A, 114 (2012): 79–138.

Schmitzberger, Manfred and Pucher, Erich. "6000 Jahre Hausrinder im Alpenraum." *Streiflichter aus der Geschichte der alpinen Milchkuh. - Salzburger Bauernkalender* (2011): 71–77.

Schramm, Zdzislawa. "Long bones and height in withers of Goat." *Roczniki Wyzszei Szkoly Rolniczej w. Poznaniu* 36 (1967a): 89–105.

Schramm, Zdzislawa. "Morphological differences of some goat and sheep bones." *Roczniki Wyzszei Szkoly Rolniczej w. Poznaniu* 36 (1967b): 107–133.

Schmölke, Ulrich. *Nutztierhaltung, Jagd und Fischfang. Zur Nahrungsmittelwirtschaft des frühgeschichtlichen Handelsplatzes von Groß Strömkendorf, Landkreis Nordwestmecklenburg*, Beiträge zur Ur- unf Frühgeschichte Mecklendburg-Vorpommerns. Band 43. Lübstorf: Archäologisches Landesmuseum und

Landesamt für Bodendenkmalpflege Mecklenburg-Vorpommern, 2004.

Schülke, Hubertus. *Die Tierknochenfunde von der Burg Neu-Schellenberg. Fürstentum Liechtenstein.* Inaugural-Dissertation zur Erlangung der veterinärmedizinischen Doktorwürde der Tierärzlichen Fakultät der Ludwig-Maximilians Universität. München: Institut für Palaeoanatomie, Domestikationsforschung und Geschichten der Tiermedizin der Universität München, 1965.

Schweizer, Werner. *Studien an vor- und frühgeschichtlichen Tierresten Bayerns. IX. Zur Frühgeschichte des Haushuhns in Mitteleuropa.* München: Verlag Kiefhaber & Elbl. München, 1961.

Schwerin, Claudius von. *Leges Saxonum et Lex Thuringorum.* Hannover/Leipzig: Impensis Bibliopolii Hahniani, 1918.

Seetah, Krish. "Butchery as a tool for understanding the changing views of animal." In *Just Skin and Bones? New Perspectives on Human-Animal Relations in the Historic Past*, BAR 1410, edited by Aleksander Pluskowski, 1–8. Oxford: BAR Publishing, 2005.

Spitzenberger, Friederike. "Die Tierknochenfunde des Hausbergs zu Gaiselberg, einer Wehranlage des 12.-16. Jahrhunderts in Niederösterreich." *Zeitschrift für Archäologie des Mittelalters*, Jahrgang 11/ 1983 (1986): 121–161.

Spitzenberger, Friederike. *Die Säugetierfauna Österreichs*, Grüne Reihe des Bundesministeriums für Land- und Forstwirtschaft, Umwelt und Wasserwirtschaft Band 13. Wien: Austria-Medien-Service, 2001.

Stampfli, Hans R. "Wisent, *Bison bonasus* (LINNÉ 1758), Ur, *Bos Brimigenius* BOJANUS 1827, und Haurind, *Bos taurus* LINNÉ, 1758." In *Seeberg Burgäschisee-Süd. Die Tierreste. Acta Bernensia* II, Teil 3, edited by Joachim Boessneck, Jean-Pierre Jéquier and Hans R. Stampli, 117–169. Bern: Stämpfli, 1963.

Steininger, Fritz F. Waldviertel – Kristallviertel. *Die Steinerne Schatzkammer Österreichs-Gesteine und Mineralien des Waldviertels*, Schriftenreihe des Waldviertler Heimatbundes 49, Horn: Waldviertler Heimatbund, 2008.

Stöllner, Thomas. "The Economy of Dürrnberg-bei-Hallein: An Iron Age salt-mining centre in the Austrian Alps." In *The Economy of Dürrnberg-bei-Hallein: An Iron Age salt-mining centre in the Austrian Alps.* With contributions, edited by Thomas Stöllner, The Antiquaries Journal 83 (2003): 164–170.

Strid, Lena. *To eat or not to eat? The significance of the cut marks on the bones from wild canids, mustelids, and felids from the Danish Ertebølle site Hjerk Nor.* MA Dissertation (Osteoarchaeology). University of Southampton, 2000.

Sykes, Naomi. *Beastly Questions. Animal answers to archaeological issues.* London: Bloomsbury, 2015.

Tecchiati, Umberto. "Die Tierknochen aus der bronze- und eisenzeitlichen Siedlung auf dem Kiabichl bei Faggen (Tirol, Österreich)." *Annalen des Naturhistorischen Museums in Wien*, Serie A, 114 (2012): 79–138

Teichert, Manfred. "Osteometrische Untersuchungen zur Berechnung der Widerristhöhe bei vor- und frühgeschichtlichen Schweinen," *Kühn Archiv* 83 (1969): 237–292.

Teichert, Manfred. "Osteometrische Untersuchungen zur Berechnung der Widerristhöhe bei Schafen." In *Archaeozoological studies*, edited by Anneke Clason, 51–69. Amsterdam, Oxford/New York: North Holland/ Publishing Company, 1975.

Teichert, Manfred. "Berechnung zur Ermittlung der Widerristhöhe des Ures *Bos primigenius* Boj., nach drei bedeutenden Skelettfunden aus dem 19. Jahrhundert." In *Historia animalium ex ossibus. Beiträge zur Paläoanatomie, Archäologie, Ägyptologie, Ethnologie und Geschichte der Tiermedizin. Festschrift für Angela von den Driesch*, edited by Cornelia Becker, Henriette Manhart, Joris Peters, and Jörg Schibler, 447–454. Rahden/Westf: Marie Leidorf, 1999.

Teichert Manfred, May Eberhard and Hanneman Klaus. "Allometrische Aspekte zur Ermittlung der Widerristhöhe bei Schweinen auf der Grundlage der Daten." *Anthropozoologica* 25/26 (1997): 181–191.

Teichert, Lothar. "Die Tierknochenfunde von der slawischen Burg und Siedlung auf der Dominsel Brandenburg/ Havel (Säugetiere, Vögel, Lurche und Muscheln)." In *Veröffentlichungen des Museums für Ur und Frühgeschichte Potsdam* Band 22, edited by Bernhard Gramsch, 143–220. Berlin: VEB Deutscher Verlag der Wissenschaften, 1988.

Telldahl Ylva, Svensson Emma, Götherström Anders and Storå Jan. "Osteometric and molecular sexing of cattle metapodial." *Journal of Archaeological Science* 39 (2012): 121–127.

Walcher, Claudia. *Die Metallfunde der Burganlage auf der Flur Sand.* Dissertation zur Erlangung des Doktorgrades der Philosophie aus dem Fachgebiet Ur- und Frühgeschichte, eingereicht an der Geistes- und Kulturwissenchaftlichen Fakultät der Universität Wien, 2004.

Watson, Mary Jane. "The effects of castration on the growth and meat quality of grazing cattle." *Australian Journal of Experimental Agriculture and Animal Husbandry* 9, 37 (1969): 164–171.

Wawruschka, Celine. *Frühmittelalterliche Besiedlung in Niederösterreich, Mittteilungen der prähistorischen Kommission.* Philosophisch-historische Klasse Band 68. Wien: Österreichische Akademie der Wissenschaften, 2009.

Wiedemann Ulrike. "Tierknochefunde vom Burgstall Hummertsried." Sonderdruck aus HENJA. Das Schlößle zu Hummertsried, *Forschungen und Berichte der Archäologie des Mittelalters in Baden-Wuttemberg* Band 2 (1974): 61–67

Wiig, Øystein. "Sexing of subfossil cattle metacarpals." *Acta Theriologica* 30 (1985): 495–503.

Wilckens, Martin. *Die Rinderrassen Mittel-Europas. Grundzüge einer Naturgeschichte des Hausrindes.* Wien: Wilhelm Braumüller K.K. Hof- und Universitäts-Buchhändler, 1876.

Wilson Bob, Grigson Caroline and Payne Sebastian. *Ageing and Sexing Animal Bones from Archaeological Sites*, BAR S109. Oxford: BAR Publishing, 1982.

Xoplaki Elena, Fleitmann Dominik, Luterbacher Juerg, Wagner Sebastian, Zorita Eduardo, Telelis Ioannis, Toreti Andrea and Izdebski Adam. "The Medieval Climate Anomaly and Byzantium: A review of the evidence on climatic fluctuations, economic performance and societal change." *Quaternary Science Reviews* 136 (2016): 229–252.

Zeder, Melinda. *Urbanism and Animal Exploitation in Southwest Highland Iran, 3400-1500 BC.* PhD Dissertation, University of Michigan, 1985.

Zeder, Melinda. "Reconciling Rates of Long Bone Fusion and Tooth Eruption and Wear in Sheep (*Ovis*) and Goat (*Capra*)." In *Proceedings of the 9th ICAZ Conference, Duhram 2002. Recent Advances in Ageing and Sexing Animal Bones*, edited by Deborah Ruscillo, 87–118. Oxford: Oxbow books, 2006.

Zeder, Melinda and Lapham, Heather. "Assessing the reliability of criteria used to identify postcranial bones in sheep, *Ovis*, and goats, *Capra*." *Journal of Archaeologial Science* 37 (2010): 2887–2905.

Zeder, Melinda and Pilaar, Susanne. "Assessing the reliability of criteria used to identify mandibles and mandibukar teeth in sheep, *Ovis*, and goats, *Capra*." *Journal of Archaeologial Science* 37, 2 (2010): 225–242.

Ziegler, Reinhard. "Tierreste aus der Prähistorischen Siedlung von Los Castillejos bei Montefrio (Prov. Granada)", *Studien über frühe Tierknochenfunde vor der Iberischen Halbinsel 12, Joachim Boessneck zum 65. Geburtstag*, Deutsches Archäologisches Institut Abteilung Madrid: 1–46. München: Institut für Palaeoanatomie, Domestikationsforschung und Geschichte der Tiermedizin der Universität München, 1990.

Fundberichte aus Österreich Fundchronik 32, 1993. Hoch und Spätmittelalter: 780-811.

Fundberichte aus Österreich Fundchronik 33, 1994. Fundchronik Hoch und Spätmittelalter: 623-648.

Fundberichte aus Österreich Fundchronik 34, 1995. Fundchronik Hoch und Spätmittelalter: 735-782.

Fundberichte aus Österreich 35, 1996. Fundchronik Hoch und Spätmittelalter: 553-587.

Fundberichte aus Österreich 38, 1999. Fundchronik Hoch und Spätmittelalter: 876-880.

Zentralanstalt für Meteorologie und Geodynamik (ZAMG) 2002. Klimadaten von Österreich: 1971-2000. https://www.zamg.ac.at/fix/klima/oe71-00/klima2000/klimadaten_oesterreich_1971_frame1.htm

Appendixes

Abbreviations for the following tables

Domesticated species: BT: cattle, O/C: sheep/goat, CH: goat, SD: pig, EC: horse, CF: dog, GGD: domestic fowl.

Wild species: BB: European bison, BP: aurochs, WB: wild Bovidae (BB and BP), CE: red deer, SS: wild boar, AA: elk, CC: roe deer, UA: brown bear, LU: European otter, MP: European polecat, CA: beaver, MA: European pine marten, SV: red squirell, MM: European badger, EE: European hedgehog, LE: European hare, CL: wolf, CR: European hamster, RR: black rat, FS: wild cat.

Skeletal element: Pf: processus frontalia, Cv: calvaria, Mx: maxilla, Md: mandible, Hy: hyoid, Vt: vertebrae, Co: costae, Corac: coracoideum, Sc: scapula, Hu: humerus, Ra: radius, Ul: ulna, Ca: carpalia, Cmc: Carpometacarpus, Pa: patella, Se: sesamoidea, Mc: metacarpus, Pe: pelvis, Fe: femur, Ti: tibia, Fi: fibula, Om: Os malleolare, Tita: tibiotarsus, Tl: talus, Cc: calcaneus, Ta: tarsalia, Mt: metatarsus, Tmt: tarsometatarsus, Mp: metapodia, Ph1: phalanx 1, Ph2: phalanx 2, Ph3: phalanx 3.

Antlers were excluded from the total quantification.

Sex estimation: f: female, f?: female?, m: male, m?: male?, c: castrated, c? castrated?

Appendix A. Tables of Quantification

Sand 1 – Domesticated species – Number of identified specimens (NISP)

Element	BT	O/C	CH	SD	EC
Pf	6		18		
Cv	39		8	53	
Mx	73	23		62	2
Md	143	24		95	2
Hy	3	1			1
Vt	201	3		28	7
Co	166	12		49	6
Sc	40	6	1	27	7
Hu	47	5	3	37	5
Ra	40	6	3	10	2
Ul	22			11	1
Ca	31			2	3
Mc	44	1	1	2	1
Pe	69	1	1	17	4
Fe	36	2		6	4
Pa/Se	9				5
Ti	56	10		10	2
Fi/Om	2			4	
Tl	26	1		1	4
Cc	23			3	4
Ta	11			0	
Mt	46	3	2	3	1
Mp				3	1
Ph1	41	1		6	2
Ph2	24	1		2	
Ph3	6			4	3
Total	1204	100	37	435	67

Element	GGD
Corac	3
Sc	1
Hu	6
Ra	1
Ul	1
Cmc	2
Pe	2
Fe	5
Tita	8
Tmt	4
Total	33

Sand 1 – Wild species – Number of identified specimens (NISP)

Element	BB	SS	CE	CC	AA	LU	MP	MA	SV	MM	CA	UA	EE
Pf			10*	1*									
Cv	3	31	17	6	2		1	3		2			
Mx		36	27	8							5		
Md		87	38	5	1	2		3			14	3	
Hy			1										
Vt	20	50	34	5							1		
Co	21	54	55									1	
Sc	14	20	15	4								1	
Hu	7	25	25	6							3	2	1
Ra	10	18	41	8					1		3	2	
Ul	8	24	19		1					1	3	2	
Ca	10	5	5									1	
Mc	2	26	20										
Pe	12	15	20	1						1	7		
Fe	6	8	14	2				2	2		5		1
Pa	2	1		1									
Ti	11	9	23	5				1			4		1
Fi/Om	3	6	1										
Tl	2	12	12	4									
Cc	6	7	10		1								
Ta	1	7	1	1									
Mt		17	12	4							1	1	
Mp		3			1								
Ph1	15	28	28		2							1	
Ph2	11	19	17		2								
Ph3	3	10	11		1							2	
Baculum						1							
Se		1											
Total	167	519	446	60	11	3	1	9	3	4	46	16	3

Sand 2 – Domesticated species – Number of identified specimens (NISP)

Element	BT	O/C	CH	SD	EC	CF
Pf	2		6			
Cv	44	8		43		
Mx	59	12		41		
Md	104	17	1	100		
Hy	4	1				
Vt	81	15	2	30	1	
Co	69	20		53	3	
Sc	48	5		25		
Hu	46	4		29	2	
Ra	38	4	3	8	1	1
Ul	19	3		6		
Ca	7			4	2	
Mc	19	1	6	2	1	
Pe	36	2		14	2	
Fe	38	14		11		
Pa	1					
Ti	28	11		22	3	
Fi/Om	1			3		
Tl	16			6	1	
Cc	7			5		
Ta	7			2		
Mt	18		2	3		
Mp	4			8		
Ph1	26		1	3		
Ph2	15			2	1	
Ph3	1			1		
Se	7					
Total	745	117	21	421	17	1

Element	GGD
Corac	1
Sc	1
Hu	2
Ul	1
Tita	7
Total	12

Sand 2 – Wild species – Number of identified specimens (NISP)

Element	BP	BB	WB	SS	CE	CC	AA	MA	SV	CA	UA	CL	LE
Pf		1				3*							
Cv			1	4	5		2	2					
Mx		1		3	12		9			3	1		
Md	2	13		15	20	8	2	1		5		1	
Hy													
Vt			10	9	3	4							
Co			36	2	16					2			
Sc		2	4	3	1	2							
Hu				2	7	7					2		
Ra		1	1	1	6	5	2			1	1		
Ul		3	1	5	3	1				2			
Ca			1	4	5	2							
Mc				2	3	1					1		
Pe			3	4	5	1	2						
Fe			3	7	1	1			1	2			1
Pa				2		1							
Ti			4	11	11	8	1		1	1			
Fi/Om				1									
Tl		2	1	2	9	1				1	2		
Cc		2	1	2	2	2					1		
Ta													
Mt				1		4					1	2	
Mp					3								
Ph1			16	2	8	4					1		
Ph2			9	4	2	1							
Ph3			2	2	2								
Se													
Total	2	25	93	88	124	53	18	3	2	17	10	3	1

Sand 2 – Domesticated species – Weight

Element	BT	O/C	CH	SD	EC	CF
Pf	103.0		131.0			
Cv	638.0	34.0		239.0		92
Mx	853.0	59.0		188.0		
Md	1677.2	235.0	53.0	936.0		
Hy	15.0	0.1				
Vt	1851.4	77.0	30.0	312.0	40.0	
Co	715.0	42.0		208.0	53.0	
Sc	1034.2	15.0		279.0		
Hu	2404.5	34.0		464.0	52.0	
Ra	1794.0	19.0	28.0	94.0	84.0	3.0
Ul	369.0	4.0		62.0		
Ca	60.0			18.0	33.0	
Mc	910.0	7.2	24.0	9.0	37.0	
Pe	883.0	4.3		237.0	47.0	
Fe	1258.1	76.0		155.0		
Pa	19.0					
Ti	1252.0	94.0		261.0	497.0	
Fi/Om	5.0			8.0		
Tl	402.0			71.0	49.0	
Cc	327.0			42.0		
Ta	170.0			4.0		
Mt	903.0		30.0	12.0		
Mp	25.0			15.0		
Ph1	392.0		6.0	14.0		
Ph2	134.0			5.0	23.0	
Ph3	17.0			0.0		
Se	21.0					
Total	18232.4	700.6	302.0	3633.0	915.0	3.0

Element	GGD
Corac	0.0
Sc	0.5
Hu	2.6
Ul	1.8
Tita	16.3
Total	21.2

Sand 2 – Wild species – Weight

Element	BP	BB	WB	SS	CE	CC	AA	MA	SV	CA	UA	CL	LE
Pf		124.0				71.0*							
Cv			8.0	63.0	65.4		208.0	13.0					
Mx		28.0		165.0	106.5		146.0			12.0	12.0		
Md	857.0	280.0		365.0	233.5	79.0	226.0	1.0		6.0		5.2	
Hy													
Vt			706.0	238.0	58.0	24.0							
Co			754.0	22.0	165.0					1.0			
Sc		125.0	201.0	110.0	30.0	24.0							
Hu				186.0	373.0	86.0					323.0		
Ra		79.0	30.0	5.0	277.0	24.0	56.0			3.0	18.0		
Ul		271.0	22.0	130.0	92.0	0.0				7.0			
Ca			15.0	37.0	37.0	3.0							
Mc				49.0	108.0	17.0					6.0		
Pe			193.0	77.0	202.0	7.0	90.0						
Fe			140.0	168.0	16.0	4.0			0.2	34.0			0.0
Pa				31.0		4.0							
Ti			380.0	190.0	336.0	117.0	125.0		0.3	5.0			
Fi/Om				4.0									
Tl		127.0	58.0	55.0	325.0	2.0				1.0	28.0		
Cc		253.0	15.0	37.0	79.0	14.0					26.0		
Ta													
Mt				16.0		34.0					10.0	20.3	
Mp					62.0								
Ph1			562.0	22.0	113.0	9.0					4.0		
Ph2			226.0	21.0	23.0	1.0							
Ph3			50.0	9.0	12.0								
Se													
Total	857.0	1287.0	3360.0	2000.0	2713.4	449.0	851.0	14.0	0.5	69.0	427.0	25.5	0.0

Sand Westwall – Domesticated species – Number of identified specimens (NISP)

Element	BT	O/C	CH	SD	EC	CF
Pf	8		29			
Cv	91	9		71		1
Mx	81	15		90		
Md	149	43	2	176		3
Hy	6					
Vt	192	15		101	3	
Co	232	21		82	13	3
Sc	48	13		65	3	
Hu	72	11	5	67	4	1
Ra	61	23	5	13	2	1
Ul	29	9		24	1	1
Ca	24			4	1	
Mc	45	4	2	16		
Pe	51	6	2	36		2
Fe	41	4	10	20	2	
Pa/Se	14	1		3	2	
Ti	55	22	1	30	3	1
Fi/Om	7			6		
Tl	27		1	6	2	
Cc	30	1	2	12		1
Ta	12	1		4	2	1
Mt	52	9	3	8	1	
Mp	18	3				
Ph1	63	1	3	12	3	
Ph2	22	1		11	1	
Ph3	20			5	1	
Total	1450	212	65	862	44	15

Element	GGD
Cr	1
St	12
Corac	10
Sc	3
Hu	15
Ra	6
Ul	8
Pe	8
Fe	7
Tita	15
Tmt	11
Total	96

Sand Westwall – Wild species – Number of identified specimens (NISP)

Element	BP	BB	WB	SS	CE	CC	AA	LU	MA	MM	SV	CA	UA	FS	LE	EE	CR	RR
Pf					11*	11*												
Cv		8		32	29	19	4		1			9	1					
Mx		3		52	33	5	5			1		14	4					
Md		8		68	38	11	1		10	1	2	18	1	1		4	1	
Hy					1													
Vt			101	29	74	32	1	2	2			15						
Co			64	36	45	21	2	1				30	7		5			
Sc		1	13	26	24	15			1			8	1		2			
Hu	1	3	2	22	31	20	2	1	2		10	14	3	1				
Ra		4	9	33	28	18	4		1	1		5	2	1				
Ul		6	4	29	13	4	1		2			6	2					
Ca			13	8	17	1												
Mc				28	15	2						2						
Pe		5	10	30	39	6	3		1	1		11	2	1				
Fe		2	13	25	19	10	1	1	1		15	22			1	1		1
Pa			2	4	6								2					
Ti		6	13	32	46	11	4	1	1		9	16			2	2		
Fi/Om		3		8	2													
Tl	1	6		17	19	5						1						
Cc	1	4	1	21	11	7			1			2	1					
Ta	1		1	8	8	2												
Mt				16	12	5	1					4						
Mp				26	10	3							1					
Ph1			25	20	42	3	8					2	1					
Ph2			17	18	27	2	2						1					
Ph3			9	5	3													
Se			4			1												
Total	4	59	301	593	592	202	40	6	23	4	36	177	31	4	10	7	1	1

Sand Westwall – Domesticated species – Weight

Element	BT	O/C	CH	SD	EC	CF
Pf	380.0		778.2			
Cv	2023.7	45.0		819.0		12.0
Mx	1.346.1	71.0		882.0		
Md	3.395.0	472.0	77.0	2076.5		19.0
Hy	26.0					
Vt	4701.3	114.0		978.0	198.0	
Co	3284.6	90.0		410.0	222.0	7.0
Sc	1699.2	98.0		882.0	143.0	
Hu	4360.1	91.0	73.0	1185.6	561.0	12.0
Ra	3220.0	213.0	112.0	132.0	197.0	6.0
Ul	633.0	37.0		327.0	32.0	12.0
Ca	201.0			18.0	12.0	
Mc	2773.0	39.0	25.0	66.0		
Pe	1774.1	27.0	19.0	590.0		28.0
Fe	2593.2	36.0	75.0	226.0	158.0	
Pa/Se	92.0	0.5		13.0	23.0	
Ti	3055.0	263.0	16.0	492.0	311.0	1.0
Fi/Om	45.0			19.0		
Tl	824.0		5.0	52.0	61.0	
Cc	1157.0	3.0	14.0	157.0		1.0
Ta	222.0	5.0		14.0	24.0	7.0
Mt	2974.0	56.0	23.0	26.0	201.0	
Mp	159.0	0.5				
Ph1	1161.3	0.5	9.0	31.0	68.0	
Ph2	242.0	0.8		26.0	38.0	
Ph3	277.0			14.0	11.0	
Total	42618.6	1662.3	1226.2	9436.1	2260.0	105.0

Element	GGD
Cr	1.7
St	15.3
Corac	10.8
Sc	1.4
Hu	25.4
Ra	2.7
Ul	8.0
Pe	15.4
Fe	12.2
Tita	35.9
Tmt	13.6
Total	142.4

Sand Westwall – Wild species – Weight

Element	BP	BB	WB	SS	CE	CC	AA	LU	MA	MM	SV	CA	UA	FS	LE	EE	CR	RR
Pf					431.5*	185.0*												
Cv		502.0		1028.0	990.0	154.0	554.0		7.0			61.0	16.0					
Mx		56.0		1496.7	460.0	30.0	119.0			1.0		46.0	62.0					
Md		348.0		2498.3	937.0	77.0	49.0		18.0	11.2	2.0	378.0	29.0	1.9		0.1	0.1	
Hy					5.0													
Vt			6018.2	758.0	2572.3	197.0	54.0	6.0	0.0			72.0						
Co			1709.1	351.0	637.0	43.0	19.0	0.0				44.0	128.0		3.1			
Sc		158.0	817.0	859.0	1020.4	122.0			0.0			40.0	23.0		4.0			
Hu	257.0	690.0	128.0	1112.0	1998.2	249.0	122.0	6.0	4.0		5.8	140.0	162.0	6.8				
Ra		599.0	827.0	810.0	1363.5	140.0	188.0		1.0	4.7		16.0	54.0	3.2				
Ul		674.0	102.0	988.0	363.0	23.0	14.0		1.0			43.0	226.0					
Ca			287.0	47.0	176.0	1.0												
Mc				274.0	789.0	23.0							20.0					
Pe		667.0	600.0	865.0	1369.0	76.0	157.0		1.0	0.0		222.0	219.0	2.4				
Fe		673.0	1114.6	933.0	780.0	90.0	284.0	3.0	1.2		11.0	450.0			1.0	0.1		0.0
Pa			96.0	59.0	113.0								24.0					
Ti		988.0	1386.0	1124.2	2842.0	176.0	290.0	4.0	0.8		7.0	230.0			9.0	0.1		
Fi/Om		29.0		60.0	12.0													
Tl	116.0	466.0		349.0	745.0	28.0						4.0						
Cc	202.0	318.0	17.0	560.0	464.0	55.0			0.7			9.0	28.0					
Ta	96.0		43.0	71.0	162.0	5.0												
Mt				121.0	1363.0	44.0	337.0					17.0						
Mp				196.0	111.0	6.0							23.0					
Ph1			929.0	146.0	757.0	7.0	241.0					2.0	4.0					
Ph2			456.0	33.0	359.0	3.0	34.0						6.0					
Ph3			208.0	21.0	35.0													
Se		32.0					0.0											
Total	671.0	6168.0	14769.9	14760.2	20423.4	1549.0	2462.0	19.0	34.7	16.9	25.8	1774.0	1024.0	14.3	17.1	0.3	0.1	0.0

Sand Westwall – Wild species (? Anatidae) – Number of identified specimens (NISP)

Element	Anatidae
Ul	2
Cmc	1
Tmt	2
Total	5

Sand Westwall – Wild species (? Anatidae) – Weight

Element	Anatidae
Ul	2.7
Cmc	0.4
Tmt	3.6
Total	6.7

Sand – Number of identified specimens (NISP) and Weight

	Sand 1		Sand 2		Westwall area	
	NISP	Weight	NISP	Weight	NISP	Weight
Domesticated species	1876	5567.8	1334	23807.2	2749	57457.3
Wild species	1296	3925.1	444	12057	2131	63766.5
Total	3172	9492.9	1778	35864.2	4880	121223.8

Sand – Number of identified specimens (NISP-%) and Weight-%

	Sand 1		Sand 2		Westwall area	
	NISP%	Weight%	NISP%	Weight%	NISP%	Weight%
Domesticated species	59.1	58.7	75.0	66.4	56.3	47.4
Wild species	40.9	41.3	25.0	33.6	43.7	52.6

Appendix B. Tables of Measurements
(based on Driesch 1976)

Bos primigenius f. *taurus*

Bos: Processus frontalis

Nr.	99/04	73/03	45/06	60/99	71/00	115/96	115/96
Horncore basal circumference	130.0	150.0	110.0	130.0	115.0	105.0	103.0
Greatest diameter of the horncore base	45.0	51.0	37.0	44.5	40.5	34.5	32.5
Least diameter of the horncore base	33.5	38.0	31.5	35.0	29.5	28.0	27.0
Length of the outer curvature of the horncore	-	-	-	140.0	-	-	120.0
Sex	f	f	f	f	f	f	f

Bos: Processus frontalis

Nr.	115/96	54/07	120/97
Horncore basal circumference	104.0	170.0	169.0
Greatest diameter of the horncore base	26.5	46.5	48.0
Least diameter of the horncore base	39.5	56.5	59.5
Length of the outer curvature of the horncore	113.0	-	-
Sex	f	c	c?

Bos: Cranium

Nr.	115/96+89/96+103/96
Greatest mastoid breadth: Otion-Otion	161.0
Greatest breadth of the occipital condyles	80.0
Greatest breadth at the basis of the paraoccipital processes	120.0
Greatest breadth of the foramen magnum	37.0
Height of the foramen magnum (Basion-Opisthion)	37.0
Least occipital breadth	97.5
Least breadth between the bases of the horncores	126.5

Bos: Maxilla

Nr.	115/96+89/96+103/96
Length of the cheektooth row (measured along the alveoli)	110.5
Length of the molar row (measured along the alveoli on th ebuccal side)	69.5
Wear stage (M^3)	(++)

Bos: Mandibula

Nr.	71/96	71/96	54/03	42/06	79/02
Length of the angle: Gonion caudale-Infradentale	335.0	336.0	-	-	-
Length: Gonion caudale-aboral border of thr alveolus M_3	101.0	103.5	-	-	-
Length of the horizontal ramus: aboral border of the alveolus M_3-Infradentale	230.5	232.0	-	-	-
Length: Gonion caudale-oral border of the alveolus of P_2	232.0	232.5	-	-	-
Length: Gonion caudale-the most aboral indentation of the mental frontale	280.5	285.0	-	-	-
Length of the Diastema: oral border of the alveolus P_2-aboral border of the alveolus of I_4	85.5	82.0	83.0	98.0	-
Length of the premolar row, measured along the alveoli on the buccal side	44.0	44.5	44.0	47.5	42.0
Length of the molar row, measured along the alveoli on the buccal side	79.5	80.5	-	-	-
Length of the cheektooth row, measured along the alveoli on the buccal side	127.0	128.5	-	-	-
Length of M_3	35.0	35.0	37.5		
Breadth of M_3	14.0	13.5	16.5		
Wear stage of M_3	(++)	(++)	(++)		
Aboral height of the vertical ramus: Gonion ventrale-highest point of the condyle process.	128.0	-	-	-	-
Height of the mandible behind M_3	57.5	62.5	-	-	-
Height of the mandible in front of M_1	42.5	46.5	-	-	-
Height of the mandible in front of P_2	32.0	32.5	-	-	-

Bos: Mandibula

Nr.	41/07	107/03	41/05	119/03	43/02
Length of the premolar row, measured along the alveoli on the buccal side	44.5	-	-	-	-
Length of the molar row, measured along the alveoli on the buccal side	80.5	-	-	-	-
Length of the cheektooth row, measured along the alveoli on the buccal side	125.5	-	-	-	-
Length of M_3	-	34.5	36.0	37.0	-
Breadth of M_3	15.0	11.5	16.0	16.0	14.5
Wear stage of M_3	(++)	0	(++)	(+++)	(+++)

Bos: Mandibula

Nr.	41/05	119/03	43/02	51/08	75/03	195/98	25/00
Length of M_3	36.0	37.0	-	33.0	32.5	32.5	-
Breadth of M_3	16.0	16.0	14.5	15.0	14.0	14.5	16.5
Wear stage of M_3	(++)	(+++)	(+++)	(++)	(+)	0	(+)

Bos: Mandibula

Nr.	66/96	55/94	115/96	22/95	220/97	211/97	94/97
Length of M_3	32.0	39.0	36.0	32.5	39.0	37.0	34.5
Breadth of M_3	13.0	13.0	12.5	13.0	12.5	15.5	13.0
Wear stage of M_3	(+)	(+)	(+)	(++)	(+)	(++)	(+)
Height of the mandible in front of P_2	38.5	-	-	-	-	-	-

Bos: Mandibula

Nr.	163/97	220/97	217/97	207/97	196/97	68/96	(20/2/97)
Length of M_3	37.5	32.0	33.0	31.0	-	-	35.0
Breadth of M_3	14.0	13.5	12.5	11.0	12.0	12.0	12.5
Wear stage of M_3	(+)	(+)	(+)	0	(+)	(+)	0

Bos: Atlas

Nr.	79/02	71/00	1/00
GL	81.5	-	-
GLF	-	80.0	64.5
BFcr	99.5	101.0	83.0
BFcd	96.5	84.0	67.5
H	85.0	-	69.0
LAD	-	38.5	33.0

Bos: Axis

Nr.	(6/03)	103/96	91/96	45/94	89/96
BFcr	95.5	89.0	-	66.5	75.0
SBV	-	46.5	-	40.0	-
Bpacd	-	-	73.0	-	-

Bos: Sacrum

Nr.	62/04
BFcr	55.0
HFcr	26.0

Bos: Scapula

Nr.	207/97	(30/05)	99/04	51/03
GLP	66.0	-	-	-
LG	54.0	-	58.0	-
BG	-	44.0	-	-
SLC	-	46.0	48.5	51.5

Bos: Scapula

Nr.	115/96a	115/96b	(30/05)	42/06	67/00	217/97	(11/03)
GLP	66.0	73.5	62.5	74.5	65.0	75.0	65.0

LG	55.0	62.0	52.5	61.0	52.5	62.5	54.0
BG	45.0	52.0	41.0	54.0	44.5	49.5	-
SLC	50.0	53.5	50.0	54.5	54.0	58.5	50.0

Bos: Scapula

Nr.	67/00	217/97	97/97	76/02	158/98	115/96c	129/97
GLP	65.0	75.0	72.0	66.0	66.0	67.5	52.0
LG	52.5	62.5	58.5	55.5	54.0	56.5	46.0
BG	44.5	49.5	50.0	46.5	45.0	45.5	38.0
SLC	54.0	58.5	55.5	-	-	-	-

Bos: Humerus

Nr.	42/06	(19/05)	31/98
SD	29.0	30.0	37.0
Bd	67.0	78.5	84.0
BT	61.0	69.5	77.0

Bos: Humerus

Nr.	0	127/03	82/04	(28/05)	65/00	78/99	121/03
Bd	69.0	85.5	73.5	86.0	77.5	74.0	85.5
BT	63.0	71.5	65.0	75.5	72.0	70.0	78.0

Bos: Humerus

Nr.	107/96	115/96	76/96
Bd	80.0	88.5	87.0
BT	74.5	79.0	76.0

Bos: Humerus

Nr.	84/95	44/95	107/96	56/94	(20/2/97)	97/97	120/97
Bd	85.5	77.5	66.5	72.0	77.5	82.5	77.0
BT	76.0	70.5	60.5	64.5	72.0	72.0	67.0

Bos: Humerus

Nr.	22/95	83/00	77/99	44/02	47/02	48/06	(10/08)
BT	70.5	80.0	71.0	69.0	74.5	68.5	49.0

Bos: Radius

Nr.	31/98	115/96	115/96	74/03	74/96 + 66/96	111/04	(16/04)
GL	305.5	274.0	288.0	249.0	-	-	-
PL	-	-	-	234.5	-	-	-
Bp	85.5	84.5	85.0	-	84.5	76.5	71.5
BFp	78.0	75.5	76.0	62.5	78.5	66.5	65.0
SD	42.0	40.5	-	35.5	43.5	-	-
Bd	77.0	74.5	-	-	-	-	-
BFd	68.0	-	-	-	-	-	-

Bos: Radius

Nr.	39/03	36/07	43/08	60/99	106/99	48/00	58/00
Bp	65.5	75.0	73.5	77.5	67.0	86.0	78.0
BFp	62.0	68.5	66.5	71.0	61.5	77.0	71.0

Bos: Radius

Nr.	32/93	89/96	115/96	115/96	141/97	44/95	207/97
Bp	76.0	64.0	70.5	76.0	62.0	57.0	78.0
BFp	70.5	59.5	64.5	-	-	-	-

Bos: Radius

Nr.	47/99	48//99
BFp	62.5	63.5

Bos: Ulna

Nr.	43/08	115/96	74/03	31/04	177/98	(27/01)	106/96
LO	91.5	73.0	-	-	-	-	-
DPA	57.0	54.0	53.0	63.0	61.0	50.5	60.0
SDO	47.5	43.0	-	-	-	-	-
BPC	43.0	39.0	39.5	45.0	46.0	39.5	41.5

Bos: Ulna

Nr.	102/97	172/97	31/98	59/00	60/99	71/95	225/97
DPA	60.5	56.5	64.5	63.0	63.0	64.0	53.5
SDO	-	-	53.5	-	-	-	-
BPC	45.0	42.0	50.0	-	-	-	-

Bos: Ulna

Nr.	75/01	207/97	25/93	(9/03)	49/06
LO	110.5	-	-	-	-
BPC	-	38.5	38.0	42.5	40.0

Bos: Ulna

Nr.	68/99	58/00	39/05
BPC	51.5	43.0	46.5

Bos: Os carpale (radiale)

Nr.	115/96	31/94
GB	45.5	43.5

Bos: Os carpale (intermedium)

Nr.	?
GB	39.0

Bos: Os carpale (ulnare)

Nr.	41/94	119/96	88/95	55/94	115/96
GB	35.0	32.0	32.5	34.0	33.5

Bos: Os carpale (II+III)

Nr.	127/04	82/03	115/96	88/96a	88/96b	66/96	103/96
GB	35.0	29.0	35.5	36.0	32.5	30.5	33.0

Bos: Os carpale (II+III)

Nr.	68/96a
GB	34.5

Bos: Os carpale (IV)

Nr.	68/96b	115/96a
GB	28.0	30.0

Bos: Metacarpus

Nr.	31/04	78/03	(13/03)	117/03	99/04	83/04	93/03
GL	174.0	172.5	165.0	-	-	-	-
Bp	48.0	47.0	44.0	51.5	46.5	43.5	-
SD	28.0	29.0	25.0	25.0	-	-	22.5
DD	19.5	20.0	18.0	-	-	-	16.0
Bd	51.0	-	47.0	-	-	-	-
Dd	27.0	26.5	25.0	-	-	-	-
Sex	f	f	f	f	f	f	f

Bos: Metacarpus

Nr.	91/03	117/03	62/04	(14/07)	115/96	115/96	93/95
Bp	-	51.5	-	-	48.0	48.0	-
SD	-	-	-	-	26.0	26.5	-
DD	18.0	-	-	-	-	-	-
Bd	47.0	-	49.0	56.0	-	-	47.0
Dd	25.5	27.0	24.5	25.5	-	-	-
Sex	f	f	f	f	f	f	f

Bos: Metacarpus

Nr.	115/96	103/97	75/02	110/97	217/97	74/03
GL	179.5	175.0	-	171.0	-	-
Bp	48.0	-	-	50.5	57.5	-
SD	26.0	23.5	29.0	28.0	-	-
DD	-	-	-	-	-	18.5
Bd	50.0	-	-	52.5	-	-
Sex	f	f	f	f?	f?	

Bos: Metacarpus

Nr.	(30/05)	42/03	80/02	89/96	41/95	114/96	124/97
GL	201.3	196.0	-	-	-	-	-
Bp	55.5	55.5	56.5	65.0	58.0	62.0	-
SD	31.0	27.5	29.0	33.0	-	-	35.0
DD	22.0	20.5	-	-	-	-	-
Bd	61.0	57.0	-	-	-	-	-
Dd	32.0	31.0	-	-	-	-	-
Sex	c	c	c	c	c	c	c

Bos: Metacarpus

Nr.	32/98	82/00	83/00	89/00	38/95	54/95	184/97
Bp	59.0	57.0	58.5	57.0	60.0	-	-
Bd	-	-	-	-	-	58.5	58.5
Sex	c	c	c	c	c?	c?	c?

Bos: Metacarpus

Nr.	102/96	97/97	56/95	(12/04)	62/02	(29/05)	70/08
Bp	56.0	57.0	51.0	-	-	54.5	55.0
SD	-	-	28.5	-	-	-	-
DD	-	-	-	-	24.0	-	-
Bd	-	-	-	61.0	62.0	-	-
Dd	-	-	-	32.0	31.0	-	-
Sex	c?	c?	c?	c?	c?	c?	c?

Bos: Metacarpus

Nr.	115/96	112/96	99/04	68/99	96/00
GL	-	190.5	-	-	-
Bp	57.0	56.5	53.0	-	59.0
SD	29.5	30.5	-	30.0	-
Bd	-	56.5	-	-	-
Sex	c?	c?	c?	c	c

Bos: Metacarpus

Nr.	98/04	85/03	47/99	67/00	97/97	76/96	111/97
GL	182.5	175.0	-	-	178.5	174.5	185.5
Bp	58.5	56.5	-	-	55.0	52.5	-
SD	34.0	32.0	32.0	-	32.5	30.0	33.5
DD	22.0	23.0	-	-	-	-	-
Bd	61.5	61.5	-	63.0	55.0	56.5	61.0
Dd	31.0	30.0	-	-	-	-	-
Sex	m	m	m	m	m	m?	m?

Bos: Pelvis

Nr.	135/04	126/03	54/07	115/96	68/96	54/95	102/96
LA	-	-	60.0	70.0	73.5	70.0	70.5
SB	20.5	23.5	-	-	-	-	-
LAR	-	-	49.0	-	-	-	-
Sex	c	c	c	c	c	c	c

Bos: Pelvis

Nr.	102/97	112/96	112/96	68/96	63/03	141/97	63/03
LA	73.0	71.5	67.5	60.5	62.5	75.0	59.0
LAR	-	-	-	-	-	-	52.0
Sex	c	c	c	c?			

Bos: Pelvis

Nr.	134/04	115/96	59/96	115/96	103/96	78/03	76/03
LA	56.0	70.0	66.5	64.5	67.0	-	-
SB	-	-	-	-	-	27.5	19.0
LAR	53.0	-	-	-	-	-	-

Bos: Pelvis

Nr.	65/00	88/00	107/3
LA	71.0	-	-

SH	-	33.5	-
SB	-	19.0	17.0
LAR	59.5	-	-

Bos: Femur

Nr.	121/03	55/03	66/03	34/04	109/04	(5/04)	59/00
Bd	79.0	71.0	-	-	-	-	-
DC	-	-	37.0	40.5	46.0	45.0	41.0

Bos: Patella

Nr.	127/03
GL	60.5
GB	53.0

Bos: Tibia

Nr.	(6/03)	79/02	121/03	124/03	0	(19/04)	127/03
Bp	87.0	-	91.0	-	-	-	-
SD	-	30.0	-	35.5	-	-	-
Bd	-	-	-	61.0	61.5	61.0	61.5

Bos: Tibia

Nr.	(29/04)	(16/04)	120/03	34/02	(17/05)	(6/03)	54/03
SD	31.0	-	-	34.5	-	-	-
Bd	-	61.5	57.0	63.0	57.0	52.5	50.0

Bos: Tibia

Nr.	54/04	106/03	49/07	?	89/00	96/00	159/98
GL	-	-	-	354.0	-	-	-
Bp	-	-	90.0	-	-	-	-
SD	-	35.5	-	35.0	-	34.0	-
Bd	60.0	-	-	58.0	61.5	57.5	58.0

Bos: Tibia

Nr.	36/99	88/96	78/97	102/96	43/93	115/96	69/96
SD	39.5	-	-	-	-	-	-
Bd	62.5	63.5	60.5	55.5	57.0	60.0	56.0

Bos: Tibia

Nr.	97/95	83/97	21/97	54/95	115/96	26/95	108/95
Bd	60.0	63.5	65.0	57.5	60.0	47.5	53.0

Bos: Tibia

Nr.	38/94	163/97	23/97
Bd	62.5	62.5	61.5

Bos: Os malleolare

Nr.	52/06	61/02	83/04	(6/03)	62/04	36/07	43/07
GD	33.5	35.0	32.5	29.0	32.0	36.0	34.5

Bos: Os malleolare

Nr.	97/95
GD	34.5

Bos: Talus

Nr.	99/04	62/02	(11/04)	(19/05)	106/03	83/04	54/03
GLl	62.5	57.0	58.5	58.0	62.0	62.0	61.0
GLm	59.0	51.5	53.0	53.0	59.0	57.0	55.5
Dl	37.5	33.0	33.0	33.5	36.5	35.0	33.0
Dm	35.0	31.0	-	-	34.0	36.5	34.0
Bd	41.0	38.5	35.0	36.5	39.0	39.0	39.5

Bos: Talus

Nr.	34/02	54/03	111/04	111/04	63/03	35/08	67/08
GLl	65.0	58.5	54.5	54.5	59.0	63.0	55.5
GLm	58.3	53.0	49.5	49.5	54.0	57.5	50.0
Dl	35.0	33.5	30.5	30.5	32.0	35.5	30.0
Dm	36.0	33.0	30.5	30.5	31.5	31.0	28.0
Bd	42.0	38.5	37.0	37.0	38.0	40.5	35.0

Bos: Talus

Nr.	43/08	40/99	29/98	93/99	68/99	81/00	51/01
GLl	65.0	63.0	63.0	59.5	53.5	62.0	60.0
GLm	58.0	57.0	57.5	55.5	48.0	55.5	56.5
Dl	35.0	35.0	34.5	34.0	30.0	33.5	33.0
Dm	34.0	35.0	35.5	33.0	28.5	32.5	34.0
Bd	41.0	44.0	39.5	39.5	34.0	40.0	39.0

Bos: Talus

Nr.	106/99	86/96	115/96	69/96	78/97	97/95	23/97
GLl	62.0	69.0	66.5	66.0	63.5	64.0	64.5
GLm	56.0	63.5	61.0	58.5	57.0	56.0	57.5
Dl	34.0	37.5	36.5	35.5	35.5	34.5	35.5
Dm	34.0	38.0	37.5	35.5	36.0	34.0	35.0
Bd	39.0	43.0	41.5	43.5	43.5	42.5	42.0

Bos: Talus

Nr.	220/97	66/96	115/96	129/97	49/95	66/96	176/97
GLl	60.0	60.5	59.0	55.0	58.0	59.0	66.5
GLm	54.5	55.5	53.5	50.5	-	53.5	59.5
Dl	33.0	33.0	32.5	29.0	31.5	33.0	36.0
Dm	-	33.0	32.5	29.5	-	32.5	36.0
Bd	37.0	40.0	36.5	33.5	36.0	36.5	-

Bos: Talus

Nr.	112/97	(6/96)	129/97
GLl	67.5	56.5	75.0
GLm	62.0	50.5	68.0
Dl	-	-	-
Dm	39.5	29.5	-
Bd	46.5	33.0	-

Bos: Talus

Nr.	184/97	97/95	(1/01)	159/98	35/07	102/96	44/08
GLl	62.5	63.5	59.0	57.5	-	-	-
GLm	57.5	57.5	55.5	53.5	58.5	70.0	-
Dl	33.5	34.5	32.5	31.0	-	-	-
Dm	36.5	34.0	-	-	-	42.0	-
Bd	39.5	43.0	36.0	34.5	39.5	-	40.0

Bos: Talus

Nr.	17/00	24/99	42/07
Bd	35.0	34.5	34.5

Bos: Calcaneus

Nr.	76/02	88/03	126/03	102/04	158/98	76/99	184/97
GL	123.0	124.0	137.0	135.0	124.0	134.0	117.5
GB	44.5	39.5	44.0	47.0	43.5	42.0	39.0

Bos: Calcaneus

Nr.	35/04	43/08	43/03	121/03	144/04	116/04	99/04
GB	40.5	41.5	44.5	41.0	37.5	36.5	44.0

Bos: Calcaneus

Nr.	89/00	93/99	115/96	23/97	68/96	92/95	76/96
GB	41.5	45.0	43.0	37.5	39.5	42.0	38.0

Bos: Calcaneus

Nr.	31/93
GB	38.0

Bos: Os centroquartale

Nr.	(30/05)	62/03	(?)	(18/08)	43/07	1/00	91/99
GB	51.5	43.0	46.0	51.0	50.0	57.0	54.0

Bos: Os centroquartale

Nr.	193/98	83/00	76/96
GB	48.0	54.0	51.5

Bos: Metatarsus

Nr.	95/03	118/03	54/03	127/03	127/04	193/98	80/00
GL	187.0	187.5	224.0	-	-	-	-
Bp	40.5	37.0	48.5	-	-	42.0	42.0
SD	20.0	21.5	28.0	23.5	22.5	-	-
DD	20.5	20.5	26.0	-	23.0	-	-
Bd	43.0	43.5	55.5	-	46.5	-	-
Dd	24.5	24.0	31.3	-	27.0	-	-
Sex	f	f	f	f	f	f	f

Bos: Metatarsus

Nr.	31/04	73/02	158/97	66/96	21/97	34/94	19/95
Bp	-	-	42.5	39.5	43.5	43.5	38.0

SD	23.5	-	-	-	-	-	21.5
Bd	-	24.0	-	-	-	-	-
Sex	f	f	f	f	f	f	f

Bos: Metatarsus

Nr.	60/93+55/94	(20/2/97)	73/02	39/04
GL	202.5	-	-	-
Bp	41.5	-	-	-
SD	20.0	-	-	-
Bd	44.5	47.5	-	45.5
Dd	-	-	24.0	27.0
Sex	f	f	f	f?

Bos: Metatarsus

Nr.	41/03	(11/03)	(28/05)	(29/04)	(30/05)	54/03	(9/08)
GL	-	-	-	-	228.0	-	-
Bp	-	47.0	48.0	-	45.0	47.5	51.5
SD	26.5	26.5	-	-	22.5	25.0	-
DD	24.0	-	-	25.0	24.5	-	-
Bd	54.0	-	-	58.5	53.0	-	-
Dd	-	-	-	32.0	31.0	-	-
Sex	c	c	c	c	c	c	c

Bos: Metatarsus

Nr.	1/00	1/00	66/95	163/97	115/96	41/95	110/97
GL	-	-	212.0	224.0	208.0	-	-
Bp	49.0	-	48.5	49.0	-	45.5	-
SD	-	-	26.5	28.0	26.0	-	27.5
DD	-	25.5	-	-	-	-	-
Bd	-	59.0	58.0	-	53.0	-	55.0
Dd	-	32.0	-	-	-	-	-
Sex	c	c	c	c	c?	c?	c?

Bos: Metatarsus

Nr.	(9/08)	78/99	116/97	40/05	(9/03)	38/04	50/08
Bp	51.5	-	46.0	49.5	-	-	-
DD	-	26.0	-	-	-	-	-
Bd	-	57.5	-	-	52.0	56.5	55.0
Dd	-	32.0	-	-	28.0	31.0	30.5
Sex	c	c	c?	c?	c?	c?	c?

Bos: Metatarsus

Nr.	41/03	(11/03)	(28/05)	(29/04)	(30/05)	52/93	42/95
GL	-	-	-	-	228.0	-	-
Bp	-	47.0	48.0	-	45.0	-	50.0
SD	26.5	26.5	-	-	22.5	-	-
DD	24.0	-	-	25.0	24.5	-	-
Bd	54.0	-	-	58.5	53.0	61.5	-
Dd	-	-	-	32.0	31.0	-	-
Sex	c	c	c	c	c	m	m?

Bos: Metatarsus

Nr.	59/01	83/00
Bp	51.5	51.5

Bos: Phalanx 1

Nr.	127/04	45/05	42/06	55/03	88/03	120/03	36/04
Glpe	51.0	55.0	53.0	51.5	52.5	49.5	49.0
Bp	26.0	26.5	24.0	27.0	25.0	27.5	29.0
SD	23.5	22.0	22.5	24.0	24.0	24.0	26.5
Bd	25.5	23.0	24.5	24.5	24.5	25.5	29.5

Bos: Phalanx 1

Nr.	54/03	54/03	42/03	(4/03)	121/03	54/03	80/04
Glpe	47.5	48.0	48.0	49.0	54.0	56.0	58.5
Bp	23.5	24.0	24.0	30.0	28.0	31.5	30.0
SD	22.0	21.0	20.0	24.5	25.5	30.0	27.0
Bd	22.0	22.5	22.0	27.5	28.0	29.5	29.0

Bos: Phalanx 1

Nr.	(30/05)	73/03	66/03	34/02	55/05	42/03	131/04
Glpe	59.0	52.5	58.0	60.0	53.0	56.0	54.5
Bp	30.0	27.0	29.5	29.5	28.0	28.0	31.0
SD	27.0	24.0	28.5	28.5	23.0	23.5	26.0
Bd	29.5	26.0	30.0	30.0	25.0	28.0	29.0

Bos: Phalanx 1

Nr.	55/03	48/06	50/03	144/04	(26/05)	33/05	137/04
Glpe	58.5	58.5	58.0	64.0	62.5	58.0	59.0
Bp	28.0	28.5	30.0	29.5	30.0	29.0	28.5
SD	26.0	25.5	26.0	25.0	25.0	25.5	25.5
Bd	28.5	26.0	29.0	27.0	26.5	27.0	27.5

Bos: Phalanx 1

Nr.	65/03	(28/05)	127/04	92/04	62/02	(20/07)	67/08
Glpe	58.5	62.0	51.0	53.5	48.0	59.0	52.5
Bp	31.0	29.5	21.5	19.5	24.0	25.5	27.0
SD	27.0	27.0	18.0	15.0	18.0	23.0	24.0
Bd	30.5	19.0	19.0	18.0	25.0	24.0	26.0

Bos: Phalanx 1

Nr.	50/07	78/99	93/99	175/98	17/00	24/99	24/99
Glpe	59.0	59.5	60.5	55.0	57.0	54.5	54.5
Bp	30.5	29.5	31.5	28.0	30.5	29.5	29.5
SD	27.0	24.5	27.0	24.0	23.5	23.5	24.5
Bd	29.0	28.0	30.0	27.5	26.5	27.0	27.0

Bos: Phalanx 1

Nr.	43/99	88/00	50/98	205/98	89/96	115/96	56/95
Glpe	56.0	50.5	54.5	47.5	60.0	57.0	54.5
Bp	29.0	28.5	25.5	22.0	30.0	25.5	26.5

SD	24.5	23.0	21.5	17.5	24.5	21.0	22.5
Bd	25.0	25.5	24.0	20.0	28.5	26.0	25.0

Bos: Phalanx 1

Nr.	112/96	101/96	112/96	54/96	94/97	158/97	21/97
Glpe	51.0	49.5	49.5	51.5	63.0	66.0	52.5
Bp	26.5	28.5	25.5	28.0	29.0	30.5	27.0
SD	22.0	25.0	20.5	22.5	25.0	27.5	21.0
Bd	25.0	26.5	22.5	26.0	27.5	32.0	26.0

Bos: Phalanx 1

Nr.	23/97	102/97	110/97	78/97	180/97	110/97	68/96
Glpe	51.5	57.0	51.5	57.5	47.5	53.0	59.5
Bp	26.0	33.5	30.5	24.5	23.0	28.0	32.0
SD	22.0	29.0	26.5	20.0	20.0	22.0	26.0
Bd	25.5	31.5	30.0	23.5	23.5	27.5	29.0

Bos: Phalanx 1

Nr.	115/96	65/95	115/96	119/96	115/96	32/95	38/95
Glpe	61.0	61.0	57.0	57.0	57.5	61.0	58.5
Bp	30.0	29.5	27.5	27.5	29.0	28.5	26.5
SD	25.0	25.0	22.5	22.5	26.0	24.0	22.0
Bd	28.0	29.0	29.5	27.0	29.5	29.5	25.0

Bos: Phalanx 1

Nr.	115/96	68/99	43/99	?	115/96	66/03	32/98
Glpe	56.5	66.0	61.0	55.0	60.0	-	61.5
Bp	27.5	31.5	31.5	29.0	30.0	27.0	32.5
SD	22.0	27.0	27.0	24.0	25.5	23.0	24.5
Bd	27.5	29.5	29.5	26.5	-	25.0	-

Bos: Phalanx 1

Nr.	(23/07)	48/07	(10/08)	43	159/98	51/04	0
Bp	30.0	29.5	32.0	-	-	-	28.5
SD	24.0	27.0	-	-	25.0	24.0	24.0
Bd	-	-	-	27.5	-	-	-

Bos: Phalanx 1

Nr.	47/05	127/04	65/00	37/98	35/01	75/00	35/01
Glpe	45.5	-	-	-	52.5	-	-
Bp	21.0	21.0	-	-	-	27.5	30.0
SD	-	-	22.0	24.5	21.0	21.5	-
Bd	-	-	29.5	27.5	-	-	-

Bos: Phalanx 1

Nr.	48/00	74/99	103/96	97/95
Glpe	-	-	56.5	-
Bp	-	31.0	30.0	32.5
Bd	22.0	-	-	-

***Bos*: Phalanx 2**

Nr.	(19/04)	76/02	144/04	51/03	127/03	(19/03)	127/04
Glpe	30.0	28.5	31.0	-	27.0	28.0	30.0
Bp	22.0	23.0	19.0	18.5	20.5	19.0	19.0
SD	15.0	15.5	14.5	13.5	13.0	13.0	13.0
Bd	16.0	13.5	16.5	14.0	17.5	15.5	15.0

***Bos*: Phalanx 2**

Nr.	51/04	102/04	79/02	127/04	51/02	75/00	89/00
Glpe	25.5	27.0	24.5	25.0	28.0	34.0	32.5
Bp	18.0	17.5	18.0	15.5	15.5	28.0	28.5
SD	11.5	10.5	13.5	10.5	10.0	22.5	21.0
Bd	13.5	13.0	14.0	11.5	10.0	24.0	24.0

***Bos*: Phalanx 2**

Nr.	78/99	65/00	115/96	89/96	37/95	90/96	44/95
Glpe	38.5	41.0	36.0	35.0	34.0	43.5	38.5
Bp	30.0	29.0	25.5	25.0	23.0	31.5	28.0
SD	24.0	23.0	20.0	19.0	18.0	23.5	21.5
Bd	25.5	23.5	21.5	21.0	18.5	27.0	22.5

***Bos*: Phalanx 2**

Nr.	35/07	1/00	101/96	90/96	59/96	159/98	73/03
Glpe	38.0	39.0	40.5	40.0	37.0	38.5	-
Bp	28.0	33.5	30.0	30.0	27.0	-	22.0
SD	21.5	26.5	24.0	23.5	22.0	26.0	-
Bd	22.0	28.5	25.5	25.5	23.0	25.5	-

***Bos*: Phalanx 2**

Nr.	57/06	48/07	(27/01)	(3/93)	108/96	49/95
Bp	15.0	32.0	-	-	-	-
SD	-	24.5	21.5	23.5	23.0	24.0
Bd	-	-	-	-	-	25.0

***Bos*: Phalanx 3**

Nr.	61/02	(21/05)	(6/03)	(19/05)	31/04	82/04	80/02
DLS	53.0	55.5	53.5	-	70.0	68.5	74.0
MBS	19.0	18.5	16.0	22.0	22.5	21.0	23.5
Ld	41.0	45.0	44.5	49.0	57.0	55.0	58.0

***Bos*: Phalanx 3**

Nr.	79/02	144/04	141/04	(4/03)	61/01	35/08	31/04
DLS	-	65.5	62.0	54.5	71.0	55.5	66.0
MBS	23.0	22.0	20.0	17.5	25.5	18.0	20.0
Ld	49.5	53.0	52.0	42.5	55.5	41.5	47.5

***Bos*: Phalanx 3**

Nr.	(11/08)	35/08	71/00	43/93	115/96	76/96
DLS	71.0	77.0	58.0	60.5	63.0	-
MBS	22.0	23.0	22.0	24.0	22.0	17.5
Ld	54.0	56.5	46.5	47.5	51.5	47.0

Capra aegagrus f. *hircus*

Capra: **Processus frontalis**

Nr.	127/04	116/04	88/03	42/03	(31/03)	69/03	35/03	115/96
Horncore basal circumference	110.0	95.0	100.0	95.0	100.0	100.0	110.0	90.0
Greatest diameter of the horncore base	40.0	33.0	35.0	35.0	33.0	36.0	37.0	34.0
Least diameter of the horncore base	23.0	21.5	21.0	21.0	25.0	23.0	27.0	20.5
Sex	f	f	f	f	f	f	f	f

Capra: **Processus frontalis**

Nr.	115/96	108/96	103/96	103/96	44/93	163/97	142/97	163/97
Horncore basal circumference	95.0	-	100.0	-	90.0	90.0	85.0	85.0
Greatest diameter of the horncore base	32.5	33.0	37.0	34.0	33.0	32.5	32.0	32.0
Least diameter of the horncore base	19.5	21.0	23.5	22.5	23.0	20.5	20.0	21.5
Lenth of the horncore on the front margin	-	-	163.0	-	-	-	-	-
Sex	f	f	f	f	f	f	f	f

Capra: **Cranium**

Nr.	205/98
Greatest breadth at the basis of the paraoccipital processes	37.5
Greatest breadth of the foramen magnum	53.5
Height of the foramen magnum	18.0

Capra: **Mandibula**

Nr.	127/04	(15/01)	48/99	81/00	32/98	115/96	114/96	86/96
Length of the angle: Gonion caudale-Infradentale	158.0	159.0	-	-	-	-	-	-
Length from the condyle: aboral border of the condyle process-Infradentale	168.0	166.5	-	-	-	-	-	-
Length: Gonion caudale-aboral border of thr alveolus M_3	52.0	41.0	-	-	-	-	-	-
Length of the horizontal ramus: aboral border of the alveolus M_3-Infradentale	110.0	114.0	-	-	-	-	-	-
Length: Gonion caudale-oral border of the alveolus of P_2	118.0	119.0	-	-	-	-	-	-
Length: Gonion caudale-the most aboral indentation of the mental frontale	135.0	132.0	-	-	-	-	-	-
Length of the cheektooth row, measured along the alveoli on the buccal side	68.0	74.5	72.5	68.5	64.5	73.0	69.0	68.5
Length of the molar row, measured along the alveoli on the buccal side	45.0	50.0	47.5	46.0	42.0	50.0	45.5	45.0
Length of the premolar row, measured along the alveoli on the buccal side	22.5	23.5	25.0	22.0	22.5	23.0	23.5	23.0
Length of the Diastema: oral border of the alveolus P_2-aboral border of the alveolus of I_4	37.5	-	-	-	-	-	-	-
Aboral height of the vertical ramus: Gonion ventrale-highest point of the condyle process.	70.0	66.5	-	-	-	-	-	-

Middle height of the vertical ramus: Gonion venyrale-deepest point of the mandibular notch	64.0	65.5	-	-	-	-	-	-
Height of the mandible behind M_3	35.5	-	34.0	35	33	-	-	-
Height of the mandible in front of M_1	21.5	22.0	21.0	21.0	23.0	-	-	-
Height of the mandible in front of P_2	17.5	18.0	14.0	18.0	18.0	-	-	-
Length of M_3	20.0	23.0	17.5	21.5	20.0	23.0	23.0	22.0
Breadth of M_3	8.0	8.5	7.5	8.0	8.0	8.5	9.0	9.0
Wear stage of M_3	(++)	(++)	0	(+)	(++)	(++)	(+++)	(+++)

Capra: Mandibula

Nr.	115/96	48/02	92/04	54/04	116/04	121/03	35/07	50/07
Length of the cheektooth row, measured along the alveoli on the buccal side	72.5	-	73.0	-	-	-	-	73.0
Length of the molar row, measured along the alveoli on the buccal side	49.5	-	46.0	-	-	-	-	47.0
Length of the premolar row, measured along the alveoli on the buccal side	23.0	28.5	25.5	-	-	-	-	24.5
Height of the mandible in front of M_1	-	19.5	19.5	-	-	-	-	-
Height of the mandible in front of P_2	-	15.0	17.0	-	-	-	-	-
Length of M_3	23.0	21.5	18.0	24.0	23.0	-	22.0	18.5
Breadth of M_3	8.0	7.5	7.0	9.0	8.0	8.5	9.0	7.5
Wear stage of M_3	(++)	(+)	(+)	(++)	(+)	(++)	(+)	0

Capra: Mandibula

Nr.	(28/01)	88/00	45/05	54/04	(4/03)
Length of the cheektooth row, measured along the alveoli on the buccal side	73.0	-	-	-	-
Length of the molar row, measured along the alveoli on the buccal side	47.5	47.0	-	-	-
Length of the premolar row, measured along the alveoli on the buccal side	24.0	-	24.0	25.0	-
Length of the Diastema: oral border of the alveolus P_2-aboral border of the alveolus of I_4	-	-	36.0	-	-
Height of the mandible in front of M_1	21.0	20.5	22.0	23.0	-
Height of the mandible in front of P_2	16.5	-	16.0	14.5	15.0
Length of M_3	20.5	-	-	-	-
Breadth of M_3	8.0	8.0	-	-	-
Wear stage of M_3	(+)	(++)			

Capra: Axis

Nr.	64/00	55/00
LCDe	53.0	-
BFcr	33.5	44.5
SBV	19.0	23.5
BFcd	17.5	23.5

Capra: Scapula

Nr.	66/96	116/4	83/04
GLP	34.5	-	-
LG	28.0	-	-

BG	22.5	-	-
SLC	21.5	21.5	19.0

Capra: Humerus

Nr.	121/03	40/05	118/03	116/04	62/02	34/04	17/00	48/00
SD	16.5	-	-	-	-	14.5	-	-
BT	30.5	29.0	29.5	29.5	27.5	-	28.0	30.5
Bd	31.0	30.5	30.5	30.5	28.5	-	31.0	-

Capra: Humerus

Nr.	98/97	19/97	?
BT	27.0	29.5	29.0
Bd	29.5	32.0	31.0

Capra: Radius

Nr.	76/02	73/02	35/04	62/04	121/03	160/97	88/95
Bp	30.5	32.5	30.0	30.0	30.0	31.0	32.5
BFp	29.0	30.0	29.0	28.0	29.0	29.0	31.5
SD	17.5	18.0	-	-	-	-	-

Capra: Radius

Nr.	13/98	102/96	51/01	121/03	99/04	50/04	137/04
Bp	30.5	33.0	-	-	-	-	-
BFp	29.0	31.0	-	-	-	-	-
SD	-	-	17.0	20.0	17.0	14.5	17.5

Capra: Radius

Nr.	102/96	51/01	121/03	99/04	50/04	137/04	(11/08)	48/02
Bp	33.0	-	-	-	-	-	-	-
BFp	31.0	-	-	-	-	-	-	-
SD	-	17.0	20.0	17.0	14.5	17.5	16.5	13.0

Capra: Radius

Nr.	48/02
Bd	29.5
BFd	26.0

Capra: Ulna

Nr.	(16/04)	76/02	62/04	13/98	77/99
BPC	15.5	22.0	17.0	21.5	24.5

Capra: Pelvis

Nr.	127/03
LA	33.5
LAR	29.5
Sex	f

Capra: Femur

Nr.	48/06	(11/08)	43/99
DC	20.5	19.0	19.5

***Capra*: Tibia**

Nr.	131/04	127/04	55/03	51/08	35/01	101/98	43/93	?
Bp	-	-	40.5	-	43.5	-	-	-
SD	16.0	-	-	16.0	-	-	-	-
Bd	27.0	26.0	-	28.0	-	24.5	25.0	25.5

***Capra*: Tibia**

Nr.	?	?
Bd	25.0	26.0

***Capra*: Talus**

Nr.	42/06
GLl	31.0
GLm	29.0
Dl	16.0
Bd	18.5

***Capra*: Calcaneus**

Nr.	(29/05)
GL	59.5
GB	22.0

***Capra*: Metacarpus**

Nr.	60/02	61/04	68/00	193/98	117/03	35/94
GL	-	-	-	-	-	111.0
Bp	24.0	23.0	-	-	-	22.5
SD	15.5	16.5	-	15.0	11.5	15.5
Bd	-	-	29.0	-	-	-
Dd	-	-	16.0	-	-	-

***Capra*: Metatarsus**

Nr.	(9/03)	(12/04)	(16/04)	54/03	13/00	78/99
GL	123.0	-	-	-	-	-
Bp	21.0	-	-	-	19.0	-
SD	13.0	-	-	13.0	11.5	14.0
DD	9.0	-	-	-	-	-
Bd	24.5	24.0	-	-	-	-
Dd	15.5	15.0	17.0	-	-	-

***Capra*: Phalanx 1**

Nr.	55/03	55/03	109/00	134/04
Glpe	39.0	40.0	45.0	-
Bp	11.5	13.0	15.5	-
SD	9.5	11.0	13.0	-
Bd	12.0	14.0	15.0	12.0

***Capra*: Phalanx 2**

Nr.	31/04
SD	9.0
Bd	12.5

Sus scrofa f. *domestica*

Sus: Cranium

Nr.	41/05	127/04
Greatest inner length of the orbit: ectorbitale-Entorbitale	34.0	-
Height of the lacrimal	18.5	-
Greatest breadth of the foramen magnum	-	25.0

Sus: Maxilla

Nr.	62/02	121/03	4/105	(29/04)	51/04	(17/07)
Length of the molar row (along the alveoli on the buccal side)	61.5	-	-	-	-	-
Length of M^3 measured near the base of the crown	28.0	26.0	31.0	-	34.0	31.0
Breadth of M^3 measured near the base of the crown)	17.0	18.5	17.0	17.0	18.5	18.0
Wear stage	0	(+++)	(+)	(++)	(++)	(+)

Sus: Maxilla

Nr.	0	77/99	166/97	(20/2/97)	140/97	54/95
Length of the premolar row (along the alveoli on the buccal side)	42.0	-	-	-	-	-
Length of M^3 measured near the base of the crown	-	29.5	28.5	30.0	31.5	31.5
Breadth of M^3 measured near the base of the crown)	-	18.0	17.0	17.0	17.5	17.5
Wear stage		0	(+)	0	0	0

Sus: Maxilla

Nr.	59/96	112/96	207/97	119/97	155/97	39/95
Length of M^3 measured near the base of the crown	31.5	32.0	33.0	30.5	28.5	30.5
Breadth of M^3 measured near the base of the crown)	15.5	18.5	15.5	15.0	13.0	15.0
Wear stage	(+)	(+)	0	(+)	0	0

Sus: Maxilla

Nr.	74/95	76/96
Length of M^3 measured near the base of the crown	30.0	31.5
Breadth of M^3 measured near the base of the crown)	13.5	14.0
Wear stage	0	(+)

Sus: Mandibula

Nr.	43/99	75/02	(30/05)	(30/05)	57/02	(19/05)
Length of the cheektooth row M_3-P_1 (measured along the alveoli on the buccal side)	110.0	-	-	-	-	-
Length of the cheektooth row M_3-P_2 (measured along the alveoli on the buccal side)	89.5	-	-	-	-	-

Length of the molar row (measured along the alveoli on the buccal side)	57.5	-	-	-	-	-
Length of the premolar row P_1-P_4 (measured along the alveoli on the buccal side)	53.0	-	-	-	-	43.5
Length of the premolar row P_2-P_4 (measured along the alveoli on the buccal side)	32.0	-	-	-	-	36.5
Greatest diameter of the canine alveolus	-		-	-	-	12.0
Height of the mandible behind M_3	-	46.0	39.0	38.0	-	-
Height of the mandible in front of M_1	-	43.0	-	-	-	-
Length of M_3 measured near the base of the crown	23.5	28.5	26.0	24.5	29.5	-
Breadth of M_3 measured near the base of the crown)	13.0	15.5	13.5	13.5	15.0	-
Wear stage	0	(+)	(+)	(+)	(+)	

Sus: **Mandibula**

Nr.	129/04	37/07	(1/08)	54/7	89/00	102/00	43/99
Length of the premolar row P_2-I_3 (measured along the alveoli on the buccal side)	-	-	-	48.0	-	-	-
Greatest diameter of the canine alveolus	11.5	-	-	14.5	13.5	-	-
Length of the median section of the body of mandible	-	-	-	-	-	-	61.0
Length of M_3 measured near the base of the crown	-	28.5	29.0	-	-	27.0	-
Breadth of M_3 measured near the base of the crown)	-	13.5	14.5	-	-	14.5	-
Wear stage		(+)	(+)			(+)	

Sus: **Atlas (Vertebrae)**

Nr.	127/04	52/06	63/03
GL	40.5	-	-
GLF	39.5	-	-
BFcr	51.5	-	-
BFcd	-	63.5	-
LAd	19.0	23.0	23.5
H	48.0	58.0	-

Sus: **Scapula**

Nr.	62/04	48/06	117/03	101/04	(8/03)	102/04	31/04	99/04
GLP	35.0	33.0	30.5	-	-	-	-	36.0
LG	30.5	26.5	-	-	-	-	-	-
BG	26.0	25.0	21.5	-	-	-	25.0	-
SLC	24.5	23.0	19.0	23.5	23.0	22.5	21.0	24.0

Sus: **Scapula**

Nr.	41/05	55/03	65/03	54/07	(24/07)	55/03	(10/08)	198/98
GLP	-	-	-	33.0	32.5	-	35.0	35.0

LG	33.5	-	-	29.5	26.0	-	27.0	29.0
BG	-	-	-	20.5	23.0	-	24.0	25.0
SLC	30.5	23.0	20.5	23.0	-	23.0	25.0	-

Sus: Scapula

Nr.	68/99	68/00	77/99	81/99	76/99	188/98	163/97	25/93
GLP	38.0	30.5	-	33.0	-	31.5	-	31.0
LG	30.5	22.5	-	25.5	-	24.5	-	26.5
BG	25.5	20.5	-	23.5	-	21.0	25.5	-
SLC	26.0	-	24.0	-	22.5	20.0	25.0	23.0

Sus: Scapula

Nr.	40/94	43/93	115/96	112/96	155/97	26/93	102/96	68/96
GLP	-	-	-	-	32.5	-	-	-
LG	-	-	-	-	29.5	-	-	-
BG	-	-	25.0	22.5	-	-	-	-
SLC	27.5	26.5	24.0	-	20.0	28.5	24.5	21.5

Sus: Humerus

Nr.	144/04	55/03	33/05	(9/03)	102/04	(28/05)	127/04	55/03
Bd	37.5	38.0	36.0	37.0	38.5	-	-	38.0
BT	29.5	30.0	30.0	30.0	33.0	-	29.0	29.5
SD	15.5	16.0	-	-	-	15.5	-	15.5

Sus: Humerus

Nr.	52/03	60/02	(9/08)	54/07	106/99	71/00	106/99	88/00
Bd	36.0	37.0	37.5	37.5	-	38.0	39.5	38.0
BT	30.0	31.0	30.0	31.0	30.0	30.5	31.0	30.5
SD	-	-	16.0	15.0	16.0	-	-	-

Sus: Humerus

Nr.	115/96	(2/95)	114/96	29/95	57/94	76/96	68/96	(7/94)
Bd	41.5	39.0	41.0	37.5	36.0	36.5	36.5	38.0
BT	32.5	30.0	34.0	28.5	28.5	27.5	29.0	28.5

Sus: Humerus

Nr.	166/97	114/96	29/95
Bd	36.0	41.0	37.5
BT	29.0	34.0	28.5

Sus: Radius

Nr.	55/03	127/04	76/03	41/03	?	88/00	77/99	76/99
GL	118.0	-	-	-	-	-	-	-
Bp	27.0	27.0	27.0	27.5	28.0	30.5	34.5	34.0
SD	18.0	-	-	-	-	-	-	-
BFd	28.0	-	-	-	-	-	-	-
Bd	32.5	-	-	-	-	-	-	-

***Sus*: Radius**

Nr.	59/99
Bp	28.0

***Sus*: Ulna**

Nr.	127/03	48/06	126/03	55/03	127/03	78/03	(17/05)	(30/05)
DPA	36.5	35.0	34.0	34.0	32.5	34.0	-	-
SDO	29.0	-	26.5	26.5	24.0	-	-	-
BPC	21.0	21.0	22.0	20.0	20.5	22.0	21.0	25.0

***Sus*: Ulna**

Nr.	117/03	66/96	67/08	(10/08)	40/99	52/01	106/99	(15/01)
DPA	34.5	34.5	-	-	-	31.0	35.5	-
SDO	-	25.5	-	-	32.0	-	27.5	-
BPC	21.5	19.0	22.0	19.5	26.0	18.0	22.0	21.0

***Sus*: Ulna**

Nr.	41/99	112/97	38/94	112/97	(10/08)	40/99	52/01	106/99
DPA	-	35.0	34.5	35.0	-	-	31.0	35.5
SDO	-	28.0	-	28.0	-	32.0	-	27.5
BPC	23.5	21.5	22.5	21.5	19.5	26.0	18.0	22.0

***Sus*: Ulna**

Nr.	(15/01)	41/99	38/94	67/08
DPA	-	-	34.5	-
BPC	21.0	23.5	22.5	22.0

***Sus*: Metacarpus II**

Nr.	115/96
GL	76.5
Bd	17.5

***Sus*: Metacarpus III**

Nr.	75/02
GL	70.5
Bp	18.0
B	15.0
Bd	16.5

***Sus*: Metacarpus IV**

Nr.	75/02
GL	60.5

***Sus*: Pelvis**

Nr.	144/04	36/00	60/00	60/00	45/94	171/97	115/96	115/96
LA	-	-	-	-	34.5	36.0	34.0	35.0
LAR	-	34.0	35.0	31.0	29.5	31.0	31.0	30.5
SB	13.0	15.5	-	-	-	-	-	-
SH	21.0	23.5	-	-	-	-	-	-

Sus: Pelvis

Nr.	61/04	98/04	98/04	109/04	41/03	79/02	(29/04)	55/03
LA	37.0	-	-	-	-	-	-	-
LAR	-	36.0	-	34.0	34.0	31.5	34.0	33.5
SB	14.5	13.0	15.0	13.0	-	-	-	-
SH	23.5	23.0	23.0	21.5	-	-	-	-

Sus: Pelvis

Nr.	76/03
LAR	33.0
SB	14.5
SH	21.5

Sus: Femur

Nr.	62/04	120/04	51/04	79/02	68/99
Bd	-	-	-	43.0	42.0
DC	25.0	24.5	21.5	-	-

Sus: Patella

Nr.	76/02	61/02
GB	39.5	37.0
GL	18.0	18.5

Sus: Tibia

Nr.	92/04	(26/03)	137/04	39/04	45/05	71/00	75/99	153/98
Bp	42.5	43.0	-	-	-	-	-	-
SD	-	-	19.0	19.0	-	-	-	-
Bd	-	-	30.0	29.0	31.0	29.5	30.0	30.0

Sus: Tibia

Nr.	24/99	71/00	46/94	158/97	158/97
Bd	27.0	27.5	34.5	31.5	29.0

Sus: Talus

Nr.	55/03	75/02	127/03	52/08	48/99	75/00	68/08	25/00
GLl	41.5	43.0	40.0	42.5	47.0	40.0	34.5	-
GLm	37.5	40.0	37.0	38.5	43.0	37.5	-	45.0
Dl	20.5	22.0	20.0	22.5	25.0	20.0	18.0	-
Dm	23.5	20.0	23.0	24.5	27.5	23.0	18.5	29.5
Bd	24.5	26.0	23.5	26.0	27.5	22.5	-	28.5

Sus: Talus

Nr.	(20/2/97)	51/03
GLl	39.0	-
GLm	36.5	-
Bd	-	23.0

Sus: Calcaneus

Nr.	(26/05)
GL	74.0
GB	22.0

Sus: Metatarsus III

Nr.	115/04	78/00
Bp	17.0	15.5
B	-	13.5

Sus: Metacarpus IV

Nr.	127/04	115/04	0	48/06
Bp	15.0	16.0	15.0	14.0

Sus: Phalanx 1

Nr.	79/02	69/04	89/00	94/97	115/03
Glpe	21.0	23.0	35.0	36.0	26.5
Bp	16.0	14.0	17.0	16.0	17.5
SD	12.5	11.5	14.0	13.0	14.0
Bd	14.0	12.5	15.5	15.0	-

Sus: Phalanx 2

Nr.	52/08	(7/99)	52/08	40/95	35/96
Glpe	28.5	29.0	23.0	22.5	23.0
Bp	18.5	18.0	17.0	16.0	13.0
SD	15.0	15.0	13.5	12.5	10.5
Bd	15.0	16.0	14.0	12.5	-

Sus: Phalanx 3

Nr.	71/04	(19/04)	(30/04)	44/05	51/98	76/96	35/94	207/97
DLS	37.0	36.0	31.0	30.0	26.0	38.5	34.0	34.5
Ld	34.0	34.0	29.0	29.0	24.5	36.5	33.0	31.5
MBS	13.0	13.5	11.5	9.0	11.0	15.5	12.5	14.0

Equus ferus f. *caballus*

Equus: Mandibula

Nr.	90/96+93/96
Length of the horizontal ramus: aboral border of the alveolus of M_3-Infradentale	284.0
Length of the cheektooth raw (measured along the alveoli on the buccal side)	169.0
Length of the molar raw (measured along the alveoli on the buccal side)	81.0
Length of the premolar raw (measured along the alveoli on the buccal side)	88.0
Length of P_2	30.5
Breadth of P_2	18.0
Length of P_3	27.0
Breadth of P_3	20.5
Length of P_4	27.0
Breadth of P_4	19.5
Length of M_1	24.5
Breadth of M_1	17.5
Length of M_2	24.0
Breadth of M_2	16.0
Length of M_3	31.5
Breadth of M_3	15.0
Height of the mandible in front of P_2	59.0
Sex	m

Equus: Scapula

Nr.	54/04	55/95	220/97
GLP	87.5	91.5	91.5
LG	54.0	61.5	59.0
BG	44.0	48.0	47.5
SLC	63.5	64.5	-

Equus: Humerus

Nr.	(30/05)	51/02	42/03	217/97	255/97
SD	34.0	-	-	36.5	37.0
Bd	84.5	77.0	-	78.5	82.0
BT	77.0	73.5	68.0	72.0	-

Equus: Radius

Nr.	225/97	(30/05)	32/98
GL	333.5	-	-
PL	313.0	-	-
Ll	309.0	-	
Bp	84.0	88.0	-
BFp	76.5	83.5	-
SD	40.0	-	-
CD	115.5	-	-
Bd	78.0	-	78.0
BFd	64.5	-	67.0

Equus: **Metacarpus**

Nr.	?	105/96
Bp	50.5	-
Dp	34.5	-
Bd	-	53.0
Td	-	40.5

Equus: **Pelvis**

Nr.	115/96	102/97	119/97
LAR	68.0	64.5	66.0
Sex	m	m	m

Equus: **Femur**

Nr.	71/95	(20/2/97)
GLC	359.0	-
DC	59.0	-
SD	41.0	-
CD	145.5	-
Bd	99.0	97.0

Equus: **Tibia**

Nr.	?	71/95	78/03	48/98	124/97
GL	343.5	345.0	-	-	337.5
Ll	319.0	310.5	-	-	-
Bp	82.0	-	-	-	-
SD	39.0	41.0	-	-	40.0
CD	-	116.5	-	-	-
Bd	70.5	77.0	66.5	80.5	-
Dd	42.0	51.5	-	47.0	-

Equus: **Talus**

Nr.	78/03	59/99	115/96	13/95	90/95
GH	57.0	57.0	64.5	57.0	56.5
GB	49.5	-	66.0	60.0	-
BFd	46.0	45.0	55.0	52.5	-
LmT	56.0	55.5	64.0	59.5	-

Equus: **Calcaneus**

Nr.	(88/96)	45/96	56/94
GL	-	-	102.0
GB	57.5	53.5	51.0

Equus: **Metatarsus**

Nr.	75/08	163/97
GL	276.0	260.0
GLl	277.5	-
Ll	274.5	-
Bp	54.5	-
Dp	45.0	-
SD	32.5	31.5

CD	-	105.0		
DD	27.0	-		
Bd	50.0	-		
Dd	39.5	-		

***Equus*: Phalanx 1**

Nr.	86/96 (ant)	66/97 (ant)	(4/02)	43
Gl	89.5	88.5	-	79.0
Bp	59.5	59.5	39.0	41.5
BFp	51.5	55.0	-	38.0
Dp	40.0	38.5	-	-
SD	36.5	40.0	30.5	33.0
Bd	50.0	54.0	-	40.5
BFd	47.0	46.0	-	-

***Equus*: Phalanx 2**

Nr.	43/08	59/99
Gl	48.0	46.0
Bp	54.5	51.0
BFp	48.0	-
SD	46.5	45.0
Dp	35.0	-
Bd	48.5	50.0

***Equus*: Phalanx 3**

Nr.	219/97 (ant)	84/95 (post)
Gl	-	59.0
GB	-	74.5
LF	32.0	-
BF	-	46.5
Ld	61.5	-

Canis lupus **f.** *familiaris*

Canis: Cranium

Nr.	52/03
Greatest breadth of the occipital condyles	26.0
Greatest breadth of the paraoccipital processes	34.0
Greatest breadth of the foramen magnum	16.5
Height of the foramen magnum: Basion-Opisthion	30.0

Canis: Radius

Nr.	127/04
Bd	25.0

Canis: Ulna

Nr.	45/05
BPC	16.5

Canis: Pelvis

Nr.	(4/03)
LAR	22.5

Canis: Calcaneus

Nr.	127/04
GL	51.0

Gallus gallus f. *domestica*

Gallus: Coracoid

GL	49.5	44.0	55.0	46.5	52.5	45.0	46.0
Lm	47.0	42.0	52.0	44.0	50.0	42.0	43.0
Bd	13.0	11.0	13.5	10.0	12.5	13.0	11.0
BF	8.5	9.5	12.0	9.0	11.5	11.0	9.0

Gallus: Humerus

GL	59.0	61.0	71.0	60.0	62.0	65.5	63.0
Bp	16.0	17.0	18.0	16.0	16.0	17.5	17.5
SC	6.5	6.0	6.0	6.0	6.0	6.5	6.5
Bd	13.0	13.5	15.0	13.0	13.0	13.5	14.0

Gallus: Humerus

GL	61.0	63.5	60.0	-	-
Bp	17.0	17.0	16.0	-	-
SC	6.5	7.0	6.5	-	-
Bd	13.0	13.0	13.0	13.0	10.5

Gallus: Radius

GL	53.0	59.0	53.5	66.0	-
SD	3.0	3.0	3.0	3.0	3.0
Bd	6.0	5.5	6.0	7.0	-

Gallus: Ulna

GL	62.0	65.0	65.0	62.0	57.0
Bp	7.5	9.0	-	7.5	8.0
Dip	11.0	12.0	-	11.0	11.0
SC	4.0	4.0	4.0	3.0	3.0
Did	9.0	9.0	9.0	7.0	8.0

Gallus: Femur

GL	68.0	76.0	-
Lm	68.0	71.0	-
Bp	14.0	16.0	-
SD	6.0	7.5	-
Bd	12.5	15.5	13.0

Gallus: Tibiotarsus

GL	94.0	98.5	92.0	96.0	92.0	-	-	-
La	90.0	94.5	88.0	92.0	88.5	105.0	-	-
Dip	18.0	18.0	16.5	17.0	17.0	-	16.0	-
SC	6.0	5.5	5.5	5.5	5.5	6.5	-	6.0
Bd	10.5	10.0	9.5	10.0	9.5	11.5	-	11.5
Td	10.5	11.0	10.5	10.0	10.0	13.0	-	11.5

Gallus: Tibiotarsus

SC	6.0	5.5	-
Bd	11.5	9.5	10.0

| Td | 11.5 | 10.5 | 10.0 | | | | |

***Gallus*: Tarsometatarsus**

GL	61.5	63.0	62.5	62.5	65.0	-	-
Bp	11.0	11.0	11.0	11.0	11.5	14.0	10.5
SD	5.5	5.0	5.5	5.5	6.0	-	-
Bd	11.0	11.5	11.0	11.0	12.0	-	-

Bison bonasus

Bison: Scapula

Nr.	(99/04)	(65/00)
GLP	72.5	-
LG	65.0	69.5
BG	54.0	-
SLC	63.0	-

Bison: Humerus

Nr.	92/04	75/02	62/04
Bd	-	84.0	-
BT	84.5	80.0	79.0

Bison: Radius

Nr.	(17/05)	(19/05)	48/07
Bp	84.5	86.0	-
BFp	75.5	78.0	
Bd	-	-	82.5
BFd	-	-	69.5

Bison: Ulna

Nr.	48/07	(17/05)	43/08	(62/04)	(167/98)	(51/98)
LO	142.0	-	-	-	-	-
DPA	96.5	-	-	-	-	-
SDO	79.5	-	-	-	-	-
BPC	-	50.0	58.0	53.0	51.0	62.0

Bison: Pelvis

Nr.	(52/03)	(48/02.)
LA	93.0	70.0
LAR	83.5	-
Sex	m	f

Bison: Femur

Nr.	(28/05)	(75/02)
Bp	118.5	147.5
DC	55.0	63.5

Bison: Tibia

Nr.	(111/04)	(82/04)	(127/03)	(99/04)	(91/03)	(42/03)
Bd	73.0	77.5	67.5	63.0	71.5	77.5
Dd	58.5	58.5	49.5	49.0	51.0	59.0

Bison: Talus

Nr.	(19/08)	(99/04)	(62/04)	(48/07)	(30/05)	(47/99)	(60/99)
GLl	77.0	78.0	83.0	77.0	76.0	73.0	79.0
GLm	68.5	74.0	76.0	71.5	72.0	67.0	70.5
DL	41.5	40.5	45.0	41.0	40.5	40.0	40.5

Dm	41.5	39.0	45.5	40.5	41.5	39.0	42.5
Bd	49.0	46.0	54.0	47.5	48.0	46.5	48.0

Bison: Calcaneus

Nr.	(116/04)	(131/04)	(99/04)	(59/00)
GB	54.5	54.0	47.0	54.0

Bos primigenius

Bos prim.: Talus

Nr.	(78/03)
GLl	82.5
GLm	77.0
Dl	45.5
Dm	48.5
Bd	54.0

Bos prim.: Calcaneus

Nr.	(127/03)
GB	61.0

Bos prim.: Os centroquartale

Nr.	(127/03)
GB	70.5

Cervus elaphus

Cervus: Cranium

Nr.	52/03
Proximal circumference of the burr	145.0

Cervus: Maxilla

Nr.	115/96	115/96
Length of the cheektooth row along the alveoli)	126.5	125.5
Length of the premolar row (along the alveoli)	54.0	53.5
Length of the molar row (along the alveoli)	75.5	73.5
Wear stage	(+)	(+)

Cervus: Mandibula

Nr.	83/04	66/03	82/04	83/00	27/93	42/94	96/94	87/96
Aboral height of the vertical ramus: Gonion ventrale-highest point of the condyle process	112.0	-	-	-	-	-	-	-
Middle height of the vertical ramus: Gonion ventrale-deepest point of the mandibular notch	110.5	-	-	-	-	-	-	-
Height of the mandible behind M_3	49.5	-	-	-	-	-	-	-
Length of M_3	30.0	30.0	31.5	32.5	34.0	32.5	31.0	30.5
Breadth of M_3	15.5	14.0	13.0	15.5	13.5	12.0	13.5	13.0
Wear stage	(++)	(++)	0	0	(++)	(+)	(+)	(+)

Cervus: Mandibula

Nr.	78/97
Length of M_3	33.0
Breadth of M_3	12.0
Wear stage	0

Cervus: Atlas (Vt)

Nr.	62/04
GL	94.0
BFcd	78.5
GLF	85.0
H	68.5

Cervus: Epistropheus (Vt)

Nr.	82/04
BFcr	75.0

Cervus: Scapula

Nr.	127/03	99/04	38/04	54/04	78/97	115/96	27/93	61/04
GLP	65.0	68.0	62.0	64.0	56.5	58.5	62.0	-
LG	48.5	50.5	49.0	50.5	44.5	46.5	47.0	-
BG	48.0	48.0	47.0	47.0	38.0	43.0	43.0	45.0
SLC	43.0	43.5	45.0	40.5	32.0	34.5	35.5	39.0

***Cervus*: Scapula**

Nr.	109/4	84/96	38/96
BG	49.5	44.0	-
SLC	-	42.5	39.5

***Cervus*: Humerus**

Nr.	131/04	80/04	(19/03)	158/97	112/04	(19/04)	131/04	35/07
Bp	-	-	68.5	82.0	-	-	-	-
SD	30.0	30.0	-	-	-	-	-	-
BT	60.5	-	-	-	53.5	51.5	57.5	52.0
Bd	68.0	-	-	-	61.0	59.5	62.5	56.0

***Cervus*: Humerus**

Nr.	106/99	106/99	219/97	52/93	35/93	171/97	78/97	116/96
BT	57.0	56.0	60.5	61.0	50.0	55.0	51.0	54.0
Bd	63.0	62.0	68.0	70.5	58.0	64.5	56.5	59.5

***Cervus*: Humerus**

Nr.	161/94	115/96	115/96	137/04	(9/06)	131/04	100/04	44/02
BT	53.5	60.0	52.0	58.5	57.0	62.0	56.0	50.0
Bd	59.5	68.0	64.0	-	-	-	-	-

***Cervus*: Humerus**

Nr.	127/03	111/97	55/94
BT	55.0	52.5	58.5

***Cervus*: Radius**

Nr.	144/04	(8/06)	49/04	137/04	31/04	(15/03)	79/03	48/07
Bp	63.5	59.0	59.5	51.5	67.0	66.5	62.5	57.0
BFp	59.0	55.0	56.5	51.0	60.5	60.0	58.5	55.5

***Cervus*: Radius**

Nr.	89/00	44/01	30/95	115/96	96/98	116/96	57/94	107/96
Bp	57.5	60.5	64.0	65.5	60.5	56.0	66.5	54.5
BFp	53.5	57.0	58.0	60.0	54.0	52.5	61.5	51.0

***Cervus*: Radius**

Nr.	141/97	(3/96)	87/95	36/04	83/04	(8/03)	34/03	71/04
Bp	55.5	54.0	65.0	-	-	-	-	-
BFp	52.0	51.5	58.0	-	-	-	-	-
Bd	-	-	-	54.0	51.5	55.5	52.5	54.5
BFd	-	-	-	53.5	49.0	53.5	50.5	52.5

***Cervus*: Radius**

Nr.	51/04	79/03	82/04	76/02	(19/04)	76/99	34/99	(3/99)
Bd	49.5	58.5	50.0	-	-	55.0	58.5	-
BFd	47.0	58.0	50.0	53.5	-	53.0	-	48.0
SD	-	-	-	-	35.5	-	-	-

Cervus: Radius

Nr.	114/96	119/97	88/96	217/97	76/96	115/96		
Bd	60.0	56.0	51.0	49.5	54.0	60.0		

Cervus: Ulna

Nr.	90/98	176/97	114/96	(20/2/97)	112/04	87/95	36/07	89/00
LO	90.0	91.5	78.0	91.0	-	86.5	-	-
DPA	62.0	59.5	52.0	61.0	57.3	60.5	60.5	57.0
SDO	49.0	51.5	47.5	52.5	51.0	-	-	-
BPC	31.5	38.0	33.5	34.0	30.0	32.5	37.0	31.0

Cervus: Ulna

Nr.	86/96	79/03	115/96	172/97	47/05	99/04	66/03	?
DPA	55.0	63.0	54.0	49.0	-	-	-	
BPC	33.0	35.5	32.0	28.5	34.0	36.0	31.0	35.0

Cervus: Metacarpus

Nr.	131/04	127/04	120/04	79/00	(11/03)	75/03	62/04	127/03
Bp	-	-	41.0	43.5	43.5	48.5	45.0	48.0
SD	25.0	27.0	-	-	-	-	-	-
DD	21.0	23.0	-	-	-	-	-	-
Bd	45.0	-	-	-	-	-	-	-
Dd	31.0	-	-	-	-	-	-	-

Cervus: Metacarpus

Nr.	115/96	(3/94)	115/96	89/95	114/04	115/96	66/96	115/96
Bp	48.0	48.0	48.5	44.5	-	-	-	-
DD	-	-	-	-	19.5	-	-	-
Bd	-	-	-	-	42.0	47.0	48.0	49.0

Cervus: Os carpale II+III

Nr.	92/04	120/04
GB	26.5	27.5

Cervus: Pelvis

Nr.	(27/07)	114/96	90/96	115/96	102/96	115/96	138/04	(19/04)
LA	57.0	62.5	63.0	62.0	63.0	62.0	54.5	56.0
Sex		m	m	m	m?	m?		

Cervus: Pelvis

Nr.	111/04	95/03	121/03	(27/07)
LA	59.5	57.0	54.5	57.0

Cervus: Femur

Nr.	220/97	138/04	52/03	65/03	45/05	(15/01)	(4/94)	74/97
Bp	82.5	-	-	-	-	-	-	76.5
DC	34.5	34.5	41.5	39.0	36.0	37.5	37.5	-

Cervus: Patella

Nr.	47/05	61/02	51/08
GL	61.0	56.5	53.0
GB	47.0	43.0	46.5

Cervus: Tibia

Nr.	(26/05)	42/03	79/03	(23/08)	(9/95)	38/94	34/94	98/04
Bp	85.5	77.0	87.0	72.5	87.0	81.0	81.5	-
Bd	-	-	-	-	-	-	-	51.0
SD	-	-	-	-	-	-	-	32.0

Cervus: Tibia

Nr.	79/02	83/04	(6/03)	137/04	83/04	112/04	(6/03)	83/04
Bd	52.5	59.5	57.5	56.0	56.5	53.0	54.0	54.0
SD	31.0	-	-	-	-	-	-	-

Cervus: Tibia

Nr.	82/04	131/04	42/03	35/07	(10/08)	4/00	51/98	116/97
Bd	54.5	52.0	49.5	54.0	54.0	51.0	51.0	56.0

Cervus: Tibia

Nr.	101/96	53/94	119/96	89/96	54/96	213/97
Bd	56.0	56.5	58.0	56.0	52.5	50.0

Cervus: Metatarsus

Nr.	53/06	131/04	99/04	82/04	111/04	112/04	55/03	127/3
GL	315.0	300.5	287.0	-	-	-	-	-
Bp	43.0	36.5	38.0	42.0	-	-	39.0	38.0
SD	28.5	22.5	20.0	24.0	-	-	23.5	-
DD	25.5	23.0	22.5	25.0	24.0	25.5	-	-
Bd	47.0	44.0	-	46.0	50.0	47.0	-	-
Dd	33.0	29.5	31.0	32.0	-	32.0	-	-

Cervus: Metatarsus

Nr.	76/02	207/97	112/97
Bp	38.0	38.5	43.0

Cervus: Talus

Nr.	98/04	92/04	83/04	(17/04)	126/03	42/03	62/03	78/08
GLl	59.0	62.5	60.5	58.5	60.0	54.0	62.5	57.5
GLm	54.0	58.0	58.0	56.0	54.0	51.0	57.0	53.0
Dl	31.0	33.0	33.0	31.0	31.5	28.0	34.0	31.0
Dm	32.0	34.0	34.0	34.0	31.0	30.5	35.0	31.0
Bd	36.0	38.0	39.5	37.0	35.5	33.5	39.0	34.0

Cervus: Talus

Nr.	102/00	116/98	89/00	(5/98)	55/95	94/97	55/95	96/96
GLl	59.0	58.0	57.5	58.5	59.0	57.5	60.5	56.5
GLm	56.0	54.0	54.5	53.5	54.5	54.0	54.0	53.5
Dl	31.0	32.0	31.0	31.0	32.0	31.0	32.5	31.5

Dm	32.5	31.5	33.5	32.5	32.5	32.0	33.5	31.0
Bd	37.0	35.5	35.5	38.0	37.0	35.5	37.0	36.5

***Cervus*: Talus**

Nr.	**141/97**	**80/95**	**16/99**	**68/01**	**47/96**	**27/95**	**66/96**	**73/02**
GLl	53.5	61.5	59.0	-	57.5	57.5	58.5	55.5
GLm	49.5	58.0	54.5	54.0	53.0	54.5	56.0	-
Dl	30.5	32.5	32.0	-	30.0	33.0	32.0	-
Dm	31.0	34.0	-	32.5	-	-	-	-
Bd	36.5	40.0	36.5	37.0	36.5	-	-	-

***Cervus*: Talus**

Nr.	**36/04**
Bd	41.0

***Cervus*: Calcaneus**

Nr.	**98/04**	**42/03**	**83/04**	**51/01**	**41/95**	**115/96**	**141/97**	**207/97**
GL	128.0	117.0	137.0	135.0	123.5	118.0	117.5	119.0
GB	43.5	38.0	44.5	42.5	37.5	38.0	38.5	38.5

***Cervus*: Calcaneus**

Nr.	**115/04**	**76/02**	**38/95**	**18/97**	**66/96**
GB	38.0	38.5	40.0	42.5	37.0

***Cervus*: Os centroquartale**

Nr.	**83/04**	**131/04**	**76/02**	**116/04**	**48/07**
GB	47.5	44.5	45.0	44.5	40.5

***Cervus*: Phalanx 1**

Nr.	**62/04**	**126/03**	**61/04**	**119/04**	**(17/05)**	**116/04**	**120/03**	**62/04**
Glpe	65.5	66.5	63.0	66.0	65.5	61.0	60.0	59.0
Bp	25.5	26.0	24.0	24.5	25.0	25.0	23.0	25.0
SD	20.0	20.5	19.5	22.0	20.0	20.5	18.5	20.0
Bd	23.0	23.5	22.5	23.0	22.0	23.0	22.0	23.0

***Cervus*: Phalanx 1**

Nr.	**61/02**	**127/04**	**127/04**	**116/04**	**(16/04)**	**55/03**	**99/04**	**34/04**
Glpe	63.0	59.0	59.0	62.0	63.0	60.5	63.0	60.0
Bp	22.5	22.5	22.0	23.0	22.0	24.0	25.0	24.5
SD	19.5	18.0	18.0	20.5	19.0	18.5	19.5	21.0
Bd	23.0	22.0	21.0	21.5	22.0	22.5	23.0	23.5

***Cervus*: Phalanx 1**

Nr.	**42/03**	**137/04**	**88/03**	**51/01**	**65/03**	**134/04**	**111/04**	**83/04**
Glpe	60.0	60.5	64.5	65.0	62.0	63.0	61.0	59.5
Bp	23.0	23.0	23.0	23.5	24.5	24.0	25.0	21.0
SD	18.5	20.0	19.0	19.0	20.0	19.5	21.0	18.5
Bd	22.0	22.0	22.0	22.5	22.0	23.0	25.0	25.0

Cervus: **Phalanx 1**

Nr.	114/04	55/03	97/04	99/04	99/04	141/04	42/03	127/04
Glpe	59.0	58.0	57.0	60.0	60.0	58.0	55.5	58.5
Bp	22.0	21.0	21.0	24.0	24.0	22.5	21.0	21.0
SD	18.5	18.0	17.5	18.5	19.0	18.5	17.0	17.0
Bd	21.0	20.5	21.0	22.0	22.0	21.5	19.5	20.0

Cervus: **Phalanx 1**

Nr.	59/06	73/02	25/97	35/04	53/04	76/03	62/04	127/04
Glpe	56.5	67.5	56.5	-	-	-	-	-
Bp	20.0	-	21.0	-	-	-	-	-
SD	16.0	19.0	17.0	-	-	-	-	20.0
Bd	19.5	23.5	-	22.5	23.0	20.0	22.0	25.0

Cervus: **Phalanx 1**

Nr.	95/00	121/3
Bd	22.5	21.5

Cervus: **Phalanx 2**

Nr.	83/04	114/04	111/04	116/04	99/04	82/04	79/02	127/04
GL	50.0	45.5	47.0	48.0	47.0	45.0	45.0	47.5
Bp	26.0	24.0	23.0	25.0	24.0	24.5	22.5	22.5
SD	18.5	18.0	16.5	17.5	17.0	17.5	16.5	17.0
Bd	23.0	21.0	21.5	20.0	20.0	21.0	19.5	19.5

Cervus: **Phalanx 2**

Nr.	111/04	98/04	99/04	(26/05)	83/04	82/04	111/04	48/02
GL	48.0	45.5	45.5	42.5	40.0	43.0	43.5	41.5
Bp	24.5	22.5	23.0	21.5	20.5	22.5	22.0	20.0
SD	18.0	17.0	16.5	15.5	15.0	17.0	15.5	15.5
Bd	20.0	19.0	20.5	18.5	17.0	18.0	20.0	19.0

Cervus: **Phalanx 2**

Nr.	210/98	177/98	129/03	115/04	62/06	107/03	38/04	92/04
GL	46.5	43.0	44.0	42.5	41.0	50.0	45.5	48.0
Bp	20.5	21.5	-	-	-	23.5	22.5	23.0
SD	15.0	15.0	16.0	15.0	-	-	-	-
Bd	18.0	19.0	18.0	17.5	16.5	20.0	18.0	20.0

Cervus: **Phalanx 2**

Nr.	(19/05)	111/04	(19/07)
Bp	-	21.0	21.5
Bd	21.5	-	-

Cervus: **Phalanx 3**

Nr.	61/02	115/04	63/03	68/99	37/99
Ld	50.5	-	-	-	-
MBS	15.0	15.0	13.5	13.5	15.0

137

Capreolus capreolus

Capreolus: Cranium

Nr.	141/04	74/02	57/03	125/03	71/00	129/98
Proximal circumference of the burr	-	-	85.0	50.0	70.0	50.0
Distal circumference of the burr	-	-	-	-	65.0	-
Greatest breadth of the foramen magnum	18.5	19.0	-	-	-	-

Capreolus: Mandibula

Nr.	112/04	96/00	60/99	96/00	60/99	0	59/96
Length of the cheektooth row along the alveoli)	69.5	67.0	62.5	67.0	62.5	-	-
Length of the molar row (along the alveoli)	40.5	39.0	36.0	39.0	36.0	-	40.0
Length of the premolar row (along the alveoli)	29.0	27.5	26.0	27.5	26.0	30.0	-
Length of the diastema (oral border of the alveolus of P_2-aboral border of the alveolus of I_4)	40.5	-	-	-	-	42.0	-
Height of the mandible behind M_3	27.0	28.5	25.0	28.5	25.0	-	-
Height of the mandible in front of M_1	18.0	19.5	17.5	19.5	17.5	-	-
Height of the mandible in front of P_2	15.0	18.5	18.0	18.5	18.0	-	-
Length of M_3 measured near the base of the crown	15.5	16.0	15.0	16.0	15.0	-	-
Breadth of M_3 measured near the base of the crown)	8.0	7.5	7.5	7.5	7.5	-	-
Wear stage	(+)	(+)	(++)	(+)	(++)		

Capreolus: Scapula

Nr.	62/04	51/03	89/00	111/04	45/05	80/02	69/04	42/06
GLP	30.0	31.0	28.0	27.0	30.0	28.0	28.5	-
LG	29.0	25.0	23.0	22.5	24.0	24.0	23.0	23.0
BG	23.0	22.5	22.5	21.0	23.5	20.0	21.5	-
SLC	19.5	20.0	18.0	-	-	-	-	-

Capreolus: Scapula

Nr.	137/04	65/03	36/04	67/00
BG	-	-	-	20.5
SLC	17.0	16.0	16.5	17.5

Capreolus: Humerus

Nr.	65/03	80/04	(20/05)	111/04	78/03	126/03	79/03	54/07
Bd	31.0	30.5	27.5	30.5	31.0	30.0	30.0	29.5
BT	27.0	26.0	25.0	26.0	27.5	25.5	26.0	27.0
SD	-	-	-	-	-	13.0	-	-

Capreolus: Humerus

Nr.	83/00	68/00	89/00	54/95	86/96	95/97	103/97	127/03
Bd	28.0	31.5	30.0	31.0	30.5	32.0	31.0	-
BT	25.5	26.0	27.0	24.5	26.0	26.0	-	-
SD	-	-	-	-	-	-	-	13.0

Capreolus: Humerus

Nr.	54/03	(9/03)	43/02	50/04	72/01	51/03
BT	-	26.0	27.5	-	25.0	25.0
SD	13.5	-	-	13.0	-	-

Capreolus: Radius

Nr.	36/08	69/96	30/94	220/97	83/97	0	26/93	111/04
Bp	26.5	27.0	26.0	26.5	26.5	28.5	26.5	-
BFp	25.0	25.0	25.0	25.0	24.0	27.0	-	-
SD	-	-	-	-	-	-	-	16.0

Capreolus: Radius

Nr.	60/02	82/04
SD	17.0	-
Bd	-	28.5
BFd	-	26.0

Capreolus: Ulna

Nr.	38/06	53/04	99/04	48/06
SDO	21.0	-	-	-
DPA	24.0	-	26.5	-
BPC	13.5	15.5	16.0	14.0

Capreolus: Metacarpus

Nr.	51/04	55/03
Bp	20.5	20.5
SD	11.0	13.0

Capreolus: Pelvis

Nr.	66/03	61/04	42/03	60/99
LA	30.5	29.0	28.0	28.0
SB	10.0	10.0	-	-

Capreolus: Femur

Nr.	71/04	35/02	52/08
Bp	-	-	48.0
DC	19.5	-	20.0
SD	15.5	16.0	-

Capreolus: Patella

Nr.	48/99
GB	18.5

Capreolus: Tibia

Nr.	126/03	48/06	51/02	99/04	(9/03)	42/07	129/98	79/00
Bp	43.5	-	-	-	-	-	-	-
SD	-	-	17.5	16.5	-	11.0	-	-
Bd	-	26.0	28.5	29.0	27.5	-	26.5	28.0

Capreolus: Talus

Nr.	44/05	(21/05)	80/04	127/03	(30/04)	68/96	89/96	41/94
GLl	30.0	29.0	29.5	31.5	30.0	32.5	31.0	29.0
GLm	28.5	27.0	28.5	30.0	28.0	31.5	30.5	28.5
Dl	16.5	15.0	16.0	18.0	16.0	18.0	18.0	16.0
Dm	16.5	17.0	16.0	18.0	17.0	18.0	18.5	16.5
Bd	-	18.5	19.0	20.0	19.0	20.5	20.0	18.5

Capreolus: Calcaneus

Nr.	121/03	34/04	83/99	76/02
GL	65.0	66.0	65.0	-
GB	23.0	19.5	23.0	21.5

Capreolus: Os centroquartale

Nr.	95
GB	24.0

Capreolus: Metatarsus

Nr.	76/03	68/00	90/96
Bp	-	20.0	21.5
SD	12.5	12.5	-

Capreolus: Phalanx 1

Nr.	47/05	61/02	48/06	129/98	13/98	84/99
Glpe	38.5	40.0	-	33.5	35.0	40.5
Bp	11.0	12.0	-	10.5	11.0	11.5
SD	9.0	8.5	7.5	7.5	8.0	7.5
Bd	11.0	10.5	8.5	9.0	9.0	10.5

Capreolus: Phalanx 2

Nr.	98/04	76/01	99/98
Glpe	26.0	28.0	28.5
Bp	9.5	10.5	11.0
SD	7.0	7.0	8.0
Bd	6.5	7.5	8.0

Alces alces

Alces: Mandibula

Nr.	141/04	162/98
Aboral height of the vertical ramus: Gonion ventrale-highest point of the condyle process	127.0	-
Length of M_3	-	38.0
Breadth of M_3	-	21.0
Wear stage	-	0

Alces: Pelvis

Nr.	?
LA	55.0

Alces: Metatarsus

Nr.	99/04
Bp	53.5
SD	31.5

Alces: Phalanx 1

Nr.	99/04	134/04	127/03	83/04	(23/07)	22/95	45/96
Glpe	83.0	84.5	75.0	72.0	77.5	81.0	80.5
Bp	35.0	33.5	30.0	27.0	31.0	31.0	32.5
SD	24.0	25.0	22.0	21.5	22.5	24.0	23.5
Bd	29.0	32.0	26.5	25.0	26.0	29.5	28.0

Alces: Phalanx 2

Nr.	114/04
Glpe	61.0
Bp	31.0
SD	21.5
Bd	25.0

Sus scrofa

Sus scrofa: **Cranium**

Nr.	102/04	(17/05)
Greatest inner length of the orbit: ectorbitale-Entorbitale	41.5	40.0

Sus scrofa: **Maxilla**

Nr.	34/04	112/04	(11/02)	112/04	102/04	87/03	(8/03)	(16/04)	121/03
Length of the molar row (along the alveoli on the buccal side)	84.0	-	-	-	-	83.5	-	-	85.0
Length of M^3 measured near the base of the crown	40.5	38.5	43.0	39.5	44.0	41.0	40.5	47.5	40.5
Breadth of M^3 measured near the base of the crown)	18.5	23.0	22.5	25.0	23.0	21.0	20.0	25.0	24.0
Wear stage	0	0	(+)	(+++)	(+)	(+++)	(++)	(+++)	0

Sus scrofa: **Maxilla**

Nr.	49/04	78/02	?	205/98	131/98	76/02	114/96	180/97	158/97
Length of the molar row (along the alveoli on the buccal side)	81.0	-	-	-	-	-	-	-	-
Length of the premolar row (along the alveoli on the buccal side)	-	-	-	56.0	-	-	-	-	-
Length of M^3 measured near the base of the crown	36.0	36.5	42.5	-	-	41.0	38.5	40.0	42.0
Breadth of M^3 measured near the base of the crown)	-	23.5	23.0	-	20.0	23.5	23.0	23.5	24.5
Wear stage	0	(++)	-	-	0	0	(++)	(++)	(+++)

Sus scrofa: **Maxilla**

Nr.	25/93	141/97	155/97	35/96	83/97	158/97
Length of M^3 measured near the base of the crown	42.0	44.5	49.0	40.0	41.0	44.0
Breadth of M^3 measured near the base of the crown)	21.5	24.5	24.5	23.5	23.5	24.0
Wear stage	(+)	(++)	(++)	(+)	(+++)	0

Sus scrofa: **Mandibula**

Nr.	52/03	54/03	71/04	62/04	112/04	52/03	81/04	102/04	141/04
Length of the cheektooth row M_3-P_1 (measured along the alveoli on the buccal side)	125.5	-	-	-	-	-	-	-	-
Length of the molar row (measured along the alveoli on the buccal side)	80.0	-	-	-	-	-	-	-	-
Length of the premolar row P_1-P_4 (measured along the alveoli on the buccal side)	42.0	42.0	48.0	-	-	47.0	-	-	-
Length of the premolar row P_2-I_3 (measured along the alveoli on the buccal side)	-	-	-	76.5	-	-	56.5	64.5	60.0
Height of the mandible behind M_3	51.5	-	-	-	-	-	-	-	-
Height of the mandible in front of M_1	44.0	-	-	-	-	-	-	-	-

Height of the mandible in front of P_2	50.5	63.0	-	-	-	-	-	-	-
Greatest diameter of the canine alveolus	23.5	-	18.0	36.0	27.0	-	17.5	17.0	24.5
Length of M_3 measured near the base of the crown	38.5	-	-	-	-	-	-	-	-
Breadth of M_3 measured near the base of the crown)	19.0	-	-	-	-	-	-	-	-
Wear stage	(+)								

Sus scrofa: Mandibula

Nr.	83/04	116/04	82/04	39/03	131/04	45/05	76/96	105/96	220/97
Length of the cheektooth row M_3-P_1 (measured along the alveoli on the buccal side)	-	-	-	-	-	-	153.0	-	-
Length of the molar row (measured along the alveoli on the buccal side)	-	-	-	-	-	-	86.5	85.0	83.5
Length of the premolar row P_1-P_4 (measured along the alveoli on the buccal side)	43.5	-	-	-	-	40.0	-	-	-
Length of the premolar row P_2-I_3 (measured along the alveoli on the buccal side)	47.5	62.5	-	64.0	69.0	-	-	-	-
Greatest diameter of the canine alveolus	16.0	22.0	17.0	19.5	27.5	-	-	-	-
Length of M_3 measured near the base of the crown	-	-	-	-	-	-	44.0	46.0	45.0
Breadth of M_3 measured near the base of the crown)	-	-	-	-	-	-	19.0	20.0	19.5
Wear stage							(+)	(++)	(++)

Sus scrofa: Mandibula

Nr.	117/97	219/97	88/96	66/97	170/97	0	141/97	73/97	94/97
Length of the molar row (measured along the alveoli on the buccal side)	94.5	-	-	-	-	-	-	-	-
Length of M_3 measured near the base of the crown	49.0	46.0	46.5	44.0	44.0	47.0	42.5	45.5	41.0
Breadth of M_3 measured near the base of the crown)	20.0	18.5	19.0	20.0	18.5	20.0	19.5	18.5	18.0
Wear stage	0	(++)	(+)	(++)	(+++)	0	0	(+++)	(+)

Sus scrofa: Mandibula

Nr.	(20/2/97)	102/04	(19/03)	120/03	106/03	126/03	(17/04)	(9/03)	114/04
Length of M_3 measured near the base of the crown	46.0	40.5	45.5	44.0	44.0	37.0	45.0	40.5	38.5
Breadth of M_3 measured near the base of the crown)	19.5	23.5	21.0	19.0	18.0	19.5	21.0	18.0	18.0
Wear stage	0	(+++)	(+)	0	0	0	(+++)	(+)	(+)

Sus scrofa: Atlas (Vt)

Nr.	54/03	99/04	76/02	120/04	59/00	199/97	43/93
GLF	55.5	53.0	-	-	-	55.5	54.5
BFcr	65.0	66.0	66.5	64.0	-	67.5	63.5
BFcd	66.5	64.0	-	-	-	-	-

Lad	34.0	28.0	-	26.5	29.0	-	-	
H	64.0	55.0	61.0	55.0	68.0	-	-	

Sus scrofa: Scapula

Nr.	**81/04**	**131/04**	**42/06**	**87/03**	**106/03**	**76/99**	**105/96**	**59/96**	**105/96**
GLP	52.0	41.0	42.5	46.5	45.0	47.0	51.5	48.0	45.5
LG	42.0	32.5	33.5	36.5	37.5	38.0	41.5	36.0	36.5
BG	34.0	32.0	28.5	33.5	31.0	31.5	36.5	31.0	32.0
SLC	33.5	28.0	32.0	33.5	32.0	31.0	38.0	34.5	31.0

Sus scrofa: Scapula

Nr.	**38/94**	**19/95**	**115/96**	**(29/04)**	**115/96**	**31/94**	**42/94**	**78/03**	**166/97**
GLP	46.5	47.0	44.0	44.5	47.0	47.0	-	-	-
LG	38.5	37.5	37.0	36.0	39.0	-	41.5	34.0	-
BG	34.0	33.0	34.0	31.0	-	-	36.0	-	32.0
SLC	31.0	32.5	33.5	-	30.0	38.0	36.0	33.0	31.0

Sus scrofa: Scapula

Nr.	**79/03**	**54/03**	**0**	**25/93**	**66/96**
BG	-	-	-	37.5	-
SLC	32.0	35.0	30.5	36.5	34.5

Sus scrofa: Humerus

Nr.	**71/04**	**35/01**	**65/03**	**121/03**	**0**	**82/04**	**63/03**	**115/96**	**115/96**
Bd	46.5	56.0	58.5	53.0	50.5	50.0	50.5	58.0	55.0
BT	41.0	44.0	45.5	42.0	39.5	41.5	39.5	42.0	41.0
SD	21.0	27.0	-	-	-	-	-	-	-

Sus scrofa: Humerus

Nr.	**66/97**	**105/96**	**75/96**	**116/96**	**101/96**	**115/96**	**114/96**	**(20/2/97)**	**(23/03)**
Bd	54.5	49.5	51.5	56.0	52.5	48.0	47.0	47.0	-
BT	39.5	37.0	39.5	40.5	39.0	36.0	35.5	36.5	42.0

Sus scrofa: Humerus

Nr.	**(17/05)**	**131/04**	**13/00**	**217/97**
BT	-	-	42.0	43.5
SD	19.5	22.0	-	-

Sus scrofa: Radius

Nr.	**112/04**	**(11/04)**	**55/03**	**83/04**	**42/03**	**54/03**	**43/02**	**98/04**	**112/04**
Bp	40.5	35.5	38.5	35.0	37.0	37.5	36.0	38.0	37.5

Sus scrofa: Radius

Nr.	**112/04**	**65/03**	**(12/04)**	**82/04**	**35/04**	**39/03**	**43/08**	**51/98**	**66/96**
Bp	40.0	37.5	39.5	39.0	37.5	38.0	36.0	35.0	37.5

Sus scrofa: Radius

Nr.	**86/96**	**176/97**	**27/93**	**37/94**	**176/97**	**101/96**	**114/96**	**121/03**	**(24/03)**
Bp	37.0	36.5	35.0	39.0	36.5	-	-	-	-
Bd	-	-	-	-	-	42.5	45.0	46.0	39.5

Sus scrofa: Radius

Nr.	76/02	88/03	51/04	51/04	41/03	121/03	43/02
Bd	43.0	44.5	41.0	44.0	-	45.0	45.5
SD	-	-	-	-	28.5	-	-

Sus scrofa: **Ulna**

Nr.	78/03	54/03	48/07	158/97	226/97	54/96	184/97	54/03	42/03
DPA	49.5	52.0	56.5	53.0	48.0	55.5	48.5	51.5	42.0
SDO	36.0	43.0	44.0	44.0	39.0	42.5	38.0	-	-
BPC	25.0	29.5	29.0	31.0	28.0	30.0	-	28.5	30.0

Sus scrofa: **Ulna**

Nr.	111/04	42/03	61/04	42/03	76/02	178/98	106/99	66/96	66/96
DPA	48.0	53.0	49.0	49.5	47.5	50.0	44.0	50.0	43.5
BPC	25.5	30.5	30.0	27.5	28.0	26.5	26.0	28.0	30.0

Sus scrofa: **Ulna**

Nr.	36/97	76/02	173/98	(16/04)	111/04	43/02	62/04	49/04	(28/05)
DPA	51.0	48.0	41.0	54.5	-	-	-	-	-
SDO	41.5	-	-	-	46.0	-	-	-	-
BPC	-	27.0	-	-	28.5	26.5	28.0	26.0	29.5

Sus scrofa: **Ulna**

Nr.	91/03	39/03	114/04
BPC	31.0	29.0	24.5

Sus scrofa: **Metacarpus II**

Nr.	52/03	?	(10/08)	112/96	74/97	95/97
GL	70.0	-	-	68.5	98.5	-
Bp	-	21.0	19.0	-	-	-
Bd	-	-	-	13.0	26.0	25.0

Sus scrofa: **Metacarpus III**

Nr.	67/00	55/03	83/04	(6/03)	80/04	117/03	62/04	42/03	131/98
GL	98.5	-	-	-	-	-	-	-	-
Bp	24.0	21.0	24.0	21.0	22.5	23.0	23.0	22.0	-
B	20.0	-	-	-	-	-	-	-	-
Bd	23.5	-	-	-	-	-	-	-	23.0

Sus scrofa: **Metacarpus IV**

Nr.	45/05	79/02	61/04	74/02	75/02	42/03	41/03	37/07	38/94
GL	95.0	66.0	-	-	-	-	-	-	75.5
Bp	20.5	-	20.0	20.5	20.5	20.0	18.5	23.0	-
B	16.0	-	17.0	16.0	-	16.5	-	-	-
Bd	21.0	-	-	-	-	-	-	-	15.0

Sus scrofa: **Pelvis**

Nr.	89/96	38/94	66/96	115/96	(5/95)	166/97	17/93	82/04	61/04
LA	46.0	45.0	46.0	43.5	44.0	44.0	42.5	-	-
LAR	40.0	39.0	41.0	38.0	39.5	40.0	37.5	42.5	47.0

Sus scrofa: **Pelvis**

Nr.	**(29/04)**	**138/04**	**83/04**	**(17/05)**
LAR	43.0	43.0	49.0	-
SH	-	-	-	17.0

Sus scrofa: **Femur**

Nr.	**127/03**	**(19/03)**	**62/04**	**(17/05)**	**91/99**
Bd	59.0	55.5	58.5	-	52.5
SD	-	-	-	22.5	-

Sus scrofa: **Patella**

Nr.	**144/04**	**76/02**	**117/03**	**42/07**	**71/00**	**50/01**
GL	41.0	42.5	45.5	42.5	47.0	46.0
GB	26.0	27.0	28.5	30.0	28.0	29.0

Sus scrofa: **Tibia**

Nr.	**(19/03)**	**41/07**	**(13/03)**	**(24/07)**	**51/04**	**135/04**	**39/03**	**76/03**	**87/03**
Bp	62.0	66.0	-	-	-	-	-	-	-
Bd	-	-	41.0	36.5	41.0	41.0	39.5	38.0	35.0
SD	-	-	28.0	24.0	-	-	-	-	-

Sus scrofa: **Tibia**

Nr.	**(28/05)**	**71/04**	**(12/04)**	**(4/03)**	**120/03**	**54/03**	**22/00**	**105/96**	**158/97**
Bd	35.0	34.0	37.5	38.5	37.0	37.0	36.0	40.5	38.5

Sus scrofa: **Tibia**

Nr.	**94/97**	**86/96**
Bd	42.5	36.5

Sus scrofa: **Tibia**

Nr.	**(18/03)**	**97/04**	**126/03**	**(19/04)**	**65/03**	**84/03**	**54/03**	**0**	**109/04**
GLl	51.5	49.0	52.5	53.0	55.0	45.5	53.0	45.0	49.0
GLm	46.5	43.5	48.0	47.5	48.0	42.0	48.0	42.5	44.5
Dl	27.0	27.5	28.0	29.0	27.5	24.0	28.0	23.0	26.5
Dm	29.0	30.0	32.0	32.0	26.0	-	30.5	27.0	29.0
Bd	29.0	31.5	32.0	32.0	30.5	28.5	30.0	27.5	29.0

Sus scrofa: **Tibia**

Nr.	**69/08**	**48/07**	**36/00**	**67/08**	**(30/07)**	**66/97**	**76/96**	**28/96**	**43/96**
GLl	52.0	53.5	57.5	56.5	57.0	55.0	53.5	52.5	51.0
GLm	47.0	48.0	51.5	50.5	51.5	50.5	49.5	47.5	45.0
Dl	27.0	29.0	29.5	29.0	31.0	-	-	-	-
Dm	31.0	32.5	32.5	36.5	34.0	-	-	-	-
Bd	29.0	29.0	34.5	-	-	-	-	-	-

Sus scrofa: **Tibia**

Nr.	**77/95**	**115/96**	**220/97**	**98/97**	**226/97**	**48/00**
GLl	54.0	51.5	53.0	51.0	51.0	-
GLm	48.5	46.0	47.0	46.0	46.0	-

| Dl | - | - | - | - | - | 28.0 | | |
| Dm | - | - | - | - | - | 34.5 | | |

Sus scrofa: Calcaneus

Nr.	83/04	49/06	78/03	51/04	48/02	(13/03)	49/03	115/96	184/97
GL	111.0	111.0	99.5	92.0	100.0	100.0	104.5	112.5	105.0
GB	33.0	31.0	28.0	29.0	30.0	29.5	31.0	31.0	30.0

Sus scrofa: Calcaneus

Nr.	97/95	86/96	89/96	60/02	54/03	89/00
GL	99.5	100.0	104.0	100.0	-	-
GB	31.5	28.5	29.5	-	28.5	30.5

Sus scrofa: Metatarsus III

Nr.	0	114/04	68/96
GL	79.0	82.0	-
Bd	-	-	21.0

Sus scrofa: Metatarsus IV

Nr.	51/02	59/96	45/94
GL	84.0	-	-
Bd	-	24.5	21.0

Sus scrofa: Phalanx 1

Nr.	42/03	100/04	92/03	42/06	?	75/02	41/05	99/04	(12/06)
Glpe	49.0	48.5	47.0	47.5	53.5	43.0	44.0	31.5	44.0
Bp	21.0	22.0	21.0	19.5	21.0	20.0	22.0	15.5	23.0
SD	16.5	17.0	16.0	15.0	16.5	15.0	16.0	10.3	17.0
Bd	18.5	20.5	19.5	17.5	20.0	18.5	20.0	11.5	20.0

Sus scrofa: Phalanx 1

Nr.	144/04	88/03	62/04	62/03	74/03	76/02	117/00	93/95	93/95
Glpe	51.5	30.5	33.0	32.5	28.0	30.0	50.0	50.5	50.0
Bp	22.5	15.0	13.0	16.0	13.0	13.5	22.0	24.0	24.5
SD	17.5	9.0	8.5	11.0	9.5	9.5	17.5	18.5	18.5
Bd	21.0	10.0	9.5	13.5	9.5	11.0	20.5	22.0	22.5

Sus scrofa: Phalanx 1

Nr.	155/97	180/97	158/97	87/95	176/97	59/96	141/97	57/94	38/94
Glpe	52.5	50.0	49.5	47.5	48.5	50.0	48.0	49.0	45.5
Bp	23.5	22.5	23.5	23.5	23.0	21.0	23.5	22.0	22.5
SD	19.5	17.5	17.0	17.0	17.0	17.0	17.0	17.0	16.5
Bd	22.0	21.0	24.0	21.0	20.0	20.0	21.5	19.5	19.5

Sus scrofa: Phalanx 1

Nr.	61/97	86/96	(2/93)	40/25	115/96	42	42/07	131/98	74/97
Glpe	43.0	47.5	48.5	42.0	43.5	-	46.5	-	45.0
Bp	22.5	24.5	21.0	22.0	21.5	22.0	-	-	
SD	16.5	18.0	16.5	16.0	16.0	17.0	18.0	17.0	-
Bd	19.5	21.5	20.0	18.5	19.0	-	22.0	20.5	21.5

Sus scrofa: **Phalanx 2**

Nr.	62/09	40/05	71/04	83/04	92/03	127/03	127/04	(30/09)	40/99
Glpe	34.0	31.5	31.5	31.5	28.5	29.0	31.5	30.0	30.0
Bp	24.0	21.0	18.0	21.5	21.0	19.0	22.0	19.5	19.5
SD	20.0	17.5	15.0	18.0	16.5	15.5	17.5	17.0	16.0
Bd	23.0	19.5	15.5	21.0	19.0	16.0	19.5	17.5	18.0

Sus scrofa: **Phalanx 2**

Nr.	1/00	88/00	66/96	89/96	40/95	31/94	52/97	111/97	97/95
Glpe	32.0	32.0	36.0	31.0	34.5	32.5	31.0	29.0	32.0
Bp	20.5	21.5	22.5	22.0	20.0	20.0	21.5	19.0	20.5
SD	16.5	18.0	18.5	17.5	16.5	15.5	16.5	16.0	16.0
Bd	16.0	18.5	19.0	19.0	16.5	17.5	17.5	17.5	17.0

Sus scrofa: **Phalanx 2**

Nr.	35/94	112/96	66/96	44/95	49/95	127/03	87/03	74/02	120/04
Glpe	30.5	29.5	29.5	33.0	29.5	-	-	-	-
Bp	20.0	20.5	20.0	20.5	19.5	18.5	-	21.5	21.0
SD	15.5	16.0	16.0	16.5	16.0	-	15.5	-	-
Bd	17.5	19.0	17.5	17.5	18.5	-		-	-

Sus scrofa: **Phalanx 3**

Nr.	75/02	99/04	75/02	112/97	141/97	116/96	106/96	67/00	110/97
DLS	44.0	39.0	39.0	44.5	44.5	44.5	45.0	36.0	41.5
Ld	39.5	36.0	37.0	43.0	42.0	41.5	41.5	34.5	38.5
MBS	15.0	13.5	17.0	19.0	20.0	18.5	17.5	15.0	17.0

Sus scrofa: **Phalanx 3**

Nr.	78/97	83/00	(12/04)	48/04
DLS	40.0	41.0	-	-
Ld	38.5	39.5	-	-
MBS	16.0	-	16.0	15.0

Ursus arctos

Ursus: Maxilla

Nr.	118/03
Length of M^3, measured at the cingulum	34.5
Breadth of M^3, measured at the cingulum	17.5

Ursus: Mandibula

Nr.	106/96	110/97
Length of the molar row (along the alveoli on the buccal side)	62.0	-
Length of M_2, measured at the cingulum	22.5	22.5
Breadth of M_2, measured at the cingulum	13.5	14.0
Length of M_3, measured at the cingulum	18.0	-
Breadth of M_3, measured at the cingulum	13.5	-
Height of the mandible	82.5	-
Height of the mandible behind M_2	36.0	-

Ursus: Humerus

Nr.	39/03	82/01	?
Bd	88.0	84.0	107.0
SD	-	-	32.5

Ursus: Radius

Nr.	43/99
Bp	44.5

Ursus: Ulna

Nr.	42/03
BPC	54.5

Ursus: Pelvis

Nr.	(9/05)	112/04
LA	55.0	69.0
LAR	50.0	61.0

Ursus: Patella

Nr.	73/03	(19/04)
GL	44.0	41.0
GB	34.0	31.0

Ursus: Metatarsus IV

Nr.	120/03	127/04	207/97
GL	94.5	88.5	90.5
Bd	21.0	19.0	24.0

Ursus: Phalanx 1

Nr.	88/03
Glpe	42.0
Bp	20.5
SD	12.0

Bd	15.0

Ursus: Phalanx 2

Nr.	**34/04**
Glpe	30.0
Bp	26.0
KD	10.5
Bd	13.5

Ursus: Phalanx 2

Nr.	**34/04**

Castor fiber

Castor: Maxilla

Nr.	115/96
Length of the cheektooth row along the alveoli)	33.0
Length of the diastema	50.0

Castor: Mandibula

Nr.	74/03	76/02	80/02	53/06	126/03	83/04	76/02
Length of the cheektooth row along the alveoli)	38.0	39.5	41.0	-	-	37.0	37.5
Length of the diastema	24.0	22.0	-	21.5	25.0	26.0	21.0

Castor: Mandibula

Nr.	129/03	137/04	101/96	180/97	163/97	38/95	217/97
Length of the cheektooth row along the alveoli)	40.0	34.0	38.5	35.0	39.0	36.0	36.0
Length of the diastema	-	21.5	24.5	21.5	25.5	21.5	-

Castor: Scapula

Nr.	83/04	48/06	69/04	112/04
SLC	12.5	12.5	14.0	12.5
GLP	21.0	-	-	-
LG	19.5	-	-	-
BG	13.0	13.5	13.5	-

Castor: Humerus

Nr.	83/04	38/06	(9/03)	117/03	110/04	82/04	78/0
GL	98.0	88.5	-	-	-	-	-
GLC	99.5	89.5	-	-	-	-	-
Bp	29.0	26.5	-	-	-	-	-
SD	11.5	11.5	11.5	12.5	11.0	10.5	10.5
Bd	34.0	35.0	36.0	33.0	34.0	33.0	30.0
BT	23.1	21.5	22.0	20.5	21.0	19.5	20.5

Castor: Humerus

Nr.	65/03	170/97	75/96
Bd	35.0	32.5	36.0
BT	20.0	19.5	22.0

Castor: Radius

Nr.	41/03	83/04	48/06	91/99	116/96	86/96	105/96
Bp	12.0	12.0	13.0	11.0	12.5	12.5	13.0
SD	7.5	6.5	8.0	8.0	-	-	-

Castor: Ulna

Nr.	39/04	93/99	102/96	176/97	105/96
GL	-	-	128.0	-	-
DPA	18.0	-	17.5	17.0	17.0
SDO	16.0	14.5	-	-	-

BPC	13.0	-		12.0	13.5	13.5	
SD	7.0	-		-	-	-	

Castor: Pelvis

Nr.	**126/03**	**107/03**	**82/04**	**83/04**	**40/05**	**49/04**	**115/96**
LAR	22.0	21.5	22.5	22.5	21.5	23.0	20.0

Castor: Femur

Nr.	**137/04**	**43/03**	**75/02**	**62/04**
Bp	46.0	-	-	-
DC	17.5	18.0	18.0	-
SD	24.0	-	-	26.0
Bd	-	-	-	39.0

Castor: Tibia

Nr.	**131/04**	**137/04**	**92/04**	**48/06**	**(20/2/97)**	**53/97**
GL	146.5	-	-	-	-	-
Bp	35.5	-	-	-	-	-
SD	12.0	13.0	-	12.5	-	-
Bd	23.5	23.5	23.0	22.5	23.0	23.0

Castor: Talus

Nr.	**80/02**	**178/98**	**52/08**
GL	23.5	22.5	25.0

Castor: Metatarsus III

Nr.	**61/04**
Bd	12.0

Castor: Metatarsus IV

Nr.	**49/04**	**115/04**
GL	57.0	60.0
Bd	13.5	13.5

Castor: Phalanx 1

Nr.	**31/04**	**47/05**
Glpe	28.0	-
Bp	12.0	10.5
SD	8.5	7.0
Bd	9.0	-

Martes martes

Martes: Maxilla

Nr.	135/00	135/00	88/00	88/00	105/96
Length of the cheektooth row	25.5	26.7	28.9	28.5	25.2
Length of the carnassial (Cing.)	8.1	8.2	8.6	8.5	8.9
Breadth of the carnassial (Cing.)	4.8	4.7	5.3	5.2	5.6
Length of M^1	4.9	4.8	6.1	6.2	6.1
Breadth of M^1	7.6	7.6	8.6	8.3	8.7
Sex					m

Martes: Mandibula

Nr.	15/97	112/96	68/96	68/6	121/03
Total length: condyle process-Infradentale	54.9	57.4	-	-	-
Length: angular process-Infradentale	53.5	57.3	-	49.5	-
Length: condyle process-aboral border of the canine alveolus	48.3	51.2	53.2	-	-
Length: angular process-aboral border of the canine alveolus	47.1	49.3	50.5	-	42.5
Length of the cheektooth row	30.1	31.3	32.0	-	-
Length of the molar row	13.3	13.9	14.5	-	-
Length of the premolar row	18.0	17.3	17.7	-	-
Length of the carnassial (Cing.)	10.6	11.0	-	-	8.8
Breadth of the carnassial (Cing.)	4.3	4.4	-	-	3.6
Length of the carnassial alveolus	-	-	-	-	8.8
Height of the vertical ramus	22.9	25.1	24.9	-	-

Martes: Mandibula

Nr.	(30/04)	76/02	53/04	50/04	35/04
Length of the carnassial (Cing.)	10.3	9.8	10.3	10.2	9.5
Breadth of the carnassial (Cing.)	4.2	3.9	3.8	4.0	3.6
Length of the carnassial alveolus	10.1	8.6	9.8	9.3	8.1

Martes: Scapula

Nr.	47/05
GLP	12.0
LG	10.2
BG	6.7
SLC	9.7
HS	45.9

Martes: Humerus

Nr.	(28/05)	51/01
GL	64.9	-
Bp	10.6	12.2
Dp	11.7	13.1
SD	4.3	5.1
Bd	13.2	

Martes: Radius

Nr.	47/05
GL	49.5
Bp	6.0
SD	3.3
Bd	8.1

Martes: Ulna

Nr.	47/05
BPC	8.3

Martes: Femur

Nr.	45/05	220/97
GL	81.8	80.2
Bp	16.0	16.0
DC	7.9	7.9
SD	5.5	5.6
Bd	15.3	15.4
Sex	m	f

Martes: Tibia

Nr.	127/03	103/96
GL	89.4	-
Bp	15.1	15.7
SD	4.8	-
Bd	10.7	-

Martes: Calcaneus

Nr.	?
GL	20.1
GB	9.4

Sciurus vulgaris

Sciurus: **Mandibula**

Nr.	81/04	111/04
Total length	43.0	-
Length of the cheektooth row (aboral border of canine alveolus)	21.4	23.8
Height of the vertical ramus: basal point of the angular process-Coronion	22.6	-

Sciurus: **Humerus**

Nr.	112/04	76/02	80/02	?	61/04	98/04
GL	39.6	42.6	42.0	40.4	43.1	42.2
GLC	39.8	42.7	42.1	40.7	43.1	42.3
Bp	6.8	7.1	7.2	6.8	6.9	7.2
SD	3.0	3.0	3.3	3.1	3.1	3.2
Bd	9.7	10.2	10.5	9.9	10.2	10.3

Sciurus: **Humerus**

Nr.	51/04	117/63	42/03	119/03
GL	42.2	-	-	-
GLC	42.3	-	-	-
Bp	7.0	-	-	-
SD	3.3	3.1	-	3.0
Bd	10.4	10.1	9.4	10.4

Sciurus: **Radius**

Nr.	?
GL	51.8
Bp	5.8
KD	3.1
Bd	6.1

Sciurus: **Femur**

Nr.	75/02	135/04	103/96	55/94	81/99	54/03
GL	56.3	-	57.9	54.4	-	-
GLC	55.9	56.5	-	-	54.8	54.4
Bp	9.9	10.1	10.8	9.8	-	-
BTr	11.4	10.8	11.1	-	10.0	-
DC	5.0	5.2	-	-	4.7	4.9
SD	4.0	3.7	4.3	3.7	3.6	4.0
Bd	-	9.0	9.2	8.6	-	9.0

Sciurus: **Femur**

Nr.	144/04	(19/04)	29	99/04	(19/07)	?
Bp	10.3	10.1	10.3	10.3	9.3	10.0
BTr	11.1	-	-	10.3	9.8	10.6
DC	5.1	5.4	5.2	4.9	4.6	5.0
SD	4.0	3.9	3.9	3.7	3.7	-

Sciurus: Femur

Nr.	75/02	(19/05)	137/04	(30/05)	51/04
BTr	11.0	-	-	9.8	-
DC	4.9	-	-	5.1	-
SD	3.8	3.6	3.6	3.8	-
Bd	-	8.4	9.2	-	8.9

Sciurus: Tibia

Nr.	?	76/02	?	?	112/04	144/04
GL	63.6	-	-	65.6	-	-
Bp	9.3	-	-	-	-	8.4
SD	2.8	2.8	3.1	3.0	3.0	2.9
Bd	6.0	5.5	5.5	5.1	5.9	-
Dd	4.9	4.6	5.1	5.1	5.0	-

Sciurus: Tibia

Nr.	45/05
SD	2.9

Lepus europaeus

Lepus: Scapula

Nr.	76/02	57/06
GLP	-	14.7
LG	-	13.4
BG	11.7	12.4
SLC	8.3	-

Lepus: Femur

Nr.	61/02
DC	11.9

Lepus: Tibia

Nr.	31/04
Bd	17.8
Dd	12.0

Lutra lutra

Lutra: **Mandibula**

Nr.	36/97	158/97
Total length: condyle process-Infradentale	70.3	-
Length of the cheektooth row	34.6	35.4
Length of the molar row (alveoli)	17.1	17.3
Length of the carnassial (Cing.)	13.6	13.6
Breadth of the carnassial (Cing.)	7.0	7.0
Height of the vertical ramus	34.1	-

Lutra: **Humerus**

Nr.	45/05
Bd	25.6
SD	7.3

Lutra: **Baculum**

Nr.	154/97
Total length	67.5

Mustela putorius

Mustela: Cranium

Nr.	115/96
Length of the cheektooth row (Alv.)	126.5
Length of the carnassial (Cing.)	6.6
Breadth of the carnassial (Cing.)	3.5
Zygomatic breadth: Zygion-zygion	32.7
Least breadth of skull: aboral of the supraorbital processes	15.7
Frontal breadth: Ectorbitale-Ectorbitale	21.6
Least breadth between the orbits: Entorbitale-Entorbitale	15.4
Greatest palatal breadth (Alv.)	21.2

Mustela: Mandibula

Nr.	115/96
Total length: condyle process-Infradentale	33.3
Length of the cheektooth row	15.8
Length of the molar row	7.7
Length of the carnassial (Cing.)	6.8
Breadth of the carnassial (Cing.)	3.0
Height of the vertical ramus	15.5

Cricetus cricetus

Cricetus: **Mandibula**

Nr.	?
Length: the condyle process-aboral border of the canine alveolus	28.9
Length of the cheektooth raw (M_3-P_1)	8.4
Height of the vertical ramus: basal point of the angular process-Coronion	15.0

Erinaceus europaeus

Erinaceus: **Mandibula**

Nr.	42/03	61/04	114/04	(14/05)
Length: the condyle process-aboral border of the canine alveolus	30.5	-	30.91	-
Length of the cheektooth raw (M_3-P_1)	9.9	10.7	10.8	10.5
Height of the vertical ramus: basal point of the angular process-Coronion	-	-	19.4	-

Erinaceus: **Femur**

Nr.	82/04
Bp	10.2
BTr	11.0
DC	5.5

9 781407 316376